# How to Get Stupid White Men Out of Office

## the anti-politics, un-boring guide to power

*"And by the way, it's not just stupid white men, there's a lot of stupid people of color who need to get kicked out too."*

—Sofia Quintero

*"Forget about stupid white men, it's the smart ones I'm worried about."*

—Ludovic Blain

First Edition

Library of Congress Cataloging-in-Publication Data for this book is available from the Library of Congress.

Soft Skull Press, 71 Bond Street, Brooklyn, NY 11237
Distributed by PGW, 1.800.788.3123, www.pgw.com

# TABLE OF CONTENTS

# PART 3: "Honey, We Got ISSUES!!"
## How We Changed the Laws

# PART 4: Pimping Satellites for Change:
## How We Freaked It on the Internet

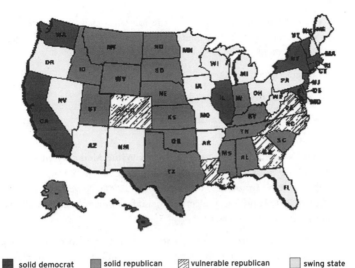

◼ solid democrat　　◼ solid republican　　▨ vulnerable republican　　☐ swing state

# Will Your State Be
# The Florida of 2004?

## By William Upski Wimsatt

This book is sponsored by the number 5.

And the number 3.

And also by . . . the number 7.

# 537.

Do you know what this number is?

It's the number of votes Bush supposedly beat Gore by in the year 2000.

Here we are in 2004.

Now pay close attention.

On the second day of November this year

—mark it in your calendar—

Stupid White Men will be stripped of the job titles they do not deserve *because of this book and the thousands of people who read it between March and October of 2004.*

I am not exaggerating.

I am not giving an inspiring speech.

I am putting my reputation on the line to tell you what's going to happen and invite you to be part of it.

On Tuesday, November 2, the gang of Stupid White Men currently occupying the White House are gonna lose their jobs. Even more Stupid White Men will be evicted from office on November 7, 2006, November 4, 2008, November 6, 2012, and every election thereafter (not to mention all the state and local ones in between).

If Stupid White Men refuse to leave, a sheriff will be forced to physically remove them and place their family photos, gun collections, liquor stashes, and MBA plaques in the street. It will be a sad day.

First, they get a hanky.

Then they get a hug. (If only they'd had more of these *earlier* in life we might not find ourselves in this situation today.)

Then they'll be taken away by nice people to a safe place where they can't hurt anyone ever again. Or maybe they'll hide in a cave.

George Walker Bush, how can you live with yourself?

Do you really have the audacity to stand on stage with NYC firefighters at your Republican convention, when it's your budget cuts that caused their stations to close? Why don't you just be honest and spit in the face of the firefighters? Why don't you be honest and kick the schoolchildren you're going to leave behind? Don't worry, by the time they're old enough to vote, you'll be retired—just in time to let them pay your Social Security. Go ahead, George, no one's looking. Just lift up that running shoe of yours and kick the kindergarteners in the chest. Watch six-year-old Brian with curly hair thud onto to the sidewalk. Watch Jennifer hit her head against a desk, your shoe imprint marking her ruffled yellow dress. That's what you're doing, George. Your tax cuts are our school cuts, our health cuts. Your six to ten trillion dollar debt is robbing us of our future. It isn't a very Christian thing to do.

And, please notice (I know some of you can be sensitive about this) the title of this book is not *All White Men Are Stupid*. I am a white man. I'm a co-author of this book. Johnny, put down the shotgun!

See, here's my picture. I look just like you, Johnny: a white American male. From the Midwest, Johnny, just like you. I like to eat pizza, play sports, go to the beach, talk on my cell–phone. And I love my country, Johnny. I'll fight to defend it if I have to. I'll even fight to defend it from *you*. America is a beautiful place, Johnny. Think of all the lakes and rivers we have! Doesn't it make you want to go swimming? There's only one problem, Johnny. We can't swim anymore because our lakes and rivers are full of chemicals dumped by your friends' companies. Since you're in charge of the "Justice Department" and polluting is a crime, would you please talk to them for me? Thanks.

I want to swim. Without getting cancer. Is that too much to ask?

I also like to play sports and, in case I get injured, I would like to have health insurance. Education is important too. It would be nice to go to school without being in debt—like my peers in Canada and Europe. But you'd rather spend my tuition money building new detention centers for random Arab-Americans.

I have one more request. I hope this isn't too extravagant. I'd like to be able to own my own home one day, Johnny. That's right, *affordable* housing. And if I do purchase a home, God willing, I don't want it to get blown up or robbed because your friend, the "president" thinks "support the troops" means "invade more countries," "cut benefits for military families," and "let homeless veterans wig out on the street" with no housing, job training, drug rehab, or mental health programs.

I am a simple person, Johnny. I have simple needs.

Oh yeah, there's one more thing. About my cell–phone. I like to talk on it. And I don't like the idea of people listening to me while I talk.

Is your stuff packed yet?

And tell Condoleezza for me: It's not just Stupid White Men who're gonna get evicted from office this year and next year and the year after that.

We're also going to pink–slip Stupid White Women (there are a few), and Stupid People of Color (we know who you are), and we're gonna provoke a sudden unexpected career change for Smart People of Any Race and Gender who shit on the rest of us in order to please their golf buddies in Big Tobacco, Big Oil, Big Prisons, Big Bombs, Big Families with Big Bank Accounts Full of Money They Didn't Earn and Small Names that begin with the letter B.

Goodbye, Johnny. Goodbye, Georgie. Goodbye, Leezza. Run along now!

I know what you're thinking. *We're fighting an uphill battle in 2004. The Democratic candidates are not all we hoped for. Bush has more money. Bush is a few points ahead in some of the polls. The voting machines are rigged. Most Americans are brainwashed by what they see on TV and* . . . um, no.

In case you don't remember, Gore was a shitty candidate too. Gore was outspent too. Gore's election was rigged too. And still, with all of that, he lost by 537 votes.

The Republicans don't believe this election is in the bag. They're tripping over themselves and pulling out all the stops because they know it's gonna be razor–close again—just like in 2000.

Let me repeat: in 2000, the presidential election was decided by 537 votes.

Well, actually it was decided by the partisan 5–4 Supreme Court vote and the Supreme Fraud of Jeb Bush and Katherine Harris. But we won't get into all that here.

Still.

537 votes. Can I make this any clearer? Would you like me to tattoo it across my forehead? What more do I have to say to get you to report immediately to your nearest swing state and start organizing?

537 VOTES!!!!!!!!!!!!!!!!!!!

I sing it in valleys and shout it on mountaintops.

I whisper it to alligators in Everglades swamps.

Because even with all the fraud, even with all the dirty tricks, 538 more votes would have done the trick to block Mr. Bush and Mr. Dick.

George Bush would not be president right now.

With 538 more votes.

The Permanent Preemptive War Against Anyone We Decide Is Bad would not have happened. Ashcroft would be Ashtray. Patriot Acts 1 and 2 would be movie sequels, not the law of the land. States would not be cutting teachers because of a tax cut for the rich–triggered financial crisis. We would not be saddled with the biggest national debt in history. The

Supreme Court would not be teetering on the brink of an anti-choice majority. We would not have cut pay and benefits for the military and their families so we could "support the troops" by dropping them off in a sandy Vietnam and leaving them there indefinitely.

538 VOTES!!!!!!!!!!!!!!!!!

What would it have taken to organize 538 more voters?

One person could've done it. What would you have done if you had known? You would've gone to Florida. You would've convinced your friends. You would've gone door to door. You would've told everyone on your pizza delivery route. You would've created an email list. You would've thrown parties on the beach. You would've written lyrics. You would've joined a campaign. You would've done it as an independent study and gotten school credit.

That's exactly what they did in New Mexico.

Check out this conversation I had with my friend from New Mexico.

Me: "Wait wait wait . . . You did *what*?"

Friend: "Well, after going to city council meeting after city council meeting with a hundred supporters and losing 2–7 each time, we thought, 'This shit is not working.' We decided that to stop this road from being built we had to get involved in the electoral scene. We developed a political action committee and a political consulting firm. In four years, we've gone from a 2–7 vote to a 5–4 vote. We replaced three of our strongest opponents with three champions. Long term, we've built a new political force led by young people of color that has reshaped Albuquerque politics."

## Double Jeopardy

My friend is Eli Lee (author of chapter 14). He used to be director of an organization called YouthAction. He realized that youth organizing is great. It's essential. But you have to build electoral power too. His company, Soltari.com, runs grassroots political campaigns.

I met Eli a couple of years ago. I had never been into electoral politics before. I think I only voted once between the ages of eighteen and twenty-eight. Even when I was a consultant for Rock the Vote in the 1990s, I didn't bother to vote. In my eyes my job was connecting Rock the Vote with "real" political activism—the grassroots kind.

Soltari's local victories had a major national impact: They swung the state of New Mexico for Gore in 2000. They turned out 2,016 "unlikely" Hispanic voters in November 2000. Gore won New Mexico by 366 votes.

The whole state. 366 votes.

"Are you serious?" says University of New Mexico sophomore Marisol Enyart, when I told her this story. "366 votes??? That's like *one* art class at UNM."

Marisol caught the bug. She decided to write about the victory in Tuscon (chapter 3) and became a co-author of this book.

Sometimes it doesn't take that many votes to swing a state. According to the Swing State Project (www.gogovernment.org/swingstate), in 2000 New Hampshire was decided by 7,211 votes; Oregon by 6,765; Wisconsin by 5,708; Iowa by 4,144—not to mention Florida.

Am I missing something here?

538 votes.

Anyone could've moved down to Florida and organized six hundred more people to vote. One person! Do you think you could've done it? The Youth Vote Coalition found in 2000 that if you remind young people face-to-face that they should vote, and you register them (which is really easy), and you tell them where their polling place is, they are 10 percent more likely to vote. On average, in the 2000 election, young adults age eighteen to twenty-four voted at a rate of 32 percent. So the goal is to increase that number to 42 percent. Sound possible?

Let's do the math.

You'd need to talk to six thousand people to get six hundred more votes. Say you hang out somewhere and you talk to fifty eligible Democratic voters per day. In one hundred and twenty days, you've talked to six thousand voters. In four months.

Do you think you could've spared four months of your life to change the course of world history?

Four months.

Where were you when we needed you?

Well, now you have another chance. In the 2000 election, only a third of young adults voted, so there are plenty of people to talk to.

Four months: I could've done it. You could've done it.

Or we could've gotten together three friends and each spent one month.

Why didn't we?

Because we weren't paying attention to electoral politics.

Now pay attention.

Your state could be Florida in 2004. Especially if you live in one of the sixteen major swing states of 2004: Oregon, Nevada, New Mexico, Missouri, Florida, Minnesota, Wisconsin, Michigan, Ohio, Pennsylvania, Arizona, Arkansas, Maine, Iowa, New Hampshire, and West Virginia.

Any of these states could be Florida in 2004.

Do you have residency in one of these states? Parents? Grandparents? A friend? An address you can move to temporarily and use to vote absentee? Young people move around a lot. You don't have to do much to prove residence in most states beyond having an address.

If half the young folks from states like Iowa and Wisconsin who attend college in Chicago or Boston would vote absentee in their home state, it could swing a close presidential election. (You can vote absentee through your state's secretary of state.)

And the New York and Cali people who attend college in Ohio and Pennsylvania need to vote where they're at. Are you following me?

So if you're from say, Missouri, and you live in Washington, D.C., you should throw a party and invite over your Missouri friends to plan how you're gonna vote absentee and call up everyone from your state.

If you don't live in these states, then we have another job for you. The Republicans will have two to three times as much money as the Democrats in 2004. So even if you're not in a swing state, your job is to make noise and force them to spend some of their TV money in your state.

Republicans are greedy. They think they can grab Illinois, California, even New York. They're also arrogant. They think they own Georgia, North Carolina, Louisiana, Virginia, Colorado, Kansas, and Kentucky. Make them spend their TV money on it!

And let's be clear: the Democrats are not our friends either.

Just before the 2000 election, my close friend told me he secretly wanted Bush to win.

"If he wins, he'll be so bad people might actually wake up."

It didn't take much to convince me. Growing up on Bill Clinton for most of my adult life, it made perfect sense.

Bring on Armageddon!

I was sick of this Clinton shit.

He pretended to be a friend to women, then kicked moms off welfare and sent them out to poke at garbage on the street for a few dollars an hour with no child care. He pretended to be a friend to people of color. Then he put eight-hundred thousand people in prison, mostly nonviolent people of color—the biggest prison expansion in world history. He pretended to be a friend to working Americans, then he passed NAFTA and GATT and shipped good manufacturing jobs overseas.

Then after he was a national disgrace and no one wanted to be seen with him, he had the nerve to move his office up to Harlem, driving up prices so families who've lived in Harlem for generations get kicked out on the street; kinda like what's gonna happen to the Bush boys, except different.

I would've voted for Nader in 2000, but Nader's name was kept off the ballot in North Carolina. Even write-ins for Nader did not count. Anyone who says Nader was a spoiler in 2000 needs to face a few facts: Clinton spoiled it with his penis. Gore spoiled with his lack of balls—he couldn't even win his own state of Tennessee! In the end, he decided he'd rather lose Florida than stand up for the fifty thousand voters (mostly blacks and Jewish grandmothers) who were deprived of their right to vote.

How did the Democrats get so fucked up?

According to *The Emerging Democratic Majority* by John Judis and Ruy Teixeira, in the 1970s and early '80s, the Democrats actually used to have a lot more spine than they do today. In 1980, Ted Kennedy ran on a platform of universal health care and a massive government jobs program. In 1972, McGovern ran against Nixon on an antiwar, pro–civil rights, pro-women agenda, and he lost every state except Massachusetts and D.C.

Part of what happened to the Democrats is that they got tired of losing. Now, that's partly their own fault. And it's partly *our fault* for not working our asses off to get them elected. In 1984, Walter Mondale ran against Ronald Reagan, talking about liberal issues. He got slaughtered. He lost every state except D.C. and his home state of Minnesota. The right-wing had successfully tarred Democrats as financially irresponsible "tax-and-spend liberals" who were controlled by "special interests" (read: African-Americans, man-hating feminists, corrupt union bosses, campus radicals, and tree-huggers). So Democrats lost much of the white middle and working class, and the South, to the Republicans. Let's be clear: they lost in part because they were trying to do something right.

In response, in 1985, the Democratic Leadership Council (DLC) was born. They said, "Hey, we're getting our asses kicked. We need to co-opt the Republicans' rhetoric." In and of itself, this wasn't a bad idea. The plan was to talk more about "family" and being "tough on crime"—like Republicans—but to legislate like "moderate" Democrats (and pursue incremental instead of sweeping change) which was also, in and of itself, not such a bad idea given the political climate. But then they drifted, and drifted and drifted . . . and soon they had lost their way. In 1992, Clinton intentionally picked public fights with Sister Souljah and Jesse Jackson as a way of distancing himself from African-Americans in the eyes of "moderate" (a.k.a. bigoted) white voters.

So wait, why are we voting for the Democrats again?

The harsh reality that we young whippersnappers hate to face is that most people in America actually *don't* think like us and our friends. The revolution is *not* going to happen tomorrow. Winona LaDuke will *not* become vice president of the U.S. or even governor of Minnesota. The system will *not* magically crumble into a multi-racial ecological paradise. We actually have to do the hard work of winning over and mobilizing another ten or twenty million or so skeptical American voters to build a solid progressive majority so that we can actually have dangerous revolutionary things like health care and affordable tuition; jobs that pay enough to live on; Social Security for when we're old; and an economy based on ecological sustainability instead of permawar. And maybe even a seat at the table for people who are not multimillionaires.

Getting there will take a thirty-year plan.

We need to study the Right. While we were busy screaming that Democrats and Republicans are all the same, the right-wing understood very well that they're not the same. They mapped out a thirty-year plan to take over the Republican Party. They had patience. They were disciplined, and they were persistent. People are so amazed by the political power of the Christian Right. Back in the 1960s, right-wing Christians were just like us. They believed electoral politics was dirty and they didn't want to go near it.

Then God Himself appeared in the form of Pat Robertson. And at the same time, there were these scary minorities, homos, pop culture, and well, women. It was all too much to take. So that's when you got conservative "fusionism." The People of God would unite with the People of Money and Weapons against the scary women, minorities, and gays. According to a fascinating book about the right wing, *Mobilizing Resentment* by Jean Hardisty, "Fusionism represented an agreement by [conservative leaders] to emphasize their commonalities, rather than their differences." It was a "political compromise arrived at in the 1960s that united the traditional conservative economic agenda with the right-wing social issues agenda by merging two formerly distinct branches of conservatism. Fusionism created a politically appealing, ideological package that provided the grounding vision for the rise of the New Right in the later 1970s."

The Republicans then used "wedge issues" like welfare, affirmative action, and taxes to split the Democratic voter base along race lines. They played on the economic resentment, racial fears, and cultural insecurity of white working and middle class people—especially men—and got them to vote against their own economic self-interest. The classic book on this is Thomas and Mary Edsall's *Chain Reaction: The Impact of Race, Rights and Taxes on American Politics.*

The Republican strategy worked beyond their wildest dreams. Now they're drunk with power, looting the country in a two-fisted fashion. To make matters worse, now that they've got *their* game down, they're learning *our* game.

You might not be interested in actually getting out and doing something this election cycle. But believe me, the right wing is *very* interested. They're reading this book right now, studying everything we do.

(Hey guys! Why so mean-spirited? Deep down you just need a hug, don't you?)

They're organizing a whole subculture of white "Christian" rock and hip-hop groups that are musically talented, attract thousands to their own network of venues, register, and organize their audiences to vote and run for office.

There's this thing called campus activism which the Left invented. It accomplished a few things like helping end the war in Vietnam, helping bring down apartheid in South Africa, forcing sweatshops to allow unions, and providing the vast majority of the training for the entire progressive movement. But it gets next to zero funding. The liberal and progressive money folks take it for granted. Campus activism: isn't it quaint?

There used to be a thing called the Center for Campus Organizing. The idea was to actually provide resources, training, and support to progressives on campus. It died. Not enough support.

Conservatives took our model and ran with it. (Check out campusconservatives.com, leadershipinstitute.org, yaf.org and http://campusnonsense.blogspot.com.) If one conservative student on a campus decides she wants to start a paper, presto! Suddenly she has funding, a huge support network, strategy advice from the big shots, and more than likely a job in the conservative movement once she graduates. I'll never forget the time I was speaking at UC Santa Cruz and this young woman came up to me in a panic: "The conservatives are trying to take over student government. They've been trained, they're motivated. They're attacking us like crazy. They have this newspaper that gets outside funding. They've been trained dude, they're scary, and they have a serious chance of winning."

Me: "Wait, conservatives might take over the student government *at Santa Cruz?*"

Her: "Yeah, they've already done it at Davis, Irvine; they defunded the gay student group. They're on a rampage, and no one even knows this is going on. Everyone thinks Santa Cruz is so liberal. They think they don't have to do anything."

On campus after campus, I hear the same story.

A lot of the recent Republican takeover has been masterminded by a man named Karl Rove, a.k.a the most manipulative man in America. He is the person who is single-handedly responsible for George Bush's presidency, and until last year, he was totally unknown. There are two big books out about him now. One is called *Bush's Brain* (which argues that Rove is Bush's brain). The other is called *Boy Genius*—on the cover, it has one pic-

©2003, David Rees

ture of George that says "Boy" and next to it a picture of Rove that says "Genius." Are you getting the picture here? Texas used to be a solidly Democratic state until Karl Rove got his hands on it. The man knows no boundaries in his quest for power over others.

He has a "Hispanic strategy," an "Arab strategy," and a "Jew strategy" to co-opt all of these groups into the Republican Party. As Nicholas Lehman discovered in his *New Yorker* profile on Rove, the Democratic Party has three main funding bases: unions, trial lawyers (these are the good kind of lawyers who sue big corporations that screw people), and wealthy liberals. Rove has a plan to yank the funding rug out from underneath the Democratic Party: (1) Bust the unions. (2) Defund the trial lawyers with "tort reform" (that's what those anti-lawyer billboards you see are all about). (3) Woo wealthy liberals with tax-cuts.

They are not playing.

There was an article in the *New York Times* by economist Paul Krugman called "Toward One-Party Rule." Think about it. One-party rule. Just because we grew up under a two party system doesn't mean it has to stay that way. I can remember my political science teacher saying: "The pendulum swings one way, then it swings back. It goes in cycles." That's the way it has always been during the twentieth century. Not only are Republicans trying to roll back the social programs of the twentieth century, they are actually trying to *stop the pendulum.*

Krugman refers to today's Republican Party as "an unprecedented national political machine, one that is well on track to establishing one-party rule in America. Republican leaders often talk of 'revolution,' and we should take them at their word."

This is what's about to happen if the Republicans are able to elect Bush this November. They're building a machine. And if y'all Greens think you have a fucking prayer in hell of changing shit in *that* America, y'all need to take some Dexedrine and open them eyes. I like Greens. My heart is with y'all. I think you have the power to destroy the Democratic Party. And I think you're generally good people.

Like most good people, I don't think you understand the art of war. You can't fight on two fronts at once. First you have to get together with the Democrats to beat the Republicans. If you fend off the Republican threat, it buys you slack to move the Democrats in a more progressive direction *over a period of decades as people of color become a majority.* If you kill the Democrats first, then the Republicans control everything and they can yank the floor out from under all of us and shift the whole playing field to the right. You think things are bad now? You think the two-party system is bad? Say hello to the one-party system.

Here's the good news. Republicans have a long–term problem: People of color are going to be a majority in the U.S. by 2052. And they don't tend to vote Republican. The Republicans know this and they're shitting in their pants. Karl Rove acknowledges: "If the 2000 election were held today, we'd lose because there are more Hispanics in the population." The GOP is terrified, which is why they are so vicious—exactly like the White Afrikaaners under apartheid South Africa. The Republicans know if they don't lock down their political machine in the next few election cycles, their reign is history. They realize that the 2004 election may be their last chance to consolidate power.

What we need over the next thirty to fifty years is Progressive fusionism. We need to begin the long, painful process of healing the wounds between us, rebuilding those bridges, and emphasizing our common ground.

This is a book for regular people who are upset about Bush or our local politicians, but don't believe we can actually get them out. This is a book for people who have never voted, people who can't vote because they're under eighteen, they're an immigrant, or because they've had their voting rights stripped due to felony convictions in Alabama, Arizona, Delaware, Florida, Iowa, Kentucky, Maryland, Mississippi, Virginia, or Wyoming.

It's also a book for people who don't know who our local politicians are.

This book is a prayer that through all our efforts and little victories, we can create a world that makes sense.

Where to start?

Make a list right now of everyone you know who lives in swing states. Get your friends together, have everyone bring address books, and start brainstorming.

It's estimated that the average American adult knows around a thousand other people. Remember that guy you went to high school with who moved to Arizona?

Call them. Find them on the Internet. Dial the phone. Buy them this book. Tell them they need to read this book RIGHT AWAY or you can't be their friend anymore. Write them an email. Tell them the future of the world may depend on how many voters they can mobilize in their state over the next few months. Tell them they're gonna need to use every talent they have, every relationship.

That's what Piper, Adrienne, Annie, Jackie, Davey, Malia, Mattie, Aya, Bouapha, Marisol, Alma Rosa, and I are doing.

Each one of us had something special to add to the soup. Creating this book together in five months was kind of like a reality TV show. We all barely knew each other beforehand. And now look at us . . . mmmmm Tasty—except Lalo who's all by himself in L.A. with the Cucaracha aftertaste. When we started, none of us except Malia knew electoral politics. We had to learn fast. Now we're all touring the book, teaching our people to Smackdown the Liarman like a special edition of WWE.

Invite us to your college, organization, or house party. We will teach you our secret Professional Wrestling Techniques.

Then we won't have to wake up on the morning of November 3 and groan, *"If only I had known it was gonna be this close, I would have . . . "*

No. No. No. Instead we can wake up on the morning of November 3 and feel joyful. We can curl up under the covers with a big smile.

"We did it. We did it. WE DID IT!!!"

Hmm, what should we do next?

It's with great pleasure that I introduce Adrienne Brown, my friend, co-editor, and the person who I'm going to dance in the streets with when Stupid White Boys get kicked to the curb . . . Ladies, Gentleman, and Trannies, please welcome Ms. Adrienne Brown.


# I Hate Politics
## Confessions of a Pleasure Activist
### by Adrienne Maree Brown

Everything I know about electoral politics I know from working on this book.

I've only voted once, and my one vote was for . . . Ralph Nader. I know, I know. But I was living in a really polluted part of New York and the idea of anything green seemed intensely appealing.

And if it makes you feel better, I immediately felt guilty because the media convinced me I had voted for "President" Bush.

I tried to make amends by voting locally two years later, but I had injured my knee and when I got to the polling place in my neighborhood they told me I had to go up the block like two miles to vote in my district. I hobbled home instead, grumbling about how people should be able to vote whenever and wherever they want.

Four years later, I've learned that my Green vote in New York was all good cuz New York isn't a swing state. I've learned what a swing state is. I've learned that Gore's loss was more a lesson in election stealing than third–party challenges. I've learned what Billy was telling y'all about how if more people had voted, the election would have been unstealable.

I've also learned that those of us who hobbled home when the voting machine didn't work for us played right into the hands of the Right. Everyone foiled by the electoral system in 2000 and 2002 contributed to a radical Right takeover of Congress, giving near total power to the biggest bullies of them all, George W. Bush and the Oilspillers (repping Old Money Millionaires, ya heard?).

Four years later, I wake up some mornings and it literally feels like Brown vs. Bush. Why?

Plain and simple: this administration has gotten all up in my face by getting all up in my bank account—and yours, y'all—on some old deficit wackness. These knuckleheads are taking our paychecks and retirement plans and using the cash to blow up people, lock up people, and completely destroy the planet!

I'm kinda pissed about it.

© 2003, Abe Menor

Our nation is in a right-wing nosedive. And please don't get me wrong: I don't want to spin us into a left-wing nosedive—I just want a new balance.

I'm not talking about a sneaker y'all.

(Is that too corny? My bad.)

But you might ask, just who is this novice hot mama politico trying to balance the decks?

Well, you've never heard of me, so it's cool to ask that—once.

I am the Virgo first–child of a black army officer born and raised in poverty and a white nurse-homemaker raised in comfort, both rooted in the deep plantation South. I am the seed blown far from the tree, through Texas, Georgia, Kansas, Germany, and New York. I was raised in a very loving household, but like all kids I stepped into the real world and was immediately besieged by insecurity, boredom, violence, drugs, sex, and media.

I grew up to be a harm reduction youth activist, working to ensure that people who have sex or use drugs, legal and illegal, are seen as people first, and know how to do these things safely. Rather than just working towards abstinence (a mere 15 percent of the population over sixteen is abstinent from either sex or drugs), we teach folks to reduce the harm that the other 85 percent of people do to themselves and others—thus the term harm reduction.

Some people think I've spent the last several years of my life working on raising awareness about HIV/AIDS, destigmatizing drug use, and ending overdose, but really it's all about breaking down barriers to pleasure.

So I'm a pleasure activist. There, I've said it.

In fact, I'm really not about politics at all. I'm about life.

To me elections, are only important insomuch as they determine how we live our lives. Really, I just want folks to get along so we can all survive and, dare I say, enjoy this whole experience. You can usually catch me on the block with olive branches and doves in my book–bag, trying to find anyone willing to make a truce with me.

I want to live in peace. I surround myself with peaceful people.

The thing I've realized is that peace is a result of good decisions in every realm of life. We must have the power to make those good decisions, or to choose people we trust to make those decisions for us. Right now, that power is withheld from us at every level: how our taxes are spent, where we go to school, what jobs are available to us, if we are watched or not, if we will make money or not—if we will feel free or not.

And so the plot thickens. To achieve peace, we who abhor fighting must gain power.

Now, I don't know about you, but I don't really want a lot of power. I would just like to have power over my own life.

And I know exactly how I want my power: I want it to be simple. I want to have power with integrity and soul. I want my friends and family to have power too. I want my power to be practical and sustainable. I want to be able to share power with everyone I meet.

And not to understate my intentions: it's true, I want a revolution, I do, and I ain't too proud to beg! But I think we can pull off a power-shifting revolution without begging, without violence, and without the chaos traditionally associated with revolution.

We outside of the Right Power Stranglehold have not yet given electoral power a try. If we all come together and vote as a collective with a clear idea of what we need, that would be akin to a revolution: an electoral revolution.

Being a pleasure activist, my first instinct is to slip my hand up your thigh and whisper suggestive voting strategies in your ear. Instead, I have decided, like many of the people in this book and many more in the League of Pissed Off Voters, to dedicate the next year of my life to electoral politics. It's so West Wing.

And I have a vision!

No, no, no—wait, I'm not crazy!

Hear me out.

When I first heard about this book I thought, "But they aren't stupid! If we come like that then we're just underestimating them and engaging in more fighting and ultimately more losing." But the thing is that the folks in power right now aren't duh-stupid, they are emotionally stupid: immature and vacuous. There's nothing more dangerous than a brilliant strategic mind with no heart. It's clear that these folks care about their bank accounts more than their kids and their grandkids, and *definitely* more than your kids or grandkids.

We need to oust the idiotocracy.

But who's left once you clear out the Stupid White Men? The options after folk who are specifically stupid *and* white *and* men are generally people who are either stupid *or* white *or* men.

We can't go tossing smart women of color into every position of power— just me. Joke alert. But seriously, we have to have a method by which we figure out who really represents us. This means we not only have to understand what we are against, we need to understand what we are *for*.

The radical Right are for using finance and fiction to keep us distracted while they tie our ankles and wrists with the shackles of the present: the Patriot Act, the unending war, manipulative foreign policies, and classist domestic ones.

Meanwhile, the grassroots Left is for pouting in the corner in a grass-stained dress, lollipop sullied by dirt, balloon deflated, occasionally sticking out its tongue. I feel like the song "Holding Out for a Hero" should be looped behind the left movement to make their apparent mission a bit more clear.

And then there's us: All these young, pissed–off voters and nonvoters who are tired of having *Boondocks* be the only touch of reality in the paper.

But what are we for?

I present to you: the Vision.

We believe in creating social support to strengthen families.

We believe in fostering a spirit of shared responsibility and community.

We believe in bringing all voices into the public dialogue.

We believe in protecting our right to privacy and our freedom of choice.

We believe in making real opportunities available to all.

We believe in using government to invest in the public good.

We believe in being respected and respectful citizens of the world.

We believe in thinking about sustainability, family, human relations, and history when making decisions.

We believe we have a right to have a vision for this country. Contrary to what conservatives have been telling us—that criticizing America in any way is unpatriotic—it is actually the very point of democracy to hold government accountable to the people.

Especially our government. The decisions our administration makes have an effect on every corner of the world. We have taken on the unwieldy international role of determining who will be safe, who will have resources, and who will live in peace. It's too much power for any single government.

Fortunately, most of us are already doing the important work of criticizing our government and calling out to our community, the progressive nation, to think before we act.

The next logical step is to start choosing the actors, rather than working with whoever happens to end up in power, or worse—the current reality—trying to work with folks who have already completely disrespected the concept of representative democracy in order to get to power.

It's no small task, but our generation has one charge: save the world for the next generation.

We—the authors of this book and the organizers of the League—are all making one promise: to bring the electoral revolution to you wherever you are. We'll bring it with this book, our brunch programs, voter blocs, progressive voter guides, parties, our amazing online network, or whatever it takes that we haven't thought of yet to make sure you know how to do just that.

All you have to do is pick the book up, or go to the party, or check out the website. If you take the step of getting on the path towards electoral power, we will point you in the right direction and give you the tools you need to create a world you want to live in.

These tools have been tested by the young people who are telling these stories, none of whom are prophets or superheroes or Einsteins. They are folks just like you who want to change the game.

Now *How to Get Stupid White Men Out of Office* is not a manual for changing the world. Rather, it's example after easy-to-follow example of how individuals have changed their worlds. From it, you will immediately be able to start changing yours.

I'm a big believer that this right here is the only moment we have, so it's imperative to go ahead and live in it. Don't forget, there's still love, devotion, flowers, babies, puppies, sex, and hope to cling to. Earth rocks and people are dope. We gots to get power so that we can focus on relaxing and enjoying reality.

In writing this book, I've gone from being the hobbling nonvoter to the empowered voter organizer.

I am moving towards power. You should too. I want you right by my side.

We, the millions voting on whether or not Bush gets to keep his stolen goods—the job, the house, the bomber jacket—cannot be afraid to flex our strength. We have to channel our ancestors who died for the right to vote, and at least this very crucial once, we must VOTE.

We can do this. If we can't, then no one can; we are young America, the inheritors of the fortune and flaws our parents have created. This book is the first step, an in-depth introduction to the new guard of electoral politics and a proposal for weaving civic power into the cloth of our daily lives.

I speak on behalf of every nonwhite, nonmale, nonwealthy world citizen when I say we cannot afford to opt out.

This electoral revolution requires the smallest, slightest commitment from you—you have to care.

Remember this: the world is always on the brink of change. We always have the power and the knowledge to impact the situation around us, at least to some small degree. Like many of you, I have long held the belief that we can be like Gandhi, Che, Malcolm, King, Dylan, Nina, Angela—be the change we wish to see in the world by any means possible and all that.

But here's the real secret: it's the normal people who make change possible. It's you and me. And now we know how.

## *Political Sex Survey* — ADRIENNE MAREE BROWN

*My first memorable experience with electoral politics:*

Let's see—we were doing mock elections in school, it was 1988 and I guess I was ten. The choice was two strangers named Dukakis and Bush. I had a major *major* crush on this guy, I really think his name was Kai something. I was constantly trying to figure out how to get his attention. The thing is, he was super dorky, much dorkier than me—protractors and sharpened pencils and his hair combed just so and a button-up. Delightfully dorky. I succeeded—he wrote me a note that he liked me. *Woo-hoo.*

So we get told a little bit about the candidates and a little bit about what Republican means, what Democrat means. I, being an argumentative kid, immediately decide Bush sucks and Dukakis is boring and ask about other options, including writing myself in. I'm told that the other option was something called "independence," but they never win.

I decide, of the choices, that I'm voting for Dukakis. We're standing in line and I, trying to flirt through my big bangs, ask Kai who he's voting for.

Bush.

Bush? (I have a ten year old identity crisis.)

Why would you vote for Bush, Kai?

Well, he's very rich.

That's what important to you, Kai? (Inner monologue something like: is that how you want to raise our kids, Kai?)

Stability is very important to me.

Well I am voting for Dukakis, I personally think Bush sucks.

Oh yeah? Well Dukakis is boring. If you like him then I think you suck.

Oh. Really? Well then I don't think you need to be my boyfriend Kai!!

That's right—Kai straight *dissed* me for my mock Dukakis vote. I tried to backtrack, explain that I really didn't like him either, but it was too late. It was at that point that I decided political parties were for losers and I would join the "independence."

*Favorite thing about George Bush:*
Oh definitely my favorite thing about Bush: he was a college cokehead turned middle-aged alcoholic Yalie frat–boy who has raised two young alkies and has a pill-popping niece but, with no smirk of irony, he was down with denying federal funding to young people with a drug use history. Shame cannot catch up with him, he's so damn fast!

*Favorite Republican dirty trick:*
I think it has to be their skill at reclaiming language. Somehow the words family, God, patriotic, nation—all of those now belong to the right, where they were once everyone's words.

*What actor or public person would you like to see smackdown Ah-nold?*
Huey from the *Boondocks*. I think he could do it with historical style and a child's simple grace, meet Ah-nold on his level.

*What candidate would be best in bed?*
Ooh, naughty. My instinct is to go with Sharpton 'cause he overdoes everything which can be quite pleasant, or with Kucinich 'cause he has that gentle, determined approach. I think he'd be in for the long haul. But my final answer has to be a ten-person orgy with me, the voter, in the center, taking the best of each candidate for a thrilling long night. Ladies first: oh Carol, Moseley my Braun.

*How do you convince your Republican Uncle not to vote for Bush?*
My downstairs neighbor is a Republican. I think the best way to deal with Republicans is first and foremost to not think of them as Republicans. That party mumbo-jumbo is divisive. I love my neighbor, he's a total

sweetheart of a guy. We sit down and talk about all kinds of stuff. Our last conversation was about safe injection sites and legalizing drug use. We used common terms—like for legalizing drugs we were talking about government control of access to substances. For safer injection sites we were really talking about monitored drug use, so that users weren't out on the street endangering themselves and others. We felt the same way on it, even though we were using different terms. The Republican view and the Democratic view on those topics are probably polar opposites, but two people talking in terms of common sense can usually find a common ground.

*A slept-on group of voters you'd like to see organized?*
Progressive Republicans. Drug users. 50 Cent listeners. Prisoners. A lot of people don't know which states ex-felons can actually vote in. My girl Dani is organizing around this in Cincinnati.

*How do we get a progressive majority? How long will it take?*
We have a progressive majority. We need to get instant runoff voting in this country, so that progressives can support third–parties without giving their vote to the Right.

*A young person I know who should run for office?*
It's a tie: Sofia Santana or Janine de Novais—the two smartest political women I know. Thinking logically about every aspect of the world comes naturally to them, and the number one reason they should both run is that neither of them would ever think to do so, neither of them hungers for the power, they're just brilliant.

*Future trends to watch out for:*
Republicans trying to rap.

# How We Got Our People Into Office

*"And so we shall heave to do more than register and we shall have to do more than vote; we shall have to create leaders who embody virtues we can respect, who have moral and ethical principles we can applaud with enthusiasm."*
— Martin Luther King Jr., 1967

# The Hip-Hop Generation's Deputy Mayor

## From Rallying Outside Newark's City Hall to Governing Inside

By Yahonnes Cleary

 I knew hardly anything about Ras Baraka when I was asked to write this chapter. The first thing I heard about Ras (pronounced like *jazz*) is that he speaks in quotes. Some of my favorites are from a campaign speech during his third attempt at elected office. Referring to his youth-driven campaign, Ras preached to his mostly adult audience:

(Our future begins now. It's the hip–hop generation's time. Don't get upset. Be a part of it! . . .) You should be happy that your kids want to hang around us. Cause if we don't organize them, the streets are gonna organize 'em. If we don't get 'em, drugs gon' get 'em. If we don't get 'em, the cops gon' get 'em, the jails gon' get 'em, the statistics gon' get 'em . . . Hell, you wanna get your kids out the gangs? Send them to Bergen and West Market! You don't need to call the police, just call us! We ain't afraid to come on the block! We from the block. We ain't afraid, we ain't afraid.

The father of three daughters, Ras is deeply committed to nurturing youth. He has spent the past ten years organizing, teaching, and coaching basketball at public schools in Newark, his hometown.

The son of poet-activists, Amiri and Amina Baraka, Ras also has close ties to the hip–hop and spoken word communities. It is his voice that introduces the Fugees' sophomore album, *The Score*. He is the teacher on Lauryn Hill's album who asks students about love. He co-edited *In the Tradition: An Anthology of Young Black Writers* with Kevin Powell (1992), and released a spoken word album, *Shorty for Mayor* (1998). He also recently appeared on HBO's Def Poetry Jam where he recited his "American Poem," a passionate people's history–style plea for more stories that are told from the perspective of unheard and unrepresented Americans:

I wanna hear an American poem, an American poem about sharecroppers on the side of the road or families in cardboard boxes, not about kings or majestic lands or how beautiful ugly can be. I wanna hear some American poetry about projects and lead poison, poverty and children in jail . . . I just want to hear an American poem, something native like the Trail of Tears, Wounded Knee, or small pox in blankets. You know, American, something that represents us: a colorful rainbow, a big black fist, an uncorrected sentence, improper English. As American as COINTELPRO . . .

Ras's roots in hip-hop have led many writers such as Bakari Kitwana and Davey D to cite him as evidence that hip-hop's massive following combined with its inherent political messages can be used to advance a progressive agenda in the mainstream political realm.

Ras has run for office in Newark three times since 1994. Two years after graduating from Howard University, he ran and lost against Newark's current mayor, Sharpe James. Ras also ran for council member at large in 1998 and again in 2002. He won the 1998 general election, but lost in a run-off. He lost again in 2002 by 114 votes. Despite these losses, Ras has built increased credibility and support among Newark residents. His commitment and backing, particularly among youth and low-income voters, led his former opponent Mayor James, now in his fifth term, to appoint Ras deputy mayor for youth and community development.

It's not hard to understand why he's so relentless if you ever heard him on the campaign trail in 2002. "That's what the election is about, it's about seizing power," Ras proclaimed

> the power to give money to a school system or take it away; the power to allow kids to have a recreation center in their neighborhood or not; the power to put police on the street; the power to give us a civilian police review board; the power to control the police; the power to build these buildings and to take away these buildings; the power to say, No more projects! Decent housing for people! That's power— giving jobs and contracts to people in your neighborhood, to your mothers and fathers, to get your kids off the corner. It's about seizing and taking power.

## Shorty for Mayor

Ras's first run for mayor grew out of the organizing work he did at Howard and later in the Newark community. The organization that he founded, Nia Freedom Organization for Racial and Cultural Enlightenment (FORCE) challenged political apathy on campus. The organization was originally conceived as a nationalist, militant organization in the tradition of the Nation of Islam and the Black Panther Party.

In addition to campus activism, Nia FORCE organized food and clothing drives in the local community, and Black history classes for local youth. On campus it's most well-known victory was in 1989, when Nia FORCE members led the student protest that resulted in the resignation of Lee Atwater, Chairman of the Republican National Committee, from Howard's Board of Trustees. A year later, Ras ran for and won his first political office—vice-president of the student government.

After graduation, Ras helped establish Nia FORCE chapters in Harlem and Newark. The Newark chapter continues to do community service and political education targeted especially at Newark's youth. Concerned about an increasing gang presence, Nia FORCE organized Newark's first gang summit. They gathered representatives from Black political organizations together-with local gang members to discuss the social problems that lead youth to join gangs. They encouraged political activism as an alternative response to these problems.

Soon after beginning their work in Newark, Nia Force realized that rallies, protests, and other strategies that characterized their student activism were not adequate for genuinely addressing their concerns in Newark. "We came to the decision that instead of complaining to these politicians over and over again, we needed to do something else in addition to just protesting and going down to city hall," said Trevor Phillips, a Nia FORCE member since 1993. "And that we can't really as organizers say that we're trying to lead the community but are afraid to step up and officially lead the community."

In other words, elected officials would never take Nia FORCE's concerns seriously unless they were directly challenged. Sharpe James, who has been Newark's mayor since 1986 and was city council member for sixteen years prior, had run unopposed in the 1990 election, so Nia FORCE decided to run a candidate against him in 1994. Ras was the natural choice.

With little experience or familiarity with electoral politics, Nia FORCE organized a mostly young, entirely volunteer staff to support Ras's bid for office. The campaign attracted hundreds of, mainly youth, volunteers from Newark, as well as friends and supporters from across the country. In January 1994, they began collecting the thousand signatures they needed to put Ras on the ballot, allowing themselves fewer than four months to campaign for the May election. They also tried to raise money, ultimately collecting ten thousand dollars, including a thousand-dollar donation from Ras's grandmother.

Meanwhile, Sharpe James had raised over a million dollars.

Nia FORCE spent evenings and weekends going door-to-door to distribute campaign literature, organizing rallies and driving through the streets with a bullhorn. Of the four candidates running for mayor that year, Ras placed third.

Although passionate and energetic, the 1994 campaign was too inexperienced and financially strapped to displace Mayor James. "Our strategy was to win," Ras says now. "We didn't focus on who would vote for me, why would they vote for me, how do we attract new voters. We didn't cultivate our message. We didn't do anything. We thought people would vote for us because we were right, because we were right and they were wrong. In fairyland, that would be the right thing to happen. But in the real world it doesn't have anything to do with right and wrong, especially in politics."

## Shorty for Deputy Mayor

After the election, Nia FORCE's membership continued to grow as many of the campaign volunteers enrolled. The organization also continued its community organizing and direct service work. They learned that the community service work in particular expanded their constituency for future campaigns.

As Phillips puts it, "The feeding and clothing drives, the Freedom Schools and the Liberation schools, those are things we did in order to give us access to and gain familiarity with the regular working class people. I wish we could have did some more. We should have had a basketball team . . . It took Nia FORCE a little too long to understand the need of basic material programs in order to win people over."

Reflecting on the first campaign, Ras is critical of the organization's failure to organize and mobilize voters through existing organizations in the communities that they targeted. He says now: "We didn't go to tenant association meetings . . . senior citizen cook outs, PTA meetings, or block association meetings or any of those things that working people attend, that they're a part of, that they're concerned about. We go to work and we go to the free Mumia rally . . . And most of the people who we're trying to win over, a lot of them don't even know about Mumia."

In 1998, rather than run again for mayor, Ras ran for one of four council member-at-large positions. Ras and his campaign supporters applied earlier lessons to this second, more successful, campaign.

First, they were much more strategic about targeting voters. Rather than use the phone book to contact potential voters, they used a list of registered voters and targeted those who had previously voted for Ras. The 1998 campaign also placed much more emphasis on mobilizing voters through existing local organizations and structures such as tenant associations and local district leaders. They especially targeted the city's well-organized elderly population.

The campaign focused more on fundraising this time around, raising a total of thirty-five thousand, which they again used mainly for campaign literature and publicity. They also campaigned and raised money through "coffee klatches"—meetings organized by local residents at their homes to introduce their neighbors to candidates. This larger financial base allowed Nia FORCE to publicize their campaign more widely and to pay small salaries to some of their campaign staff.

The new approach paid off. Ras placed fourth in the general election, well enough to win one of the four councilmember-at-large seats. That night, Ras and his campaign staff celebrated in the streets—literally. To their dismay, they were told hours later that there would be a run-off. None of the candidates won a majority of the votes. Nobody on the campaign staff knew about the run-off rule, and they did not have the money for additional campaigning.

Ras received an offer to join a ticket with two of the other winning candidates who also had the backing of an influential local union. Ras rejected them on ideological grounds, so they invited the candidate who placed fifth, Bessie Walker. In the runoff, Walker placed fourth and Ras placed fifth.

Ras now regrets not joining the ticket: "I was really hesitant about that because . . . I didn't like these people and so forth and so on, which I think was a little immature politically . . . Some of them people on the same ticket get into the council and fight each other like cats and dogs. It's not even about that, it's about the strategy in terms of winning . . . If in '98, I got on the ticket with Gail Chaneyfield, and Luis Quintana and Local 617, I would have been the councilperson–at–large in the city of Newark."

The next time he ran for council in 2002, Ras aligned with Hector Corchado who helped increase Ras's support among Latinos. With ten years of experience, Ras and Nia FORCE had a sharper strategy. They door-knocked and canvassed most heavily in districts where Ras had done well before. In districts where support was weaker, they relied more on phone calls and mailings. They also continued to organize through local organizations, particularly those representing senior citizens.

Ras's campaign began to look more like a mainstream political campaign. He started earlier than he had in the past, about a year before the election. The campaign acquired a larger, more central headquarters. They developed a condensed platform that placed greater emphasis on economic development. They also came up with the slogan "Take It Personal"—encouraging voters to take what the government does to them as a personal affront.

Ras changed too. As David Muhammad, the manager of Ras's third campaign, remembers, "In 1994, Baraka campaigned in his jeans and Timberlands and a cap. In 1998 he mixed it up a bit. But in 2002, he was suited down." Or as Rahman Muhammad, a local union president, put it, "In later campaigns he got more conservative about his dress and actually looked like a candidate."

The campaign also raised much more money in 2002—about ninety thousand dollars—with the help of celebrity supporters such as Danny Glover, Lauryn Hill, Al Sharpton, Pharoah Sanders, and Russell Simmons. The bulk was raised, however, through small fundraisers and individual donations. This larger financial base allowed the campaign to buy more TV ads and send out a thirty thousand–piece mailing. But like previous campaigns, the 2002 campaign was volunteer-driven, built around face-to-face contact with voters.

In the end, 30 percent of voters gave one of their four votes to Ras in the general election. In the run-off, 40 percent did. He finished fifth in a field of ten. Although he didn't win a seat, it was clear that Ras commanded a great deal of support among Newark's voters, particularly those in the predominantly Black South Ward, where Ras got the third highest number of votes.

Mayor Sharpe James was well aware of Ras's widespread support and, being the seasoned politician that he is, asked Ras to endorse him during the 2002 campaign even though he could not officially endorse Ras in return. As mayor, he had to endorse incumbents but couldn't afford to lose Ras's endorsement to challenger Corey Booker. The desire to have Ras on his side is also what led Sharpe James to offer Ras a position as deputy mayor for youth and community development in his new administration.

Ras has no illusions about why James offered the position. "The people in the city thought I should've won . . . They knew we fought hard, we struggled hard. Our campaign was clean. What we were saying was right. People thought that I was obviously a better candidate. And I think Sharpe felt that in order to save face he had to offer me something. Plus, how the momentum was going, we could've got with the other side. And I think that's what he was concerned about, even to this day."

Regardless of Mayor James's intentions, Ras accepted the position (he says he would've refused without hesitation in 1994). As deputy mayor, his main job is to represent the city at meetings and events that the mayor cannot attend, and he often acts as an advocate for the city's residents. In addition, Ras has initiated a gang peace summit and youth development programming, including the establishment of a youth congress that will integrate youth into city government. He also retains his positions as vice principal and coach of the men's varsity basketball team at Weequahic High School.

Ras has no regrets about accepting the cabinet position, despite criticism from some that he sold-out by joining the administration of his former opponent: "People in the community, they are very grateful and very thankful that we took this job. People are happy they get calls back, that we show up at meetings and talk to people. Ask the people at 515 Elizabeth Avenue, where we're trying to get rid of this landlord for them, if they would've been happy if we didn't take the job out of some political theoretical stuff that really makes no difference."

Relentless as ever, Ras is already planning his next run. Whatever he runs for in 2006, he will campaign differently. He will most likely join a ticket with other candidates. The campaign will make contact with committed supporters earlier and then reconnect with them in the weeks before the election. They will devote more time and energy to registering new voters since those voters are most likely to support the campaign that registers them. They also hope to hire a full-time fundraiser to raise enough to have more paid staff and more effectively publicize the campaign. Even though the election is not until 2006, Ras held his first fundraiser back in October 2003. He's serious about seizing power.

Or, as Ras put it recently, "You're not running for office 'cause you just wanna have a debate about some theoretical thing. You're trying to decide who works and who doesn't . . . . You're deciding: Do we build housing or do we build recreation? Do we spend $300 million for an arena or do we put that into the school system? You decide: Are more black people going to be working on these construction sites? Do we put $1.6 billion into the school construction budget? Who builds those schools? Where does that money go, where does it stay? Who's going to be empowered by that $1.6 billion? Or does $1.6 billion come into the city and people build it who don't live here, who don't look like us and leave and we don't get none of it?"

Ras is looking forward to others seizing political power to represent the hip-hop generation: ("Our future begins now. It's the hip–hop generation's time. Don't get upset, be a part of it.")

[Editors note: Tragedy struck the Baraka family right before the interviews for this story were about to begin. Ras's sister Shani was murdered by a jealous male who was mad that she was in a relationship with a woman. The Baraka family has been devastated and they've been speaking out passionately about violence against women and the LGBT community folks. We honor their bravery and our hearts mourn their loss. Hang in there, Ras. We need you now more than ever.]

# The Tammy Baldwin Story

## By Adam Klaus

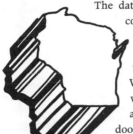 The date is Tuesday, November 3, 1998. Outside it is cold, one of the first nights where the refreshing cool of fall has yielded to the less-friendly bite of winter. Inside the campaign office, perspiration might as well be dripping from the walls. We are at the point of exhaustion where the world just keeps going out of habit, but I desperately want to run out and knock on one more door or pick up the phone and make one last call. But, in the game of absolutes that elections are, it is too late. The polls have closed.

The electricity builds as the results roll in, the percentages teetering forward as we watch in suspended disbelief, like the first ride on a two-wheeler when the fall is imminent but somehow never comes. We on the Left live with such an underdog mentality that we are always waiting for the catch; things that are good are always too good to be true.

The tension mounts until someone finally realizes that we've passed the point of no return. Whoops of excitement echo. Hugs are exchanged. And then a murmur spreads from the front of the crowd and a cheer erupts alongside the whispers of *she's here, she's here.* Tammy Baldwin—excuse me—Congresswoman Tammy Baldwin's head rises above the sardined bodies, and we see the beaming face of the woman we've made our passion for the past several months. She waits for the euphoria to boil down, and then seals the deal with three words: *We did it!*

My vision immediately blurs behind the tears, and I lean into my boyfriend for support. They are tears of relief, certainly, and tears of joy. But more important, the emotion springs from a simple language choice in the way Tammy declared victory: *We* did it. Settling into that room, I felt connected and uplifted in a way that I never had before, and the current of that empowerment stirred everyone who was there.

*We* had made history by electing Wisconsin's first female, and the nation's first openly gay, nonincumbent to the U.S. House of Representatives. We had elected a true progressive who would fight for real people's interests, especially those whose voices are often not heard in the political arena. Perhaps most importantly, *we* had created something greater than ourselves. This wasn't just an incredible candidate; it was a movement.

Let's step back for a second and look at who *we* were. On one level it was the 116,377 who cast Baldwin ballots in the election. More remarkably, it was the three thousand volunteers who for months had stuffed envelopes; walked through neighborhoods and knocked on doors in all kinds of weather; braved the wrath incurred by dinnertime phone calls to voters; baked cookies for other volunteers; raised money from friends; and stood on street corners and in highway ditches with the signature red and black Tammy signs.

To top it off, a full seventeen hundred of those volunteers were college students, mostly from the University of Wisconsin-Madison, who had organized a campaign that drove turnout numbers to 55 percent and created a landslide of 70.1 percent for Tammy in the six wards surrounding campus. Local columnist John Nichols aptly dubbed the phenomenon a "youthquake."

But is it such a surprise we got here? This is Madison, Wisconsin, right? Isn't it the unofficial tofu capital of the Midwest? Progressive miracles must happen here every day. Electing progressive lesbians is a matter of course. Routine. Old news. They're a dime a dozen.

Many publications—from *Girlfriends* to *Money* magazine—regularly rank it as one of the top places to live in the country. And against the—I'll put this nicely—"rigid" backdrop of my own hometown an hour outside of the city, the images of Vietnam War protests and all manner of march, rally, and demonstration cast our capital city in a decidedly exotic light.

Such reputations, however, are prone to exaggeration, both by the people who would like to demonize the city as a cesspit of sin, and those who cling to it as their utopia. Alongside its share of progressive activists of all ilks, the Univerity of Wisconsin also attracts many traditionally minded students. Like most large state colleges, football and frat parties are extremely popular activities. Indeed, it would be difficult to characterize a "typical" UW student.

Wisconsin's Second Congressional District, of which Madison is only a part, is also very diverse politically. Its population is divided into even thirds among rural, suburban, and urban voters. On the whole, the district breaks down into approximately 40 percent Democrats, 40 percent Republicans, and a significant 20 percent undecided or "swing" voters. It's a precarious place: definitely not a shoo-in for any candidate.

For thirty-two years, Congressman Robert Kastenmeier represented the second district in Washington. By the end of his career, he was the second-ranking member of the House Judiciary Committee. His support for civil rights, and strong opposition to the Vietnam War and Reagan's interventionist policies in Central America, earned him impressive progressive credentials.

Capitalizing on the ultimate free media publicity, Madison television news anchor Scott Klug staged a surprise upset of Kastenmeier, turning the district over to Republican hands. After eight years, he announced his intention not to seek reelection, and Tammy, among others, jumped in to the race for the district's first open seat in forty years.

Here's the official line: Tammy Baldwin isn't someone who is separate from the unique community that surrounds the UW-Madison campus. In fact, she's grown up with it. Raised on the city's near west side, hardly a stone's throw from the campus borders, she was already a leader in the student government at West High School (although she has to admit that the race for class president is the only one she has ever lost).

After attending Smith College in Massachusetts, Tammy returned to Madison for law school, and there became active in local politics, eventually becoming one of the first students to represent the campus area on the Dane County Board of Supervisors. After six years of very respected work on the county board, she launched a successful bid to represent the downtown Madison area, including the campus, in the Wisconsin State Assembly. Throughout her political career, she has been a continual champion of student issues, whether working to keep tuition down and financial aid up, committing resources to fight violence against women, or protecting students' right to have control over their student fees.

This is all fine and dandy, but great politicians lose elections all the time. Tammy has something else going for her. Julie Eisenhardt, a student volunteer from early in the 1998 campaign, describes it succinctly: "Tammy wasn't just a politician in the newspaper. She was the person who we would have a drink with at the Sunday night drag show at the bar." That is it. Besides being great on the issues, she is tied very closely into specific constituencies and communities. Continues Eisenhardt, "So when she announced her decision to run, we thought, 'That's our friend!' and we were ready to help from the start."

Tammy's relationship with her student constituents is particularly important because with forty thousand students, UW-Madison composes about 10 percent of the eligible voters in the district. She hardly had to ask. Because of her history of support for campus-based struggles, leaders of some of the most active student organizations, from the Ten Percent Society (the Lesbian Gay Bisexual Transgender group) to the Black Student Union, were in the ring from the beginning.

Says Eric Brakken, then chair of the Associated Students of Madison, the student government, "Everyone that I knew, that I trusted politically on campus, either had the same kind of chemistry or trust in her, or directly worked for her. She really permeated into the natural leadership networks among the student community and, whether by design or by accident, had a lot of key people and a lot of trust."

When Tammy entered the race in 1998, "her progressive credentials were pretty much unchallenged," Brakken says. Her platform included many items that resonated with students, including increasing Pell Grant funding; passing the Violence Against Women Act and setting aside more money for campus safety programs; defending civil rights; and working for health care for all.

There's a rare reciprocity between Tammy and her student constituents. Lobbying sessions are less about persuasion than strategy sessions, where Tammy enlists the help of her students to do the organizing to meet their common goals. To illustrate this relationship, in the 2000 race, the student campaign designed a logo in the form of a loop that read "Students for Tammy Baldwin for Students" and so forth—a moebius strip of mutual support. It's probably a chicken-or-egg game to ask who started it, but the simple fact is Tammy comes through on student issues time and again, and students continue to have her back at the voting booth.

Competing for the attention of a college student is a daunting task. It's difficult to imagine how any political candidate can pierce the muddle of exam and paper deadlines, too much pot, cafeteria food that has led to an interesting new relationship with the gastrointestinal tract, lost sleep due to the roommate's snoring problem, headaches brought on by tedious discussions of stoicism in Philosophy 101, and, if I didn't mention it, too much pot.

And that's if you can even get to the students in the first place. I still break out in a cold sweat thinking about the evil smiles of dorm desk clerks who twirl their key rings and fetishize their prerogative as gatekeeper to bar all access to prohibited political solicitations. I was with Tammy once when a resident advisor guarding her flock against our proselytizations swiftly and promptly escorted us from the building, doing all she could to keep from drop-kicking us and shaking her fist, calling, "And don't come back!"

MADISON

VICTORY: COLLEGE KIDS ELECT FIRST OUT LESBIAN TO CONGRESS

Organizing students in a successful campaign takes an aggressive strategy. The campaign saturated the campus with pro-Tammy material—making it into a virtual Tammyland—to reach every student multiple times with Tammy's message. The campaign also hired a full-time staff person to manage the huge volunteer network.

"I arrived in Madison to work on the campaign three weeks before the 1998 primary," said E. B. Nesbitt, former campus coordinator for the campaign. "I had my work cut out for me. I spent days on campus with a clipboard, begging students to get involved, to volunteer, to become dorm captains, whatever. We took Tammy to the dorms to help students move their furniture in. We went to football games. We went chalking. Tammy loved that. The students felt comfortable around her. And by the time the primary happened we had a decent-sized student crew."

The main strategy was to organize the residence halls. Because university policy prohibited outside solicitors, including candidates or their agents, in the dorms, Students for Tammy Baldwin (SFTB) recruited building captains for each dorm. This group would then be in charge of recruiting house captains for their respective units who would take charge of the people they lived with and spread the good word about Tammy.

"I was living in the dorms my first year," recalls Becky Wasserman. "I remember seeing Tammy stuff everywhere and I remember feeling like students had this big role in her campaign and were making decisions in it. And that elections could be exciting, which I didn't necessarily think before. It got folks talking to each other in a different way. I got involved in my dorm with my dorm captain. I didn't have some big role, but I was treated like I did. At the time I didn't realize that this was happening all over campus, on every floor of every dorm. I felt special. I was taken seriously as an organizer."

This strategy worked in two ways. First, while outsiders cannot campaign in the dorms, there was no rule against talking to your friends and floor mates about politics. Secondly, it built trust with voters, because word about Tammy spread between students who already knew and interacted with one another.

SFTB adopted a similar strategy to reach students in off-campus areas. We hearkened back to the days of the real grassroots political machines and recruited ward captains to be responsible for their respective voting districts. They were in charge of doing several rounds of door-knocking, dropping off literature, identifying supportive voters, and getting out the vote on election day. The elected city council and county board members who represented these wards were the first to jump at the chance to volunteer, because it gave them a chance to help Tammy and to meet their own constituents face-to-face.

Just when we thought we couldn't organize people any more thoroughly, all chaos broke out. ChaOS coordinators, that is. Developed by E. B. Nesbitt, the ChaOS plan, which stood for Changing Our State, was to give each and every student who walked into the campaign office a way to volunteer immediately. Quite simply, rather than being in charge of a dorm floor or a block, they would be responsible for getting their group of friends and acquaintances to vote for Tammy. Each ChaOS coordinator received a tracking form with twenty lines to fill, at which point the form was returned to the campaign and the names and numbers used for reminder calls on the days leading up to the election. In theory, it may sound a bit ridiculous, but in reality it produced a huge list of supporters.

Tammy spent a lot of time on campus—a major factor in garnering student support. We staged "Tammy Baldwin's Dance Party" at a local theater with local DJs. We provided fun for hundreds, as well as raising a substantial sum of money in small donations.

Tammy hit the mic for a karaoke rendition of "Girls Just Wanna Have Fun" at an Alpha Delta Phi party, thereby winning a bet that led to the brothers' unanimous support. For that party, we also created a flier that read, "In case you don't remember, you partied with Tammy Baldwin last night. Vote this Tuesday!" We tucked it into people's pockets as they stumbled home.

A huge frustration in the 2000 race was that the congresswoman was caught up in an extremely long session in Washington and couldn't make it back to the district until a scant five days before the election. Her opponent, a popular professor on campus, had all the time in the world to court the student vote, and Tammy's student support, though by no means dismal (she still won the campus area with 65 percent of the vote), was lower as a result. There is no substitute for a candidate who is willing, and able, to come to the voters.

The underlying point of all of these tactics was to build a list—the List—of the names and contact information of students who were Tammy supporters. That way, in the days leading up to the election, volunteers could contact these students on the phone and remind them to vote, and on election day itself, drag them to the polls if need be. All the enthusiasm in the world does nothing if nobody actually makes it to the polls. While the rival opponent in the 1998 primary was handing out stickers and wearing T-shirts, SFTB was talking to people, asking for their votes, and getting their names down on paper.

Free media was also important to the campaign. The two campus papers at UW-Madison have the fourth and fifth largest circulations in the district. While it has sometimes been difficult to get them to cover politics, articles like the one about Tammy chalking at midnight on campus with student volunteers (including a photo!) were very important in demonstrating her connections to the campus.

It worked. In the 1998 primary, only one week after classes started, Tammy narrowly beat her closest Democratic challenger by 1,507 votes. Her margin of victory in the campus area was 1,530 votes. Clearly, students had made the difference. The momentum only built until the general election when she bested former State Insurance Commissioner Josephine Musser by 13,600 votes, with a full 8,100 of those votes coming from the campus area.

When Tammy runs and students organize, as has happened in 1998, 2000, and 2002, there is high turnout and overwhelming student support. Because of our efforts, the residents of Wisconsin's Second District, as well as progressive people across the country, have a voice in Washington that stands up for the issues that matter—health care for all, funding for education, support of family farmers, LGBT rights, and social justice in general.

The impact of Tammy's election in 1998 was felt beyond her own race. Even Republican Governor Tommy Thompson publicly credited Tammy's effort for the narrow margin that re-elected Senator Russ Feingold.

Eric Brakken sums it up: "To be from a campus, from a community that put the first open, out lesbian in Congress, you felt like there was something that was precedent-setting in that campaign. Getting Tammy elected was more than getting just another progressive person in Congress, another Democrat in Congress, and taking that seat away from the Republicans. It felt like we were going into uncharted territory."

© 2003, Amy Woloszyn

# Sweatshops, Hip-Hop and A Whole Lot Of People For Grijalva

By Marisol Enyart

Politics has always been like the spawn of the devil for me. Or not the devil, but the spawn of something! You, know, just the spawn. Like don't touch it. Voting doesn't do crap for you. It's just gonna screw you. It's not how you get stuff done.

When I rolled down to Tuscon to write a story on the Grijalva campaign, I knew virtually nothing about it or electoral politics. I just recently found out this website Progressivepunch.org rated him as the "#1 Most Progressive" person in Congress.

I started doing interviews. Damn, the things people had to say and the stories people brought to me were just—shit, I don't want to be all corny, but it was inspiring. Especially because Tuscon is a lot like my hometown, Albuquerque. So, I don't know, something was just saying to me: Don't lose hope Marisol. Anything worth fighting for is never easy. But there are victories. That's what keeps your mouth wet.

The first person I met when I got to Tuscon was Maritza Broce, age twenty-nine. I didn't know where to go when I first got there so I just had my friend drop me off at the Democratic campaign office. A ton of people who worked on the Grijalva campaign decided to stay with electoral politics. So now they're working on getting other good people into office.

Maritza saw the Grijalva campaign as a place where her passion for politics would be put to good use. "When I moved to Tucson, I worked with an organization called the Coalición de Derechos Humanos. They have worked with Raùl for years, so I know him in the context of being a strong supporter for immigrant rights. When I was in the office I saw a lot of people that I knew and loved dearly."

The next person I talked to was eighteen–year–old Celeste Espinoza, which was really exciting cuz I knew her through my work with United Students Against Sweatshops, and we danced it up at a conference in Atlanta—adding a little Latin spice to the crowd. I called her up in Chicago where she lives, and she was extremely enthusiastic. I had a really hard time trying to get down everything she was saying. She was describing how Raùl is like a father to her. Everyone in the campaign, it was like this big family.

When Celeste walked into Raùl Grijalva's 2002 congressional campaign office for the first time, she was bombarded by "all these crazy signs reminding you to call back your volunteers, along with a general vibe of really actually caring about who was going to be put into office and the impact on our district." Celeste had just graduated from high school and wanted to work on social justice issues affecting her community.

The Grijalva campaign attracted volunteers from a wide range of ages, interests, and backgrounds. It arrived as local activist groups in the Tucson area were marginalized, as their needs and demands were ignored. The campaign slogan was: "A Whole Lot of People for Grijalva" and it was true. Headquarters was a place "where the Chicano community went, where the environmentalist community went, where the social justice community went. The community organizations working on the campaign stressed over and over how this was a campaign for the comunidad of Tucson," remembers Maritza.

Grijalva was born in Tucson in 1948. His father had come to the U.S. as part of the infamous Bracero Program, which brought over four million Mexicans to offset labor shortages during World War II. In the 1960s, Grijalva founded the El Rio Community Center, which houses everything from from quinceañeras (a Mexican right of passage ceremony for fifteen-year-old girls) to after school programs. The city tried to convert the building into a police substation, but Raùl and other Chicano activists fought to keep it open. Grijalva was most recently known for his leadership in the protracted battle to establish a Cesar Chavez holiday. Before running for Congress, Grijalva served twelve years on the school board, where he built close working relationships with many of his future constituents.

Over half a million people live in Grijalva's District 7, one of the most diverse in the nation. District 7 is the second largest in Arizona—larger than Rhode Island, Delaware, Hawaii, Connecticut, and New Jersey combined. Its boundaries include a large portion of Tucson, a vast stretch of the Mexican-American border and the lands of seven different Native American tribes. Almost 30 percent of Grijalva's constituents are under eighteen and half are Latino.

The big issues are immigration, water preservation, sovereignty for Native Americans, poverty, illiteracy, drug trafficking, and unemployment.

When Grijalva arrived on the scene he was rich with ideas, but his campaign was poor in pocket. He had to face a field of seven Democratic candidates, including Elaine Richardson, a prominent and politically connected realtor who was able to spend twice as much money and who had the backing of the business community and the daily newspapers.

Where Richardson had funds, Grijalva had to rely on volunteers, and more than five hundred people volunteered on a regular basis. It was clear that they had to make the campaign a success. The reason so many people were accountable to Grijalva was because Grijalva was accountable to them. "He would return our calls. A lot of the community has his home and cell phone numbers. You can always get a hold of him when you need him," says Camiliano Juarez.

Camiliano, the son of farm workers from Yuma, grew up in California, but has lived in Tucson for thirteen years. "Part of me is the hard–core chicano that doesn't want to have anything to do with the system. I didn't know too much about green politics or women's politics. After the campaign, I got involved in a lot of things that I would typically say 'I don't have time for that.'" This last year Camiliano was elected on to the Board of Directors at a domestic violence shelter.

Then I talked to Daniel Brito (who I also knew through USAS). He went to the University of Arizona and was the People of Color Caucus representative for USAS before he graduated. He got involved with Grijalva's campaign and became so engrossed he put everything into it. "We sent a lot of people door to door because that's what we had: people," says the twenty-six-year-old Tucson native who now works in D.C. on Grijalva's staff. And so they walked. Every volunteer in this campaign can attest to going out to "walk," or "supporting the walkers."

"Weekend to weekend, Raùl could count on forty to fifty people every Saturday to come out and walk," says Tom Castillo. "You have to maintain people's spirits, which you really need a lot of in Tucson and Yuma, where the temperature is always on its way to a hundred degrees or beyond."

"I was not able to walk because I'm disabled," remembers Samuel Newsome, who came from the carpenters union. "My job was to drive the truck and supply the water and supply materials to the various people that were walking."

**TUSCON**

VICTORY: ELECTED A
GRASSROOTS ORGANIZER
TO U.S. CONGRESS

With so many volunteers in the field, the campaign was built on face-to-face contact. "I was going back to the same household the third or fourth time and they remembered me and we would have small, pleasant conversations and I would bring their requests back to Raùl and the campaign," remembers Castillo. "On the first visit people would say, 'Yes, we know about Raùl. He was on the school board and on the county board of supervisors, we think he's okay, we may vote for him.' Then, the sec-

ond visit, they would say, 'Yes, we're pretty certain we're going to vote for Raùl.' By the third visit, [they would say], 'Raùl, he's our guy, that's who we're voting for.' The magic number is always three contacts."

On the day of the primary election, it rained. Bad news. Republicans usually have more money and are more likely to have cars. Rain has killed many a grassroots campaign by lowering turnout of poor people.

But A Whole Lot of People was prepared. "It was pouring," said Celeste. "We were out there until the last second giving people rides in the rain to get them to vote. People who normally wouldn't vote felt impassioned by people that walked through a flooding city to find them and give them rides to the polls."

"That day was insane," says Maritza. "It wasn't just rain. It was heavy hail. But there was also this amazing response from people because they understood that we were out there with our signs at the polling places, at the street corners, holding up signs the entire day. Passersby were nodding their support for us, so we knew before the votes were counted that we had won."

In the primary, Grijalva beat Richardson two to one despite the fact that she spent twice as much money. In the general election, Grijalva trounced his Republican challenger.

Since taking office, Grijalva has been coming through for his community. Grijalva opposed the U.S. intervention in Iraq and drilling in the Alaskan reserves. He opposed Bush's $550 billion dollar tax cut and managed to allocate $1.5 million in grants to begin building affordable housing in his district. "He even brought John Ashcroft to District 7 and had him tour the border in the middle of the summer to raise his awareness about border issues," says Camiliano Juarez.

It made me wish there was a Raùl in Albuquerque to inspire people. Honestly, I think there are Raùl's in every place, and Tuscon just got lucky 'cuz theirs was just handed to them. He was ready and he was willing to do the crappy-ass job you have to do to be a politician. I really do believe there are people like that all over the nation, but they just need to be found and then supported.

I imagine that a lot of people are like me when it comes to politics. They're cynical or apathetic or both. And sometimes it takes somebody to believe in you enough to reinforce your confidence in yourself, you know? I mean there are so many amazing, smart, capable people that would do such a great job in Congress or the Senate or the White House. Raùl just stands as a reminder that grassroots people of color can do it too, and they don't have to change when they get into office. He very much stands by the things he promised to Tucson when he left.

## *Political Sex Survey* — MARISOL ENYART

*How many potential Raùl's do you think there are?*
I can think of so many. There are people in Albuquerque who everyone respects—like Alma Rosa. That's all Raùl was. He'd been around Tucson and organizing for so long, *everybody* knew Raùl. I really don't think it's a matter of having some sort of politics background or wanting to hold office. I think it's a matter of being passionate. Seeing the crap that's going on in your city. Getting pissed off about it and getting inspired to change it. You'd be surprised what people can pull off when they give a shit about something.

*What actor or public person would you like to see smackdown Ah-nold:*
Damn, I'll do it myself.

*A slept-on group of voters you'd like to see organized?*
College students of color

*What candidate would be best in bed? (please explain)*
Kucinich is a crazy boy—I'm sure he'd be creative.

*Favorite thing about George Bush?*
When he tries to speak Spanish.

*What do you think about the way Republicans are using the war to appeal to Latinos to be Republican?*
I have three cousins in Iraq right now. My boyfriend Robert was gonna be sent. My best friend's dad just got called to duty—all these people that I love in my life that don't have anything to do with this war. They're all

minorities. They're all on the front lines—and it's been proven that the military targets Latinos and other minorities. If that doesn't piss you off . . . well, it *has* to piss you off. And then Latinos are supposed to for some reason *like* Bush? The Republicans and the Bush administration are trying to sabotage everything we care about: education, immigration, health care, labor rights. I personally don't know any Latinos who are Republican. I'd really love to talk to Latinos who are Republican and see where their mind set is. Because if there's something appealing about this Bush administration, I want to know about it. I have yet to find something!

*What are your goals for 2004 on this book tour? Where are you touring this book?*
Hopefully anywhere that will have me. I want to travel the nation. I really want to meet a million people and have conversations with them about the things they think are jacked–up about the world. I hope to spark passion in people. I don't think I have the power to empower people. But I want people to feel empowered. The potential's there, man. We could do some amazing–ass shit. Blow your mind kinda shit. Like "Where did that come from?" It's just a matter of letting people believe in themselves, that despite what people see on the news every day, despite what goes on in their neighborhoods everyday, there is much to be done that is well within our reach. It's just a matter of doing it. And having the confidence and skills to do it. Which we already have really. We just need to be reminded.

# Two Greens

## By Miriam Markowitz

Since the 2000 election, it hasn't been easy being Green. Party members have suffered the slings and arrows of outraged Democrats, as well as the smirks of smug Republicans. The Greens didn't get their 6 percent, or Ralph Nader, or even Al Gore. Many miffed political pundits predicted the Greens' retrenchment into the nether regions of Berkeley and Vermont, where they think election-stealing, tree-hugging wackos belong.
The retrenchment is nowhere in sight.

Over the past several years, Green Party membership has increased by 24 percent while other party's numbers are falling. As of July 2003, Greens held 178 elected offices across the country. Young people continue to flock to the only party that seems willing and able to stand up against corporate corruption, unjust military action, and the big, bad Dubya Bush.

Green-leaning voters—like young people and racial minorities—are taken for granted by Democrats because they mistakenly believe the Greens have no real alternatives. Any number of eminent Democrats have wagged their fingers at the Greens and other Naderites, reminding them how much their bad behavior cost everyone last time around. They assume that Greens are so scared of Bush, they'll take any pittance the Democrats offer them.

The same Democrats who whined about the spoiled election are spending little to no energy courting Green support, making a repeat of the 2000 debacle all the more likely. George W. Bush has proved that there is a difference between Republicans and Democrats (not to mention Republicans and rabid right-wingers), yet many Greens would rather go line dancing with the devil than vote for a Democratic nominee they don't believe in.

Increasingly, the Greens are realizing that local elections provide the best opportunities to build up their base and mount a real challenge to the two-party system. Progressive people across the country are parlaying activist energy into electoral victories. For David Segal twenty-two-year-old city council member in Providence and for Jason West—the twenty-six-year-old mayor of New Paltz, New York—it wasn't enough to vote Green, lead some protests, and call it a day. They ran for office, they won, and now, they're doing their jobs with high energy that seems inversely related to their low pay.

Jason makes eight thousand dollars a year as the mayor of New Paltz. He spends one day a week in his office and the other four supporting himself at the job he's worked for the past ten years: painting houses. In his spare time, he expresses his creative activist urges as an environmentalist puppeteer. He moved to New Paltz to attend college at the State University of New York (SUNY), and has been organizing the six thousand–person hamlet ever since.

When he isn't attending town meetings or researching policy initiatives, David Segal works as a substitute teacher. David moved to Providence's East Side and quickly assimilated into the community fostered by Brown University. The Columbia University graduate and Maryland native won a city council seat in November 2002 despite having lived in Providence for fewer than two years.

Both guys are young Greens who ran against multiple candidates in a college town. Both victories inspired some of their disgruntled elders to issue the younger candidates verbal bitch-slaps. New Paltz's outgoing mayor Tom Nyquist was so chagrined by Jason's May 2003 victory that he refused to help the junior politician in any way. "I'm sorry to see the Green Party win," Nyquist told the *New Paltz Oracle*. "They were spoilers in the presidential election. And now they have used the students, most of whom are ill-informed on the New Paltz community issues, to get themselves elected."

A column from the *Providence Journal* derided David's victory an "Election Stunt from Brown." Another resident told the *Providence Phoenix*, "The students are really guests in the community. A kind way to say it would be to say that they're not taxpayers."

If you look carefully at these statements, you'll see that these bitter adults aren't just attacking their young opponents, but the "ill-informed" "guests" who voted for them. Translation: students are too young, too stupid, and too irresponsible to elect representatives that speak for the entire community.

Rather than prove their haters right, David and Jason may have taken their criticisms to heart. They look like they've grown up real fast, and consistently emphasize their politics over their age. "I guess I never thought of myself as a young politician," said Jason. "It's everyone else who thinks of me that way."

In both elections, the skeptical point to the other factors—a vote split by more established candidates, support from transient college students—and ignore the fact that's staring older, lazier politicians in the ass: these guys ran great campaigns, both on and off campus. David didn't just send his volunteers canvassing. "*He* spent a lot of time going door to door," said Peter Asen, David's campaign volunteer coorindator. In the end, only 438 of David's 1,068 votes came from the two precincts where students tended to vote.

Jason ran along with twenty-three-year-old Julia Walsh and Rebecca Rotzler—a thirty-nine-year-old woman of Eskimo descent—who were both elected to one of four trustee positions (trustees share legislative power with the mayor). Their campaign came complete with folk songs and shuttles to drive voters to the polls. Rotzler says that their ticket got a lot of support not only from students, but also from small-business owners and senior citizens. Rotzler said that one opponent prophesied that after the Greens won, there would be a mass exodus of young families and senior citizens from New Paltz. There wasn't.

Just before President Bush attacked Iraq, it became obvious to Rotzler that New Paltz progressives needed to run someone in the May 6 mayoral election. Jason had run for state assembly once in 2000 and again in 2002, and was also a recognizable presence in town meetings and social demonstrations, so he seemed the natural choice.

© 2003, SFifty1

Even before the war, Jason's desire to wreck the status quo was a strong one. Jason says that he ran in 2000 because the local Democratic assemblyman wasn't pushing Green issues, and the guy had even accepted campaign money from the union-busting management of a local manufacturing company. Rumor has it that Jason made such a stink about the ordeal that the assemblyman eventually came out for the workers, finding half a million dollars in state money to help settle their contract negotiations. Although he didn't win a seat, he still had a positive impact.

So in 2003, Jason leapt into an election for the third time. It's a mistake, Rotzler notes, to think that Jason, Walsh, and herself succeeded only as antiwar candidates. While antiwar sentiment certainly factored into their appeal, the three also garnered support on social justice issues and environmental protection. A major part of their platform focused on opening up town government to the citizens through experiments like televised town meetings. Rotzler says their campaign really spoke to people "who felt like they weren't a part of their local government—and we found plenty of them."

Jason thinks that most people in New Paltz support the initiatives he's implementing, even though there is a vocal minority who aren't supporters. One plan is to cut the cost of shipping sewage sludge out of town by building reed beds that will filter it naturally. Jason also aims to purchase wind energy, create student internships in government, and institute a local currency that can be used to purchase goods in town. The currency will not only encourage people to patronize small businesses, it will also bolster low salaries to the level of a living wage when employers use it to supplement their workers' U.S. dollar paychecks.

Jason believes that he will be able to increase environmental protection without raising taxes because many of his ideas will actually save the town money. His plans have gained so much momentum that said he says with enthusiasm, "We may run out of things to do before our term is up."

David has seen his share of success too. Although his living wage proposal is stuck in committee (as of this writing), he has passed important symbolic legislation like the Providence resolution against the war in Iraq. A giant budget gap has been his biggest obstacle, and David is discovering that he has to fight flexibly. Rather than put all of his eggs in the living-wage basket, he's pushing through an initiative that will force the city of Providence to hire more minority contractors.

Rhode Island Jobs with Justice director Matthew Jerzyk, who has worked with David on the living wage campaign and the antiwar resolution, says that David has been more open and available than any politician in the city. "His presence has given courage and a renewed sense of resistance to progressive Democrats on the council," said Jerzyk.

Since he took office, David has learned that what drives politics (and policy) are personal relationships. He's pretty realistic about his stature in the community and on the council: "Some people take me seriously, some don't." David thinks the "Green Party thing puts a lot of people off."

Asen noted that some people have pressured David to switch his affiliation to Democrat. David remains adamant in his loyalty to the Green Party, explaining that in Providence, the label "Democrat" doesn't mean much. Republicans don't get elected there too often, so a lot of people call themselves Democrats regardless of what they believe. Rather than change parties, David has been organizing a Progressive Caucus to build coalitions with the council's left-leaning Democrats. The caucus is modeled on the Congressional Progressive Caucus, which is led by Democrat (and Green favorite) Dennis Kucinich.

Progressive coalitions among Democrats, Greens, and other independents make sense in Bushwhacked world, but these are few and far between. Jason thinks that such partnerships won't work. "There is a space for progressives in the Democratic party—as long as they accept that they have zero influence and zero power," said Jason. "For every Dennis Kucinich, there's a hundred DLC Democrats."

[Editors note: For what it's worth, Progressivepunch.org, which tracks Congress on 125 issues, describes 45 of the 435 members of Congress as "hard-core progressives."]

NEW PALTZ, NY
PROVIDENCE, RI

VICTORY: 22-YEAR-OLD CITY COUNCILMAN AND 26-YEAR-OLD MAYOR

Jason does think that Democrats and Greens can work together for reform of the two-party system. Right now, the two major parties get more votes in Congress than actual support warrants because third parties are handicapped by the system. While Jason avidly supports proportional representation, he is also a fan of instant runoff voting (IRV), which allows people to rank their candidates. If we had used this type of voting in the 2000 election, Bush might have lost unequivocally. Nader supporters would have had the option to rank Ralph first and Al second. Then, when Gore and Bush emerged as the leaders, second choice votes for Gore would have been added to the Democrat's total. If Instant Runoff Voting were implemented, the spoiler issue would be moot and people would be free to support emerging parties without "throwing away" their votes.

Clearly, there's a lot that Greens and Democrats could do if they worked together. Whether that's a real possibility is another question entirely. Why would a major party like the Democrats deign to share power with Green "upstarts?" And why would Green idealists care to build a coalition with "corrupt" Democrats? The answer is more than the fact that they're fighting some of the same battles. Internally, both the Democrats and the Greens need to find a way to engage the voters they claim to represent, yet often take for granted: minorities, low-paid workers, the LGBT community, and of course, young people.

For Democrats, it's not enough to be good at the politics. And it's not enough for Greens to be good on the issues. Each party has volumes to learn about making politics work for real people. They'd better learn it fast, or right-wing ideologies will haunt us for another four years—or fourteen. Or forty.

# The Liberated Logan Square: How We Beat the Daley Machine
By Alejandra L. Ibañez
(as told to Amanda Klonsky)

 Chicago is infamous for its political "machine" patronage system created by Mayor Richard Daley in the 1950s, in which every city department was run by people who owed their jobs, contracts, and other favors to the mayor. People of color were excluded from institutional power, and Dead People for Daley was a major voting bloc. What people outside Chicago don't real-

ize is that Daley's son, Richard M. Daley (who has been in office since 1988 when the city's only Black mayor, Harold Washington, died), has quietly built an even more effective machine than his father. Daley II has Chicago on lock-down to a degree that no other big-city mayor in the U.S. could even imagine. Although Chicago is two–thirds people of color, Daley manages to force support among forty-nine of the fifty aldermen (city councilmembers) for his policies which screw working class people and give handouts to big business. Any independent politician or candidate who stands up to Daley faces the wrath of his machine in the form of intimidation by police and city inspectors of all kinds (liquor, building etc) and a campaign war chest to support his stooges.

Vilma Colom was an incumbent stooge. She had been in office for eight years in the Thirty-fifth Ward. This ward was what they call a Latino super-majority ward—created after the 1990 census showed the huge growth of Latinos in Chicago.

She had been the former secretary of Dick Mell—a powerful alderman who runs his own fiefdom and has for nearly thirty years. Vilma might as well have been "placed" in that position by the Chicago political machine . . . you know . . . the old "we got ourselves a Latino majority ward let's put a Latino we can control in there" type of deal. Vilma never advocated on behalf of anybody or anything, except herself and her self-interest. Nobody ever thought we could get rid of her.

Within the first two years of her aldermanic term, she began showing her true colors with her attack on a local homeless shelter. City inspectors were sent to the shelter and a local reporter did a whole exposé on how Vilma harassed homeless people. Vilma was going to shut it down. What compassion for the poor and homeless!

It was only a few years later when Vilma and good 'ol Dick Mell took issue with the local *paleteros*, the street vendors who sell *paletas*, corn on the cob, fruit, or *aguas*. You know, working-class people—true entrepreneurs trying to make an honest living.

She was going to shut them down. She was making enemies with the homeless, working-class, middle-class, Latinos, non-Latinos . . . I mean, Chicago is known for its street vendors, our Chicago hotdogs and polishes . . . and the *paleteros* weren't any different—for her to go against them was absolutely ridiculous.

People were really fed up. There were horror stories of people who went to Vilma's office to ask for the minimal things, garbage pick-up, getting street lights to work, putting stop signs up in front of schools and high–traffic areas and—she was known for yelling at and belittling them.

For Rey Colon, who would make his first run against Vilma in 1999, it all came to a head around the issue of basketball courts for. He was working with the Park District and was told to go along with whatever the alderman said, even after the community had voted seventy to four to keep the basketball courts. For Vilma, basketball courts brought in *undesirables*: young guys—thugs or gang-bangers, in her eyes.

Another major issue was that Vilma was letting any and every developer come in to the ward and allowing them to build and demolish as they pleased. She was giving them zoning changes, which could turn a small, frame home into six-flat luxury condos. It was a development frenzy! We were losing a lot of historical buildings and the integrity of the community was being destroyed by all these developers that were coming in left and right.

So in the November 2002 election, folks put a referendum on the ballot to force the alderman to hold community hearings on all zoning changes. There was so much momentum in the community that it got to the point where even Vilma made buttons as if she was supporting it. We got all these people motivated and involved, and the referendum passed with 96 percent of the vote.

The referendum got people pumped. They felt they could actually make an impact. These are people who had given up on politics, who maybe worked on Harold Washington's campaign and in the heyday of coalition politics in the early 1980s, but left politics after Harold died and Daley II took power. There was a renewed faith in people. We had high school students, college kids, li'l old ladies, local school council moms—just regular people—getting involved. They now knew how to read a poll sheet, how to register people to vote, how to poll-watch on election day, how to pass out palm cards; they had learned everything about running an election day operation and were going to use those skills for Rey Colon's election.

In a city run completely by the political machine, it was important for the community that the candidate wasn't a political hack. Rey was a breath of fresh air. He hadn't even been involved with the few independent Latino representatives left in the city. He was just a regular schmo, who cared about kids and was dedicated to his neighborhood.

He wasn't an insider like a lot of these new young politicians, the sons and daughters of old ones. He was a kid who grew up in the neighborhood. His older brother had been brutalized by the police and later gunned down by opposing gang members. From there, Rey decided that he was gonna get involved with young people and find solutions to the street violence. He started at the local Boys and Girls Club as an eighteen-year-old and eventually became the executive director.

Rey had the lone political support of the only recognizable independent, progressive state legislator Senator Miguel del Valle. Del Valle was the first

Puerto Rican elected to the Illinois Senate. No one else had the nerve to support Rey. It would be going against the political machine and politics as usual. And in the city of Chicago, going against the machine is political suicide.

Rey ran against Vilma the first time in 1999 and lost, but got 39 percent of the vote, which was respectable considering he had no money and no experience in politics. After he lost, he mysteriously got fired from the Chicago Park District, but he was later hired as the executive director of the Logan Square YMCA. Then he decided to run against her again and, a few days after announcing his candidacy, got fired from the YMCA. It was more than mysterious. He had already discussed running for alderman with his boss and the board at the Y and they gave him the go-ahead and didn't feel it was a conflict. To this day, Vilma claims she had nothing to do with it. Yeah, right! Twice in a row?

When I got involved, the campaign was going well and they just needed someone to steer and call the shots. They had over two hundred volunteers and a strong steering committee. A lot of the volunteers were young. We had a really good group of students, a lot of students from the University of Illinois at Chicago and other universities that got wind of the election and wanted to get involved.

The campaign office was a circus. We would open up every day by 7:30 A.M., and towards the end of the campaign we were open til about 11 or 12 at night. People were coming in and out all day. We couldn't afford big jumbo signs so we reused the backs of Rod Blagojevich signs, the recently elected Democratic governor, who was from Chicago and happened to be the son-in-law to alderman Dick Mell. We bought red and blue paint and we made these big stencils that we cut out ourselves, and we would take rollers and we would roll "Rey Colon" on the back of the Blagojevich signs, and then we bought about forty jumbo-size blank boards and we used the stencils and sprayed. We got some guys to come spray paint the signs. We had these two guys that were there all weekend and they rolled for like three days straight: "Rey Colon." On election day, people volunteered to put them on their porches. If their house was right next to a polling place we would nail it up to their house or we would walk around with them on, cuz after a while we just ran out of money. Vilma spent nearly a quarter of a million dollars on her campaign. We spent less than eighty thousand dollars—which for us was tons of money.

CHICAGO

VICTORY: A CITY COUNCIL SEAT IN CHICAGO

Every day we would gauge how our precincts were doing and where we were weakest, based on our homemade formula of how many votes we needed from each precinct to win. There were days where we would just pick up our coats, leave one person in the office, and head into an area that was weak and door-knock the hell out of it for an hour and a half or two hours. It was really a day-to-day thing. You always had to be prepared to go door-knocking or to do phone banking or to use paint and markers and make homemade signs. It was like after-school camp every day. People were constantly coming in with their kids. Even the kids got involved. They would attach little posters to their bikes and draw pictures of themselves as Spiderman putting up Rey Colon signs all over the neighborhood.

In the last two weeks, we could feel the momentum—we knew we could win. We didn't need (and couldn't afford) the sophisticated election computer programs or highly paid consultants that most well-financed campaigns used to determine how well their candidate was doing. We used the tried and true methods—going door-to-door and talking to people one-on-one. It was all based on what people told us at their doorstep. If they told us they were gonna vote for Rey, then we counted them as a plus and checked them off on our low-tech photocopied poll sheet as a Rey supporter.

We were constantly strategizing about the issue of absentee voting, which is how you vote when you're hospitalized, on military leave, away at school, or out of town. See, the way it works is that you fill out an absentee application and cause it happens in the privacy of somebody's home, you have no idea whether anybody's tampered with that ballot or not. Perfect situation for major fraud. Tons of people were getting "help" filling out their absentee ballot from Vilma's people, and many of these voters were lied to and weren't even eligible to vote absentee—a federal offense. There had been record amounts of absentee voters in Vilma's last elections. So we had press conferences asking the state's attorney to please, please investigate. In Vilma's previous elections in the Thirty-fifth Ward, there were over eight hundred absentee voters and in the prior election nearly twelve hundred absentee voters.

It was ridiculous. It was rumored that Vilma's campaign manager was Dominic Longo, who had been convicted of voter fraud and had been busted stuffing ballot boxes. In press conferences we begged the city and the County Board of Elections to investigate all of the absentee voter ballots that came in. They eventually sent letters to all those who had applied for absentee ballots explaining the rules and eligibility requirements to ensure people understood the criteria. We were constantly on top of that; we never stopped fighting.

Leading up to election day, we were up for two days in a row. The night before was the only night that I actually fell asleep and slept soundly. I was at peace. We had done everything we possibly could. I told myself, you've done everything you physically and emotionally could have done for this election.

Election day came. I got up I think at four A.M. and we stacked our precincts and polling places with volunteers by six A.M. I ran from precinct to precinct to make sure our signs were up, that we had enough materials, and that no volunteer was left to cover their area alone. I had some tough precincts in the south part of the ward. We had a lot of young people aged seventeen to twenty-four volunteering there. I covered a predominantly working-class Latino area with almost all young people manning the precincts. At first they were intimidated by Vilma's people because she sent her big thugs. They were either cops or just big, scary-looking guys, and they were trying to intimidate us—especially our younger volunteers. So we brought our volunteers our homemade jumbo REY signs, and one of the kids put it on the rooftop of his car and parked it as close to the entrance to the voting place as possible and he rolled down his windows and played merengue all day. He and his friends passed out fliers and talked to voters all day—they made it into a party.

We had bought disposable cameras for election day—to document any questionable behavior. It was hilarious. Midway through election day we found out a lot of people that were working for Vilma weren't really supporting her. They were only there because they were city workers or because they owed some politician a favor for their job. So a lot of us have pictures of our volunteers and her volunteers posing together. They would tell us, "I really don't care if she loses but I'm here because I owe my job to such and such person, I owe my job to Dick Mell" or "I'm a city worker and I have to be here to keep my job." And we knew a lot of these people. I mean, a lot of Vilma's volunteers were old friends and neighbors that we had gone to elementary school with, our mothers went to the same church. At some precincts we did end up taking pictures of Vilma's people being nasty, you know, some city workers in garbage trucks trying to steal and throw away our signs. But for the most part these people didn't like Vilma and many of them showed up at our victory party.

At 7:30 when the polls closed, we all ran back to the campaign office and realized we had won. We were all crying, screaming, and cheering as massive amounts of volunteers flooded our small office onto Kedzie Avenue. It was like a parade at eight at night. It was dark as anything outside and we were screaming and people were driving past us honking their horns and we were singing and crying and laughing and just ecstatic. We were singing, "Naa naa naa naa, hey hey hey, goodbye," or "Ding dong the witch is dead," or "La bruja esta muerta."

We won twenty-seven of thirty-five precincts that day, and we only lost the other eight by a handful of votes. In the end, we won with over 58 percent of the vote.

# How We Fired Our Mayor in the Dirty South

By William Upski Wimsatt

Remember Joe Smitherman, the infamous mayor of Selma, Alabama? He's the one who called Martin Luther King "Martin Luther Coon" and ordered police to beat marchers trying to cross the Edmund Pettus Bridge on "Bloody Sunday." The ensuing outcry created pressure for the passage of the 1965 Voting Rights Act.

Joe didn't go anywhere. In August 2000, he was still mayor os Selma. In November, he wasn't anymore. For thirty years, members of the generation that led the civil rights movement couldn't get rid of Joe Smitherman in this world famous just-over-half-black town of ten thousand in Alabama's Black Belt. It took their kids' generation to do the trick.

We sometimes forget that the leaders of the voting rights movement were practically kids themselves when they started. The organizers from the Student Nonviolent Coordinating Committee (SNCC) who went to Selma in 1964 were students from Black colleges around the South. "SNCC was organizing in the projects including kids as young as eleven and twelve years old," says Selma organizer Tarana Burke. People forget these were young kids from the projects—from GWC, the George Washington Carver Homes—getting beat up on that bridge. Joanne Bland, who runs the Voting Rights Museum was a girl from the projects who got beat in the head when she was eleven years old. People had to die and people had to get hurt. It's that level of commitment that changes things."

The white power structure in Selma is something ferocious. As in most of the Deep South, there are few, if any, liberal white people in Selma. "People hear 'Selma' and they say 'Oh, the civil rights movement!' Well there was a reason why the civil rights movement chose Selma: because the oppression here is so great," says thirty-year-old Malika Sanders, former director of 21st Century Youth Leadership Movement, and one of the organizers of the "Joe Gotta Go" campaign.

In the course of 21st Century's effort to oust Smitherman, their campaign truck was fire-bombed. So was the only black radio station in the area—the major vessel of communication in the rural black community. No one was ever charged. Joe was no dummy. He had small town techniques of making sure elections went the right way. Ballot boxes turned up missing. Police were stationed at polling places to intimidate African-American would-be voters. In the year 2000, black people in Selma were afraid for the mayor to know they had gone to the polls. And on top of that, he reportedly bought people's votes, often in exchange for nothing more than a drink. "Mayor Smitherman was the mayor when I was born and he's gonna be the mayor when I die," said many Selma residents when young campaigners knocked on their doors, reflecting the deep fear and resignation.

Dr. Martin Luther King Jr. is popularly associated with "nonviolence." But the actual phrase King himself used was "creative nonviolence"—with an emphasis on creativity. In the creativity department, the young people of Selma elevated the game to new heights.

They have a song or a chant for everything. With help from the elders in the community, they have created and memorized dozens of their own original songs, which they belt out on a moment's notice. They began organizing four years before the election, holding monthly Superbirthday Tuesdays at Selma High School (on the first Tuesday of every month) for any student who turned eighteen that month. Between music and cake, new eighteen-year-olds were registered to vote.

A year before the election, they started throwing block parties all over Selma, on almost every block where black people lived. On top of that they laid hip-hop based chants: "Get Your Vote On" and for the young kids: "Bling-bling—I'll vote when I'm 18." They performed whole cheerleading routines at high school football games. The biggest hurdle was to get people excited, to make them believe it was possible. They brought in big name rappers like MC Lyte, Dead Prez, and the Outlawz to record "Joe Gotta Go" ads on the local radio station—before it was firebombed. And they got Davey D and Tracy McGregor (then political editor of the *Source*) to cover it.

November 7, 2000, may go down as the worst election day in U.S. history. The eventual outcome, and revelations of state-level fraud, would send the nation (especially African-Americans who voted 90 percent or more in favor of Gore) into rage, depression, mourning, and disbelief. But not in Selma. Even before the polls closed in Selma, on November 7, 2000, black people were celebrating. Black residents of Selma flooded by foot and by car into the three-and-a-half block downtown. "Everyone came out into the streets celebrating even before the results had been announced. So many people voted—everybody knew we had won even before we got the official word."

## Political Mentors: Rose and Hank Sanders

The usual tenants of the Alabama statehouse are out for the summer. But the fifth floor chambers are filled with eighty boisterous teenagers and kids as young as four years old. The teenagers are from all over Alabama and the rural South. They are members of an extraordinary organization—21st

Century Youth Leadership Movement—formed by lesser-known civil rights leaders who started the organization in the mid-1980s to empower the next generation. Today each 21st Century young person is playing the role of a state legislator in a special mock legislative session. They propose, amend, debate, and lobby current issues in Alabama, such as felon voting rights, school-bus safety, and teen marriage. In their normal lives, the dozen or so suit-wearing adults in the room are high-powered lobbyists, state legislators and aides. But today they have a different role. They play advisors to the teenagers.

There is a buzz in the room and a sense of possibility that young people can go into politics. Nineteen-year-old Darrell Williams, one of the older teens, who plays governor in this legislative session, is considering running for city council in his hometown of Tuskeegee. He helped to elect the first African-American woman mayor in his 98 percent black town, which is still largely controlled by the white elite, and he speaks eloquently about the police corruption in his town. Another young woman knows an eighteen-year-old who's running for city council in Montgomery. Carrie Fulgham, a 21st Century chapter leader from Sumpter County, is the mayor of her five-hundred-person town. Another chapter leader, Walter Hill, became mayor of his small town in Lowndes County at age twenty-four. And former 21st Century organizer Latosha Brown, who was instrumental in the Joe Gotta Go campaign, ran for a seat on the state board of education and came within two hundred votes.

None of this has happened by accident. An incredibly rare environment has been created and cultivated for these young people to blossom in: rural African American and African values have been holistically integrated with hip-hop culture, grassroots organizing, human spiritual development, and electoral politics. The driving force behind this culture is a tight-knit group of youth and elders in Selma. Director Malika's parents, Hank and Rose Sanders, and their friends from the civil rights movement, have spent two decades mentoring and laying the foundation for the next generation. Mr. and Ms. Sanders have a law firm in Selma. Countless African-American organizers and regular folks, traveling through town, have slept on their floor.

Rose Sanders is legendary for her songwriting, mentorship of young people, and for fearlessly taking on the local white power structure. During the "Joe Gotta Go" campaign, Joe's people staged a counter campaign: "Rose Gotta Go." Her husband Hank is the most senior black state senator in Alabama, representing all or parts of nine counties. He's the one who arranged the mock legislative session, and he has leveraged million of dollars toward black community organizing and institution building in his district over his twenty years in office. Hank and Rose have also been instrumental in building the New South Coalition, which works to elect progressive African Americans throughout the South. Movement politics in Selma, however, is currently facing a dual crisis: The Republican Party has targeted Senator Sanders's community projects for defunding. And Selma's local white elite, having been ousted from power, have packed up their toys, moved their eco-

nomic power out of Selma, and set themselves up in an unincorporated area outside of town. We asked Senator Sanders, one of the great progressive politicians of our time, to reflect on the role of elected officials in a movement:

© 2003, Chris Ho

We have to recognize that politics impacts every single thing, starting before we're born, with issues of contraception to abortion to maternal care, and it touches everything in one's life: healthcare, education, employment, religion, transportation—like driving—and even after you're dead, it impacts where you're buried, who processes your body, death certificates, everything.

It's important when someone goes into office that we not just trust them to carry out a good agenda because they're good people. Because, once they get in office, forces come after them all the time from every direction. Wherever you get the most pressure from, it's easy to go with that. Special interest groups, they have somebody to talk to you on every issue. They take you out to dinner, invite you to events all the time, trying to show you how what they want is in the best interest of Alabama. And you don't have enough staff to do the research, so they supply you with the information that proves their argument. As an elected official, you don't have the capacity to do adequate independent research or talk to all the people who might be impacted. The tendency to get swayed by special interests and money is extremely strong. And it wears you down over time. So the person you elect must have an extremely strong vision of what it is they want to accomplish.

As an officeholder, I recognize politics has severe limitations, and therefore I view it as a support mechanism for the front-line troops, which are the people in community-based organizations. And that also means we have to value—truly value—those organizations and stay committed to them. Otherwise the political process will isolate you from that base. One of the major problems is that people get into office and they think they're the most important. And some community people feel like they're the most important. And we're all spokes in the wheel. And it's so important that we understand we're all just spokes so we can have mutual respect and support each other.

Many people are mistaken in the way they judge the political effectiveness of a progressive officeholder. They look for a few big things that stand out that have media sex appeal and that's a serious problem because the media is not going to recognize what an effective politician does when it's counter to the system. Quite often our greatest contribution of progressive officeholders, particularly in a place like Alabama, is not what we pass, but what we *stop* from passing. What politicians normally do is mobilize people on the basis of emotion. That's how people get in office, by promising "If you put me in, I'll do this." You get judged on a few areas. The media, if they like you, they help you look effective. If they don't like you, they help you look ineffective, troublesome, or worse.

For progressive electoral politics to work, there must be a communications system outside of the externally controlled mass media, which includes word of mouth networks, regularly visiting community groups, doing radio programs, writing things regularly and doing email to regularly communicate with your base, and get input from people.

We have big shoes to fill.

# Georgia State Representative Alisha Thomas

## By William Upski Wimsatt

Alisha Thomas doesn't make things easy for herself.

She is a progressive black woman who won a seat in the Georgia state legislature at the age of twenty-four.

And not only did she win, she won her seat against the backdrop of the 2002 Republican "sweep," in which voters across the country went with the perceived party of patriotism. Especially in Georgia. Even popular centrist Democrats like Max Cleland and Ray Barnes lost their jobs.

On top of all that, she was elected, not from Atlanta, but from Austell, Georgia, which is located in Cobb County.

For those of you who don't know, Cobb County is the suburban district across the Chattahoochee River from Atlanta. It's 70 percent white with a median income of around seventy thousand and the heart of Newt Gingrich's former congressional district.

Cobb County is notorious for radical defenses of white flight, Christian evangelicals, and well-funded conservative political action committees (PACs). As recently as 1995, the *Atlanta Journal-Constitution* wrote: "Cobb County has become a national center for hate activities ranging from neo-Nazi skinhead and KKK recruitment to anti-Semitic revisionism."

Cobb County kept out MARTA (the Atlanta mass transit system) to insure that people who use public transportation (i.e. black people) would have no way to get there without driving. And if you do drive, you had better watch your black ass. Cobb County is where Jamil Abdullah Al-Amin (aka H. Rap Brown) was ticketed for DWB (driving while black).

Cobb County is where county commissioners passed a resolution declaring the county officially opposed to "gay lifestyles," resulting in the entire area being bypassed by the Atlanta Olympics. And to top it all off, last September the Cobb County Board of Education voted unanimously to encourage the teaching of alternative "theories of origin" to evolution in order to provide a "balanced education."

Cobb County: You know the deal.

Or do you? As in most places in the New South, there is Old Cobb County and New Cobb County. Over the last fifteen to twenty years, Atlanta's economic boom has not only lured previously migrated African Americans back south, but also Fortune 500 companies with well-established diversity programs and a vested interest in not being portrayed as having moved their headquarters to Klantown, USA. (Besides Coke, Home Depot is based in Cobb, as is NAPA Auto Parts). The many years Newt spent as Speaker of the House insured that Cobb County was cut huge, huge slabs of federal pork, with the ironic impact being an influx of technology and military-industrial corporations—IBM, Lockheed Martin, and GE Power Systems—that are required by law to adhere to some semblance of equal opportunity when it comes to hiring and contracting. The net effect has been that since 1990 the county has added more than seventy thousand black residents.

Still, how does a twenty-four-year-old progressive black woman win in the heart of the Confederacy in a district that is 70 percent white?

Does she have wings, claws, or bucks?

Alisha Thomas is originally from Miami. She first laid eyes on the Hotlanta metro area eight years ago when she arrived as a seventeen-year-old Spelman College freshman. She is a lifelong activist: joined the NAACP at fifteen and is remembered at Spelman mostly for reviving the college's moribund NAACP chapter, which she grew to a peak membership of five hundred dues paying members (nearly one quarter of the school!).

After graduation, Thomas worked for progressive organizations in the Atlanta area (such as the National Alliance for Justice, a nonprofit that tracks judicial nominations) before deciding to run for state representative.

On her first try, in November 2002, she was elected to the Georgia General Assembly, unexpectedly defeating a better funded Republican opponent by 2,144 votes.

"I moved to Austell after I graduated from college in 2000. I had only been there two years before I ran. I started getting involved in the community through the Austell Community Task force. They do a lot of service. People were very skeptical and disbelieving when I told them I was running in Cobb County and that I could actually win. I was twenty-one or twenty-two walking into a meeting saying I was running for state rep. I know in the back of their heads people were probably thinking 'that's cute.'"

And as a youth organizer from the nonprofit sector, she was able to put together a team of low-cost volunteers who engaged in an unprecedented retail political campaign. Her campaign manager was a twenty-one-year-old college student named Rashad Taylor, also a member of the NAACP from Morehouse. For Alisha Thomas' team, the campaign was an extraordinary trial by fire.

"We were out at 5:30 A.M.," recalls campaign worker Ebony Barley, part of the young team that formed around Alisha's campaign. "Alisha's campaign was so exciting. We had maps all over her house targeting precincts. Her mom and dad came up from Florida. Her dad was cooking. I organized about twenty-some volunteers. I had sent out an email to recruit people to do GOTV. We learned how to strategically target certain districts, how to hang door-knock-ers. And also what time black folks are gonna vote. Polls close at 7 o'clock. Black folks vote at 6:45. They have to pick up their kids, go to the grocery store. Georgia has laws that allow people to vote up to five days before election day. But it's not publicized. There's so much stuff we're not supposed to know. And most white progressive tactics don't necessarily work. Yelling 'Tell Bush to get out of my Bush!' Black folks don't want to hear that."

Thomas's win is also a vindication of the training and networking resources provided by mainline civil rights organizations like the NAACP. The NAACP comes in for a lot of heat, but Thomas would never have won without the networks and skills provided by the prehistoric African-American uplift organization.

Leading up to the election, Thomas and her volunteers—drawn from her contacts in Atlanta's progressive community, the NAACP, students from AU (the Atlanta University Complex which includes Spelman, Morehouse, Clark, and Morris Brown), her family, and numerous young people from Austell, went door-to-door, introducing the candidate and handing out sixty thousand leaflets with her *home phone number* printed on them along with an invitation to call anytime to ask questions.

Did a lot of people call?

No, not really. But it distinguished her as accessible at a time when a nervous electorate was looking for politicians to be more responsive in our increasingly uncertain age. For Thomas, putting her phone number out there wasn't a campaign gimmick. This is who she is.

"My home phone or my cell phone are on everything I send out," she says. "When I was running, I got anywhere from twenty to thirty calls a day. And I returned all those calls. It's just all to be accessible to my constituents. Nowadays I usually get an average of five calls a week from constituents. I do monthly town hall meetings. So sometimes I get more calls when we do those. Still, I have one hundred thirty thousand people in my district. I think the reason I don't get more calls is that people are so used to having their elected officials be inaccessible. People feel like they're bothering me by calling me. Also, people feel so disconnected from the political process that they don't realize *how important it is to tell me their views."*

Last February, her legendary openness got her embroiled in the ongoing controversy over Georgia's state flag, which had been stripped of the Confederate battle emblem. A Cobb County chapter of the Sons of Confederate Veterans invited Thomas to come before the group and explain her opposition to the emblem's reinstatement, and she (bravely or foolishly, take your pick) accepted the invitation, telling the Atlanta Journal-Constitution: "They're my constituents. I will gladly come to their meeting." She left the meeting soon after arriving, saying that the members were verbally abusing her.

When Alisha Thomas talks, you have to pinch yourself to remember you're talking to a politician. She shatters all the stereotypes of how a politician is supposed to be.

It's like what's wrong with this picture? She takes her job seriously. Means what she says. Tells the truth. Has compassion for all people. Sticks up for what she believes in. Represents her constituents. *Where's the catch?*

"About 75 percent of my calls are from people who need help on specific issues," she continues. "People know I'm very passionate about young people in the adult prison system. So I get calls from parents whose kids are in the system. I got a call recently from a parent whose young son was incarcerated. She called me to tell me about how he was being treated. A lot of the kids get raped in there and they don't even get proper counseling. It was hard to take that call because you know, as a legislator, that it isn't in your power to take that person out of that particular situation. All I could do was connect her with some other parents in the same situation. They have a group Mothers Advocating Juvenile Justice. So at least they can support one another.

"I got another call last week. I was on the phone for probably two hours talking to a parent whose son has autism. He was very upset about how the proposed changes in Medicaid and PeachCare (a state program that provides medical care for children) would harm his child. *Of course that has a huge impact on the way I will vote.* You have to listen to your constituents first and foremost. Despite what the party leadership says, or anyone else, the people who put you there are the ones you're there to represent."

When you ask Thomas questions about her views, she often manages to bring the conversation back around to her constituents. We ask her: What will it take to build a progressive governing majority in the U.S.?

"I think genuine public service is what people want. When I come to people's doors and listen to them, people see that I'm someone they can talk to.

I was speaking at a college the other day and this woman stood up and said she can't afford a car and she has to walk seven or eight miles to work every day. She said, 'How can we continuously elect these politicians who are so out of touch and who don't understand the struggles we go through?' My response was 'unelect them!' I told her, 'You need to find out who your politicians are, call them up and tell them what you need; if they don't respond to you then you need to *unelect* them. Support someone else. Or if there's no one else to support then *you* need to run.' We need more young progressive people to run for office."

And so it begins.

Alisha's campaign manager Rashad Taylor, now twenty-two, is running a school board campaign for another young person, and they're in the process of forming a PAC. "Rashad and I," says Thomas "have a passion for training more young progressives to run."

(with assistance from Gary Dauphin www.africana.com)

# The Spark and the Gas Money: Indian Country Explodes
## By Kari Lydersen

On November 5, 2002, phones were ringing off the hook in the tribal college centers on the Pine Ridge Oglala Lakota Sioux reservation in South Dakota. The centers were primarily staffed by young volunteers involved in their first political campaign; the callers were mainly voters who wanted to cast their ballot, but had no way to get to the polls.

"As soon as we'd get a dozen calls or so, we'd send someone out with our van to go and pick the people up and drive them to the polls," says twenty-one-year-old activist entrepreneur Nick Tilsen, founder of LakotaMall.com. "Everyone knows where everybody lives on the rez."

On Pine Ridge, one of the poorest stretches of land in America, the lack of a car or gas money can be a major obstacle to voting—and it's not the only one.

"We never asked the government for the right to vote—we were forced to become citizens of this country and then *told* we had to vote," says Tilsen. "Many people on this rez believe we are our own sovereign Lakota Nation, so why the hell should we vote for any state or national race? We have our own traditional way of doing things."

Indeed, many Native Americans feel jaded by elected officials who, in their eyes, are the descendants of the man who stole their land and killed their people some five hundred years ago: Christopher Columbus. Their apathy toward voting has led to a vicious cycle in which elected officials ignore Indians because they don't vote, which only makes Indians even more disillusioned about electoral politics.

But in 2002, this cycle ceased. Indians organized a campaign to support an unlikely figure: a middle-aged, straight-laced white man named Tim Johnson, the Democratic senator from South Dakota.

Though not a radical by any means, Johnson had long been credited for paying more attention to the needs of Indian Country than other politicians. Given the dire economic straits of the rez, social services like healthcare, childcare, and housing are critical to the survival of many of its residents. Johnson has secured funding for many such programs through his seats on the Senate Indian Affairs Committee and the Indian Appropriations Committee.

A lawyer and fourth generation South Dakotan, Johnson served two terms in the state House of Representatives, two in the state Senate, and five in the U.S. House of Representatives. He was elected to the U.S. Senate in 1996.
In the 2002 race, Johnson made it a point to reach out to the people of Pine Ridge and listen to their demands. He hired Brian Drapeaux, a Yankton Sioux tribal member, to coordinate his Indian Country campaign and brought in other local residents to do everything from register voters to run publicity campaigns and cart people to the polls. His office paid people for each voter they registered, and gave gas money to the volunteers picking people up on election day. Johnson and his wife Barb also met with Pine Ridge residents numerous times to talk about the reservation's needs.

"They showed a real interest in what's happening here," says Karlene Hunter, founder and president of the *Lakota Express*.

Johnson had reason to mobilize the Indian vote—or any vote, for that matter. From early on in the electoral season, it was clear his race would be one of the most hotly contested in the state's history. At the urging of the Republican Party, former Republican South Dakota Congressman John Thune gave up his original plan to run for governor to enter the senatorial race against Johnson. In a mostly Republican state, the GOP saw it as a travesty that there were two Democratic senators, and relatively liberal ones at that—Johnson and former Senate Majority Leader Tom Daschle, who is up for election again in 2004. The Republican Party made the South Dakota senatorial race a priority, and President George W. Bush visited the state four times to make speeches in support of Thune.

Johnson's campaign push began with voter registration. Tilsen and other college students went door to door and set up booths to register people throughout the rez.

Drapeaux, who has been involved in politics for twelve years as a lobbyist on Capitol Hill, a staffer for Daschle, a campaign worker for Johnson, and now economic development manager for the Lower Brule Sioux tribe, said people responded very positively to their outreach efforts.

"We incorporated all these people who don't usually get involved," he said. "We said we need your help to get the message across, and they ate it up."

While there was no official youth mobilization, Tilsen said youth played a significant part in the election (over 50 percent of Pine Ridge's population is under twenty-four). "For a lot of us who voted, it wasn't about Tim Johnson. It was about us increasing our political power as a people. That's why I was going door to door. That's why I was registering people at a Pow-Wow. That's why I was picking people up on election day. Really what got me into it wasn't Johnson or his people. It was this woman Cecilia Fire Thunder who coordinated our voting drive. Seeing how she put so much time and effort into it. She was on the radio everyday. She really helped build the momentum. Hearing your own people talk about it—that's what got me into it."

Pine Ridge youth have good reason to demand a better future from those in power. Two of the five poorest census tracts in the country are in South Dakota's reservations. Unemployment at Pine Ridge is around 70 to 85 percent, with an average per capita income of only forty-five hundred dollars per year. Indians are being hit especially hard by the welfare reform act signed by President Clinton that is making its effect felt now as many recipients are hitting the five-year lifetime limit for public aid.

"It was great to see that spark lit among the youth," says Hunter.

"As young people, the odds are really stacked against us," Tilsen says. "Our high school dropout rate is 62 percent, and we have the lowest life expectancy of anywhere in the Western hemisphere besides Haiti. But there is also a growing movement here to create jobs and small businesses. We even started a Pine Ridge Chamber of Commerce."

Between July and the November elections, according to the *Argus Leader* newspaper, about four thousand new voters were registered—21 percent more than ever before. On election day, Pine Ridge turned out the highest voter participation ever.

But for a while, it seemed that the Republicans were going to win anyway.

When people went to bed on November 5, 2002, Thune had a lead of more than three thousand votes and many pundits were already calling the election in his favor. But two counties still hadn't reported, including Shannon County, which includes Pine Ridge. People awoke the next morning to a surprise: Johnson had won 167,481 to 166,954—a margin of 528 votes.

The increase in Indian turnout had clearly accounted for Johnson's margin of victory.

In Shannon County, Johnson won 92 percent of the vote. In Todd County, which includes the Rosebud Indian reservation, he won 81 percent of the vote. In Dewey and Ziebach counties, also home to reservations, he got 75 percent and 66 percent.

"Dubya raised the hand of Thune in mock victory at every pit stop as the television cameras rolled," wrote Erthavenger on NDNAIM.com. "Bush talked Thune out of running for the Governor's office in order to challenge Tim Johnson. He spent time and money in South Dakota hoping to push Thune through the Senate doors. It didn't work."

"The Indian vote was a huge part of Johnson getting re-elected," said Drapeaux. "That's never been done before."

But the people of Pine Ridge know this is only the beginning.

They must now use their newfound political clout to pressure Johnson and other officials to keep their promises to Indian Country. For a people who ultimately want their land back and their sovereignty respected, they have no illusions that what they won in 2002 is anywhere near satisfactory.

"We know we can't win anything with Republicans, but our people are not celebrating about these Democrats either," he said. "The Democrats have become Republican and the Republicans have become extremists. We're voting for these people but then we still have to fight everything they do."

In July 2002, for instance, Senator Daschle introduced a rider attached to the defense appropriations bill that allowed logging of rare old growth trees in the Black Hills—an area that many Indians consider sacred. From an Indian perspective, the government stole the land in the late 1800s (around the time they assassinated Sitting Bull and Crazy Horse). The Lakota want their mountains back. They even turned down a 106 million dollar compensation offer mandated by the Supreme Court in 1980, saying they wanted the land instead. But the government, with the support of mainstream environmental groups, turned the Black Hills over to the Forest Service.

Native Americans are now charged a twelve dollar per car fee to get in to their own park.

"It's still the Wild West out here: cowboys and Indians. They said the reason was fire protection, but all these contracts went to logging companies, people making a bunch of money off it," said Tilsen. "They went right over our cultural rights and the burial site."

In addition to his work on business development and voting, Tilsen is part of a group called Defenders of the Black Hills (DefendBlackHills.org) which has done direct action to stop logging, mining companies, and federal officials, trying to guard the hills from deforestation and incursions by multinational companies.

"On the local level, when it comes to protecting our sacred sites, upholding our treaties and human rights, Johnson and Daschle will stand by the wayside," says Tilsen. "I voted Democrat because it is the lesser of two evils. The real reason why I voted Democrat is not so much for Johnson and my community specifically, but for the rest of the world."

Nonetheless, the 2002 election was a victory for Indian people, and a significant one. Under Johnson, residents say they are seeing more funding for Head Start programs, a childrens mental health clinic that uses Lakota spirituality, and other social service programs. Says Hunter: "This has lit a spark."

# How We Got Our People to Vote

*"One of the penalties for refusing to participate
in politics is that you end up being governed by
your inferiors."*

—Plato

*"The great thing about America is everybody
should vote."*

—George W. Bush

# Boston Vote, Baby! What!

## By Malia Lazu (as told to Seth Donley)

 *It's not often that you get to watch one of your friends being honored by having a day named after her, but that's just what was happening as I watched Boston City Councilor Felix Arroyo reading a resolution that named June 26, 2003, Malia Lazu Day. When the councilor finished, he handed the resolution to Malia, then twenty-six, who had already been presented with similar resolutions passed by the Massachusetts State Senate and House of Representatives. An aide to Mayor Thomas Menino stepped into the middle of the room and began to read yet another document honoring Malia's incredible work at Boston Vote, an organization she founded while still in college.*

*Later, I asked Councilor Arroyo when the last time that all four governmental bodies had honored one person like that. "I can't think of one," he said after a moment of thought.*

MALIA: I was always into electoral politics, although I never viewed myself as being political. I was attracted to where the power was and was pissed when I realized the power really wasn't mine. I grew up in Hawaii and I was like a typical teenager. I cut school. I was into the whole beach thing. Going to clubs. Going out. Surfing. To give you an idea, in high school, I won "most flirtatious"—I definitely wasn't on the "most likely to succeed" track. I was really passionate about black nationalism. And journalism. And debate. I was really into bell hooks. That's why I went to Emerson college; so I could be a journalist. That's how I ended up in cold-ass Boston.

I knew I wanted to get into politics. I said "I'm a Democrat," so I went to the Democratic State Committee office in Boston and tried to volunteer. I think I stayed there all of two hours before I was bored and feeling really fucking uncomfortable with the people I was with. I was like "Oh, I'm not that kind of Democrat." Those kids were doing this work so they could one day work on The Hill! I was doing this work to one day free Mumia.

I left and I came up with plan with a friend of mine to put together a get out the vote hip-hop concert on the Boston Common. When I went to the city for the permits, they wouldn't give me one. They said: "The people you are trying to bring together are not exactly like the people if you were trying to bring Barry Manilow." I decided right then that I wanted to overthrow the city government. This group called the Commonwealth Coalition gave me a job doing college outreach for a clean elections campaign. What the hell did I know about clean elections? I was only 19, but I knew I was pissed.

The Commonwealth Coalition is a statewide group in Massachusetts made up of unions, environmental organizations, and women's groups—it's pretty unique in the country. It tries to get progressive people elected to office. They train candidates. They endorse. And they train voters, which was my job. They gave me a job running their Voter Power Program to do trainings in different communities. I liked the job but it was frustrating because I would only go to a community for two days at most, then I would have to bounce, like see ya! People would get excited, but then as soon as I left the room, the energy left with me. It just wasn't working.

*What Malia realized was that people at local community organizations simply didn't have the time to add voter education to their plates. She decided to change how she was doing things. The result was Boston Vote, a three-person organization that helped to manage a coalition of 125 nonprofit organizations and churches.*

Boston Vote was built around the simple idea that community leaders are too busy to leave their posts to do voter registration. Instead of taking them away from their organizations, we brought voting to them. We provided materials and training to help them register the people that they serve or represent in the neighborhood.

We started Boston Vote to build a real network and long term relationships. To stop voting from being a once-every-four-years thing, and integrate it as a year-round activity.

For the past twenty years, most people of color saw political organizing as something for Birkenstock-wearing hippies, white labor unions, or people who marched with Martin. Not something that everyday busy people needed to do. It was a result of being continually cut down.

I'd go to bigger organizations that do voter registration and they wouldn't give me the time of day. A lot of them thought they were doing this work already, but the numbers showed that they were fucking ineffective. Instead, I'd go to a busted little health center and I'd say, "I'm not going to ask you to stop what you're doing, because what you're doing is so damn important. What I'm going to do is give you a flier with the information and when people come in for their birth control or because they have a sore throat, you can give it to them." And they'd say, "Sure," because I was giving them the tools—voter education made simple.

BOSTON

VICTORY: HUGE SPIKE IN VOTER TURNOUT AND OUR FIRST LATINO CITY COUNCILMAN

In this way, we were able to engage a lot of people. And it wasn't just about voter training or me sitting around and having lunch with people. It was about coming up with site kits, giving people the basics and then helping them to build it however high they wanted.

I also helped them with their organizations. I'd show up for people's community meetings, I would sit and do mailings with the old ladies at one organization and talk about the good old days. Shoot, I licked at least twice as many enveolpes for other people's organizations as I licked for Boston Vote. You can't go up to people's organizations and say, "Do what I say because it's for your own good." You have to be accepted as part of their team.

The other trick was getting away from the Saul Alinsky model of organizing, that seventies model that says you have to knock on every door and talk to people seven times. It's time consuming bullshit—especially if you're trying to reach young people. There are no door-to-door salesmen anymore. You wanna know why? Because they are reaching their consumers in other ways that are just as effective. I started moving instead toward the marketing model of organizing, the sexy model of organizing. I don't mean marketing on a surface level of trying to sell something. We weren't fucking voters. We were making love with voters (laughing). We would cuddle with them in the morning! We were coming up with cool shit that can be easily integrated into people's everyday lives—engaging people and communities on a very real level, not just "sign this piece of paper so you can cop this CD."

We wouldn't always ask someone to walk the block to knock on doors. Some organizations don't need to go to the block because the block is already coming to them. Young people are going to be at clubs every Friday and Saturday night. Well guess what? That's where I'm gonna be too. If you know where the people you want are going to be, you know how to reach them. I'd ask one of my girls to go to First Fridays to register young black professionals and she's say, "You're going to get me into First Fridays for free? Hell, yeah! We registered cute boys (don't worry we had some cute boys register girls too), we danced, had a few cocktails, and did democracy some *good*.

*Within a few years, the results were noticeable. In the 1999 city elections, Boston saw a 7–8 percent increase in voter turnout over 1997, while it continued to fall in the rest of the country. Malia was disappointed the numbers weren't higher.*

I was bummed but people would tell me, "What are you talking about? We stopped the decrease." And after that, I could point to how voter turnout had increased in Roxbury and Chinatown and Mattapan. The numbers spoke for themselves. Once people started seeing the results, that's when the larger groups started to ask, "So, what are you doing?" Because they weren't really doing the work they said they were; they didn't have the time. What they had never realized was that you can't start this shit in August. You have to create an energy shift in communities. At Boston Vote, we were working on this all year. We worked on this in '99, so you saw an increase in 2000. We worked on this in 2001, so you saw an increase in 2002.

*The midterm elections of 2002 were the final validation of Malia's work. The city saw the highest voter turnout rates in twenty years. Nearly thirty thousand more ballots were cast that year than just four years earlier, an impressive 24 percent increase over 1998. Even more impressive were the increases in Boston's communities of color.*

*Dudley Square saw a voting increase of nearly 30 percent through Boston Vote's partnership with the Dudley Street Neighborhood Initiative.*

*The Chinese Progressive Association (CPA) was Boston Vote's partner in Chinatown, long a politically powerless neighborhood due to being gerrymandered into the same district as the Irish-Catholic stronghold of South Boston. After the efforts of Boston Vote and the CPA, Chinatown saw a 70 percent increase in voter turnout.*

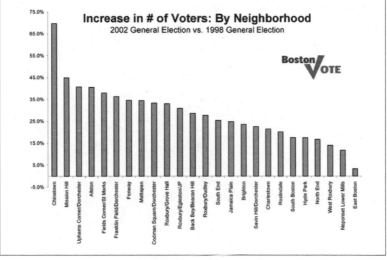

www.bostonvote.org

*Boston Vote worked with several partner organizations in Mattapan and increased voter turnout by approximately 34 percent.*

*In 2003, Felix Arroyo was the first Latino elected to City Council in Boston history. He got the second highest number of votes citywide.*

*[Editor's Note: In 2003, Malia passed on the leadership of Boston Vote and Mass Vote to a new generation of organizers.]*

www.BostonVote.org | www.TheyThinkWereStupid.com

*What politician would be best in bed? (please explain)*
Bill Clinton. Although he might be too selfish. Definitely JFK. He kept Marilyn coming so he must have been good.

*Future trends to watch out for:*
Watch out for your right to vote, man. That's the next battlefield. ID requirements are gonna be insane at the polls in 2004. Under the new Help Americans Vote Act (HAVA), it's gonna be up to the individual state or county to decide what IDs to accept. There's gonna be massive voter intimidation. We're gonna need to have community election watchers, have people at polls informing people of their rights as well as a campaign beforehand so people come to the polls with proper ID.

*Favorite thing about George Bush?*
He's a communications genius. Or his people are at least. He's the king of the soundbite.

*What superhero is needed to get us out of this situation?*
Wonder Woman! She has her Lasso of Truth, remember? She'd wrap the lasso around you and then you could only tell the truth. We need her for George Bush. I used to have Wonder Woman paraphernalia all over my office at Boston Vote.

*How do we get a progressive majority? How long will it take?*
We already have a progressive majority I believe. How do we get a progressive governing majority? We create Boston Votes throughout the fucking country. And we get out of the realm of comfortable community organizing and organize the hard to reach.

*A slept-on group of voters you'd like to see organized (who they are and how you'd do it):*
Black men definitely. With felony disenfranchisement laws and the criminal justice system, they're the group that's most under attack by this government. Whether it's being on the frontlines of this war or being the backbone of the prison industrial complex. I would take a two-pronged approach and start out integrating voting into mentoring programs where there are already successful black men. Then I would also go to halfway houses and rehabilitation centers and make voting a part of their probation and reentry programs. But I don't think I'm the best person to do that cuz I'm not a black man and it really is best to do peer to peer.

*How do you convince the brother or sister on the corner to vote?*
One conversation I'll never forget. We were going door-knocking and there were these dudes that were smoking blunts on this corner and I approached them and told them how we were registering voters and they were like "oh yeah it doesn't mean shit" and I started talking to them about going to jail and selling weed or whatever and at the end of it they registered to vote and they came to a meeting we were having that night at Roxbury Community College.

*One politician, big or small, who you think is halfway decent, other than Barbara Lee (and they have to be alive):*
Damon Lynch III, a city council candidate in Cincinnati who's gonna be the next Martin Luther King Jr. He's one of the organizers of the boycott in Cincinnati and the police accountability effort. One of the few politicians I know who has actual street credibility because he works with the hard-to-reach folks, the invisible communities, the crackheads, pimps, the boys in white shirts and saggy jeans that everyone's afraid of.

# Get On the Bus!
## By Adam J. Smith

*"The Bus Project is the most exciting thing to happen in Oregon politics in the last twenty years."* —Barbara Roberts, Oregon's first female governor (1991–1995)

*"And don't forget: the Bus is coming."*

These were the parting words of wisdom bestowed upon us by the field director before he sent my partner Karynn and me out into the wilds of Washington County, Oregon, where we were about to jump into managing a campaign for the state legislature. It was the middle of July, 2002—late in the game to switch campaign teams, but this race was one of a dozen the Democrats needed to win if they wanted to win back control of the state House of Representatives for the first time in a decade. They needed us and we, new to state politics and needing jobs and a chance to learn the ropes, needed them.

"What in the hell is the Bus?" Karynn looked a little nervous.

"How should I know?" I asked, "You're the one from Oregon." The way our new boss had said it, I'd assumed the Bus was some kind of institution that had been a part of Oregon's political establishment forever As it turned out, the Bus was only a few months old, but it was about to turn Oregon's political establishment upside down.

©2003, Adam Smith

The Oregon Bus Project was the brainchild of a group of eighteen-to-thirty-five-year-old friends, all politically progressive, who had looked around the state and realized they had to do something. Over the past twenty years, reflecting a national trend, the far Right had gained control of the Republican party in Oregon, and now most of the candidates who made it through the Republican primaries were anti-choice, anti-public services, and fiercely anti-tax. Conservative activists had also been very busy passing ballot initiatives, including several that had crippled the state's ability to raise adequate tax revenue for things like good public schools and human services.

In Portland (Oregon's largest city); Eugene (home to the University of Oregon); and some other towns, voters consistently elect progressive legislators who care deeply about issues like the environment, education and poverty. Hard line conservatives, however, were easily winning Republican primaries across much of the rest of the state. In many of those districts, particularly the more rural areas, Republicans outnumbered Democrats by wide margins, and so whomever got through the Republican primaries easily won the general elections. These right-wingers were coming to the Capitol with an ideological agenda and the backing of big business.

The result was a state legislature that was both polarized and paralyzed by ideological differences. Democrats, who dominated Oregon's largest population centers, had managed to elect their candidates to most of the statewide offices, particularly the governor's office. Republicans, who held majorities in the more numerous outlying districts, had a firm hold of the state legislature, particularly the sixty-member House of Representatives.

That left only a few districts, mostly in suburbs of the major population centers, up for grabs. In these "swing districts," voter registration is pretty much evenly divided between Republicans and Democrats. Thus, control of the legislature, and of the statewide political agenda, comes down to control of those key legislative seats.

The situation was so bad that Democratic Governor John Kitzhaber, who served two terms as governor from 1995 to 2003, earned the nickname "Doctor No" for the record numbers of vetoes he stamped on the often extremist legislation that came to his desk.

So in the summer of 2001, a group of a dozen or so friends, all from Portland and all progressive, found themselves sitting around talking about what they could do to pull their state out of its downward political spiral. Jefferson Smith, a twenty-nine-year-old lawyer who would become the driving force behind the Bus Project, had an idea.

"Let's buy a bus," he suggested, "and fill it with young people and take it around the state to help get progressive candidates elected."

The initial response was not as strong as Jefferson had hoped.

"We took a vote," he remembers. "The other suggestion was that we all just get together on Wednesday nights and watch 'The West Wing.' I had to do some lobbying. It was a pretty close call."

When we had our first meeting with the Bus People, my first impression was that they were totally insane.

As an introduction to the group and their political philosophy, they told us about the Six E's: Education, Equal Rights, Economic Justice, Environmental Sustainability, Election Reform, and 'Ealth Care.

They told us that they could basically fit every progressive issue under one of those headings. This turned out to be mostly true. They told us that they were committed to creating systemic change through the electoral process. They told us that Oregon was only the beginning.

"Insane," I thought to myself. "But a good insane."

They told us they were going to get one hundred and fifty volunteers out on a Saturday, four weeks away, to spend the day working for three legislative candidates, ours and the two in the bordering districts. The volunteers would canvass door-to-door all afternoon, hitting an average of around forty

PORTLAND

VICTORY: SWUNG UP
TO SEVEN STATE SEATS

houses per person, for a total of at least six thousand doors in one day.

They would arrive in the morning, meet the candidates, do a training on how to canvass and that we would brief the volunteers on the message that each campaign wanted emphasized. Next, everyone would eat lunch, take off to go door-to-door in the territories assigned to them, and then reassemble for a party that evening.

In addition, several volunteers would stay behind in each district to do a service project. There would be media, special guests, both in the morning when the volunteers arrived and at the party that night, and there would be a snack-mobile, driving around the districts, hooking up with the volunteers on their routes and handing out water and food.

I was exhausted just listening to them. How were they—or we—going to get more than a hundred young people to come out on a summer weekend to spend the day walking in the heat and knocking on doors for state legislative races? Young people don't even vote.

On Bus Day morning, Karynn and I showed up at the athletic field of the high school in our district that had been selected as the meeting point. Over the next hour, people began filing in. By 9:30, I counted more than eighty people, including a dozen or so people from the Bus Project itself who were busy counting out box lunches, checking off the names of new arrivals, and generally creating order out of chaos. Most of the people who had come to volunteer were under forty-years old, more than a few were under twenty. The six of us—a campaign manager and a field director from each of the three campaigns just stood and stared at the size of the event that was unfolding in front of us.

At 10 A.M., everyone's attention turned to the parking lot where The Bus was pulling in. It was an actual coach bus, silver and black. On each side of the bus was a quote, painted in big block letters..

"IT IS NOT THE HAND THAT SIGNS THE LAWS THAT CHANGES HISTORY, IT IS THE HAND THAT CASTS THE BALLOT" —Harry S. Truman

and

"A GREAT DEMOCRACY MUST BE PROGRESSIVE, OR IT WILL CEASE TO BE EITHER GREAT, OR A DEMOCRACY" —Theodore Roosevelt

As the Bus approached the field, the volunteers who had gathered, many of whom had already been to several of these events, began to applaud. Out of the Bus poured another forty or so volunteers who had made the forty-five-minute trip from Portland to canvass in the 'burbs. The gathered crowd, many of whom had also made their own way from Portland, continued to cheer them as they stepped off. The last four people to emerge from the bus, and this is what really blew me away, were two members of the Oregon House Democratic leadership, plus Congressman David Wu, and U.S. Senator Ron Wyden. Umm, fellas, good to see ya. Thanks for coming out.

The day was pretty amazing. Congressman Wu and Senator Wyden were there because, well, it's just not an everyday thing in politics to see more than one hundred and fifty young people (the final count was close to one hundred eighty volunteers) getting seriously involved in electoral politics, especially at the local level. And the Bus Project was pulling this off, in different districts, pretty much every weekend. Our best estimate is that they knocked on more than six thousand doors, and spoke with around three thousand people in the three districts in a single afternoon.

Just like the Bus People said it would happen. But better.

The party that night featured more VIP speakers, music, food, and beer. If you asked any of us, the campaign staff, who were working crazy hours, scrounging up volunteers, and watching our candidates go off each evening and weekend to walk their districts, door-to-door, often alone, it was a pretty intense day.

By the end of the 2002 campaign, the Oregon Bus Project had run thirteen full-scale bus days, and a number of smaller efforts, engaging around eight hundred individual volunteers. Those volunteers knocked on more than sixty-five thousand doors for fourteen different Democratic legislative candidates across the state. During the last days of the campaign, The Bus also provided large numbers of volunteers to staff phone banks for get out the vote efforts. About twenty extremely committed and energetic leaders drove the project. All of them were between the ages of seventeen and thirty-six, and it was, without a doubt, the most exciting thing that had happened in Oregon politics in many, many years.

How did they do this? Why did people turn out, and continue to turn out week after week to do something as geeky as knocking on doors for state legislative candidates? Most people, and especially most young people (including me until recently), don't even know who their own representatives are. How did they keep their core volunteers, the self-selected leaders who made all of this happen, engaged and involved through a long and exhausting campaign season?

It was a combination of hard work and crazy enthusiasm and positive energy.

When the core group began setting up the first event, they called everyone they knew, and then everyone else that they could think of. "We're doing this event. It's gonna rock. Lots of cool people. We're going to take back our state. It's never been done before, and we're gonna do it. There's going to be a kick-ass party afterward. We can do this. You can volunteer one day. It's gonna be a blast."

Some people got on the Bus immediately. For others, they called them for the next event and the next and then the next until they wore them down and got them to commit.

"We take our mission, and the idea of seizing political power very seriously. But we don't take ourselves too seriously" says Saul Ettlin, one of the original Bus People. "And we're never too earnest, even at our most earnest."

When the election was over, I joined up with the Bus folks as they began looking ahead to the future of the project. The first question, once they had all slept for a while, was "what do we have here?"

What they had was a network. It was a network of young, committed activists who were determined to create progressive change through the political process. It was a network that contained a fairly large number of people who could be called out to volunteer; a smaller number of people who could be counted on to do a little more; and a core of people who were committed to achieving the nearly impossible on a regular basis. The energy of the network was considerable, and it radiated out from the core group. But that energy had sparked a flame, and there would be more people to share more of the work in the next cycle.

The 2002 election results in Oregon were a mixed bag. The Democratic candidate for governor squeaked into office over a right-wing conservative in the closest statewide election in memory. Democrats gained a tie in the state senate with fifteen senators from each party, and in the house, the Republicans gained three seats, leaving them with a 35–25 majority.

The fourteen candidates that received help from the Bus went seven and seven. That was better than Democrats did across the state, and certainly better than they did across the nation in what turned out to be a huge night for the Republican Party nationally.

In the end, what we have and what we are building is a network. A network is not a hierarchy or a traditional organization, but a group of people connected to each other and to the whole on lots of different levels, doing lots of different things. We believe that networks are the organizing structures of the twenty-first century, and that our generation instinctively understands them.

We want the New Progressive Network (our new 501(c)4 organization) and The Oregon Bus Project (the Political Action Committee) to be *the* place to be in Oregon, for political action, economic opportunity, and a very cool social scene full of interesting people who are doing real things to gain real power over our lives, our communities, our state, our country, and our world.

As for Karynn and my campaign, well, we lost by just over three hundred votes. In fact, control of the Oregon House of Representatives, and thus control of the state itself, was decided by a total of around two thousand votes across eleven key races. Of course, our last presidential election in this country came down to fewer than six hundred votes in one state. When you think about it, and when you think about everything that's at stake—Education, Equal Rights, Environment, Economic Justice, Election Reform, and 'Ealth care—it doesn't make sense *not* to do something. C'mon. Get On the Bus.

# Wellstone's Secret Weapons
## By Mattie Weiss

I love Minneapolis. It's where my friends and family live. There are lakes everywhere, good salsa clubs, and the city itself is just plain beautiful. But it also makes me nuts. Sometimes it feels like drowning in a sea of whiteness. (Have you ever been to the Mall of America?!) And the "Minnesota nice" everyone is so proud of can be smothering and sometimes sinister. Tolerance is practically the state anthem, while Somali men get murdered in their taxis.

I came back to Minneapolis after college, and almost immediately wanted to get the hell out. In search of meaningful work and a political community I figured I couldn't find at home, I moved to Oakland for a job at the Applied Research Center, a racial justice "think and do tank."

Soon after I took off, my mom was hired by Minnesota Senator Paul Wellstone's reelection campaign. She had been one of Paul's advisees as a student at Carleton College, had babysat his children, and had fierce political loyalty to him. She had taken me door knocking for Paul when I was eleven, phone banking when I was seventeen.

I'd call home over the next few months to find my dad eating avocado sandwiches alone, mom still at work at 10 P.M. He said she usually came home and fell right into bed, without dinner, exhausted. He said she was ecstatic. On the rare chance when I caught her, she'd want to talk about the campaign. She said the more she got into Paul's head, the more profound she found his vision. She said the pace was nuts, that she had hired all these young people of color as field organizers, that the Hmong community was volunteering in droves. Or she had just gotten back from printing a stack of campaign literature in Somali and Oromo. One time she treated me to her rendition of the "rap" about Paul that a DJ had just recorded for a local hip-hop station—fifty-one-year-old white-lady style. My mom beat boxing. I nearly choked laughing.

But it wasn't just funny; it was baffling and intriguing. This wasn't the Minnesota I had tripped over myself trying to get away from. This was a Minnesota being energized and mobilized by people my own age, taking leadership from people of color, using hip-hop as a political tool. What? And not only was this stuff going down, but in part because of it, Paul was *winning*. Just weeks before the election in his third race for senator, major polls showed Paul four to eight points ahead of his opponent—slimy conservative opportunist Norm Coleman. This, despite the fact that Coleman had been hand-picked and groomed by the Bush administration. Despite the fact that Democrats were being wiped out in races across the country, and despite the fact that Paul had, in the middle of the race, cast the only vote among senators up for re-election against the Bush boys' war on Iraq.

Then on October 25, less than two weeks before the election, my friend Maren called from home to say that Paul had been killed in a plane crash, along with his wife Sheila, his daughter Marcia, three of his campaign staff, and the two pilots. Heartsick, I took the first flight home. This was a death in the family.

My first frigid hour back in Minnesota I rushed over to the state capitol, where a scheduled anti-war march had morphed into a giant memorial for Paul. Fiteen thousand people crying, praying, holding signs that said "Carry It Forward." In shock and belly-deep grief, the campaign leadership now had to do just this. Former Vice President Walter Mondale replaced Paul on the ballot as the Democratic candidate, leaving the campaign staff five feverish days to introduce a candidate that no one under forty had ever heard of, and who, bottom line, was not the beloved Paul Wellstone.

Coleman won. And so began the second round of mourning.

Paul's death rolled over Minnesota like a freak blizzard, blanketing everything with devastation and absurdity—strangling the political possibilities. I wrote this story, trying to make a shovel out of words, after Jasaun Boone, a beautiful person and one of the campaign organizers said to me: "We did so many incredible, innovative things. Honestly, I think some of our strategies, if they got out there, could change the face of political campaigning. But the way electoral politics works, if you lose, that's it. Nobody assesses the things you did well. To me, one of the greatest losses is the fact that a lot of what we did will probably be swept under the rug and disappear."

We need to roll back the rug.

But let's start with Paul.

## "People Power" Politics

Paul came at the political world as a community organizer. He had this deep belief that politics was about doing and about understanding people's real lives. The son of Russian immigrants, Paul took a teaching position at Carleton College in 1973. He sent his first class of political science students into the trailer parks and rural towns of nearby Rice County, to do door-to-door surveys that revealed deep poverty, isolation, domestic violence, and difficulty accessing welfare. So Paul, his students, and community members came together to launch Organization for a Better Rice County, which worked to defend the rights of low-income people.

Paul turned the next two generations of political science students into community organizers fighting for Carleton's divestment from South Africa, supporting low-wage campus staff picket lines, and organizing with local farmers against an epidemic of farm foreclosures.

Then in the late eighties, Paul got a brilliant—and frankly somewhat ridiculous—idea: he was going to run for Senate as a way to energize and cohere a progressive movement in Minnesota. He wanted to organize a base of people typically left out of the political process. He knew a lot of good people in communities across Minnesota; he wanted them to know each other. Paul believed he could not only win by working for and with these communities, but that this was the point in winning—that the energy, cooperation and base building it would take for him to get in office would give progressive Minnesotans a common focus.

Paul was an underdog of outrageous proportions, with no objective shot in hell of winning. The only people crazy and idealistic enough to believe he could actually win were young people. Wellstone's first campaign, in 1990, was run almost exclusively by folks in their twenties, many of them former students from Carleton. With laughably little money, Paul's campaign launched a "people power" operation, turning out thousands of volunteers across the state, and campaigning on a proworker, prowoman, pro–small farmer platform.

To everyone's amazement, Paul won.

I've always thought that the idea of working inside the two-party system to "tear down its walls" sounded like a fair amount of bullshit, some optimistic self-deception. I still do. But inside the Senate, Paul had this brilliant and principled ability to use a fundamentally fucked up system to do good, even occasionally radical, things.

On standard Democratic issues like education, social services, and social security, he voted with his party. Paul was extremely committed to health issues—particularly mental health; universal health coverage; and the wellness of immigrants, women, and people living on Native reservations and in juvenile halls. He authored and passed the extremely important Violence Against Women Act and its expansion, VAWA II, which protects and supports victims of domestic abuse.

But Paul also believed that when it came to challenging economic inequality in America, the Democrats were controlled by the same corporate interests as the Republicans. Paul was the only Senator in Seattle protesting corporate globalization. And he frequently went head-to-head with his own party on the Senate floor. In a move considered "political suicide," Paul voted against Clinton's 1996 welfare reform legislation—a bill with almost universal consensus among representatives, but which Paul believed would further harm poor families. He also opposed the Clinton-sponsored 1999 Juvenile Justice Reform Act because it was racist and punitive, and because it failed to acknowledge the large number of untreated mentally ill children who were incarcerated in the juvenile justice system. And, like I said, he was the lone Senator up for reelection to oppose Bush's war on Iraq.

Not that Paul was perfect. His staff will tell you how hard he could be to work with, how stubborn and inflexible, how cranky he got when he was tired. Nor was his record flawless. In 1996 he voted to support the Defense of Marriage Act, which bars same-sex marriage. And he went traipsing with virtually every other officeholder down the post–September 11 "tough on terrorism" road of no return. But in the electoral world, where most everybody sells their soul (if they had one to begin with), Paul was downright decent.

## 2002: The Comeback

Twelve years after Paul Wellstone first rolled into Senate chambers, he was running for a third term. While most Democratic campaigns were busy pumping their budgets into high-paid PR consultants and expensive television ads—dedicating an average of 3 percent to grassroots mobilization—Paul's 2003 campaign put 30 percent of its money into on-the-ground staff. Their job was to turn thousands of supporters into active, informed, and skilled volunteers, spread out over the streets of the Twin Cities, the cul-de-sacs of suburbia, and the roads of rural Minnesota.

This "people power" strategy was based on something any Friendster lover (or hater) could tell you: everybody's got a network. Emma Greenman, an energetic twenty-four-year-old and campaign organizer in the Minneapolis area, breaks it down: "Every person is a whole network of other people, and we used this as a deliberate campaign strategy. Whenever somebody came into the office asking how they could help, we would tell them to go out and get their folks." Sixteen-year-old Brendan Ballou got a taste of this when he rolled into campaign headquarters one day and told staff he wanted to volunteer and do grassroots organizing. "They looked up at me and told me to go *do it*. Just like that. They told me I should start organizing other high school students." Brendan didn't skip a beat. He started organizing students in several local schools. "But I had to get over my awe. I mean, who gives this much responsibility to, and puts this much faith in, a sixteen-year-old?"

The other critical piece of this "people power" strategy was to meaningfully and strategically involve folks typically left out of the political process. In addition to low-income people and rural folks, this meant young people, people of color, and immigrants.

## Political Virgins

Many of the young field staff and volunteers were "soft Democrats," meaning they vote Democratic but think the party is a bunch of sell-outs. That and their average age of "young," earned Paul's staff the nickname "political virgins" among campaigns around the country. Young people flocked to the campaign because Paul politicked in a way that validated them—using social networks as political tools and constantly developing new organizers. Twenty-five-year-old Hmong organizer Pakou Hang says young people had a much easier time understanding the campaign's marriage between community organizing and electoral politics than older Minnesotans. "Young people just get this. They understand the need to build a new layer of political leadership, which is what this new model is all about." On top of that, the campaign got a lot 'cause it gave a lot. It drew extremely bright, committed young people because it respected and invested resources into their ideas and strategies.

With so many young folks working early mornings and late into the night together, sardine-style, Pakou says the office quickly developed a "youth vibe." "There was always music playing—our music—and inspirational quotes all over, lots of laughing and talking." That, combined with the intensity of the work, says twenty-one-year-old Somali organizer Nimco Ahmed, made the staff feel like family, "We were like brothers and sisters. Our lives were each other. We barely saw our real families. We would work together until eight or nine at night, then go out to the clubs together until two in the morning, and then start all over the next day. We loved Paul, we loved the campaign, and we loved each other."

Not only were they holding things down within the campaign, young people—like people of color and working class people—were one of the campaign's "secret weapons" as a constituency. The campaign had an incredibly ambitious college student strategy—to identify one person from every floor of every dorm at every major college in the state to coordinate voter registration and turnout on their floor.

But it was the high schoolers that blew the campaign staff away. Emma says at first the staff thought the high school students would be good for visibility—door knocking and banner holding. "We never imagined the potential they had for organizing their own folks and turning out real numbers." Brendan, who was a St. Paul high school sophomore at the time, organized Sunday high-school volunteer nights, where students spent the first two hours doing work—phone banking, mailings, basically whatever needed doing. Then, because of the campaign's philosophy about really bringing people into the political process, the group would sit down with a different staff person each time, and talk about the work they did. Then they would have a political pizza party.

The general high school and college strategies turned out phenomenal numbers, but the majority of the people brought in through these channels were white and female. Did the campaign throw up their hands and whine about why more young people of color don't show up? No. They developed a more targeted strategy. To involve African-American college students, Jasaun, the twenty-four-year-old director of African-American outreach, sought out black sororities and fraternities. To draw Hmong students, Pakou organized a Student Summit for 150 Hmong youth. At the one-day event—sponsored by the campaign but not Wellstone-specific—Pakou taught the fundamentals of electoral campaigns, and specific skills around messaging, media, and get out the vote (GOTV) efforts. The students then split up into smaller groups and went door-knocking for a local Hmong candidate. Pakou also targeted every school in the state that had at least ten Hmong students, to bring them into the campaign. Many of them ended up coming to the city for the campaign's last few weeks, to help with phone banking and GOTV. "They were really excited about doing it. They were willing to just drop everything and come. No one had ever talked to any of these students before about elections."

In this way, immigrant youth in the campaign were bridges to their communities, developing as leaders themselves, while helping their elders take part in a political system that had never welcomed them.

## There Are Actually People of Color in Minnesota

We've all heard the moaning about the lack of participation from communities of color. They moan as if they care. And then in the next breath, they dole out blame to the communities themselves. Or they call immigrants a "low-return" effort and turn their backs. Politicians return, election after election, to the same campaign plan, playing to the people already guaranteed to vote for them. A few of them wake up a month before an election, with the genius realization that they need to involve—or at least appear to involve—a broad, diverse base of supporters. That's when they start meeting with African American church leaders and showing up at cultural celebrations with sound bites about "the colors of our community." When questioned, they apologize for not putting more than the most basic efforts towards involving communities of color, immigrants, working class people, and youth, but insist we've got to understand that electoral campaigns are too fast-paced, too high-stakes. They mumble promises about making sure to address the concerns of these communities as soon as they are elected. Please.

Wellstone 2002 was some whole other business. The campaign believed deeply and concretely that communities of color and immigrant communities needed to be engaged in Minnesota politics, and could be part of a solid progressive base. And the campaign didn't just say that; they put their money where their mouth was. The field campaign assigned at least one staff person or volunteer coordinator from each of a number of Minnesota's major racial and ethnic communities, including African Americans, Somalis, West Africans, Latinos, Hmong, and Tibetans.

Now I know you're wondering: Minnesota? Isn't Minnesota like a white colony unto itself? Isn't Minnesota basically a transplanted Sweden? Well, yeah. Kind of. Minnesota is historically an extremely white state. The 2000

Census puts us whities at nearly 90 percent. And in a lot of the suburbs and farmsteads and backwood areas you could go for a l-o-n-g time without seeing a person of color. But that doesn't mean they don't exist. Over the last few decades there has been a big migration of African Americans from other northern cities to Minneapolis and St Paul, the resettlement of large numbers of Asian refugees—mostly from Vietnam and Laos, a "Latino explosion" as a result of Minnesota's (until recently) relatively open job market, and a recent wave of East African immigrants.

Of course, most live in the Twin Cities. Minneapolis is nearly one fifth black. Asians make up 12 percent of St. Paul, and Latinos are over 7 percent in both cities.

So campaign organizing in the cities focused strongly on mobilizing these communities. But a campaign knowing it needs and wants communities of color doesn't ensure a two-way street. So why did communities of color respond? Partly it was just Paul. He had charisma and a love of people that translated across race and language. The relationship was mutual. "They even loved him in the barbershop," says Jasaun, director of African-American outreach. "And that love was there long before I came around." Unlike many of the young staff of color, twenty-four-year-old Jasaun Boone had no political or personal connection to Paul before the campaign. He had been trained in New Jersey by a group called 21st Century Democrats and donated to the campaign. Jasaun says he didn't understand the African American community's affinity for Paul until one of the early days in the campaign when he went with Paul to a black church. "I was cringing all morning, thinking, 'How's this little Jewish guy gonna do anything but embarrass himself in the pulpit?'" But when Paul took the stage, all Jasaun could do was sit wide-eyed, while Paul "preached like a Baptist and brought down the house." Says Boone, "I was sitting there with my mouth hanging open. I was completely sold."

Nimco tells a similar story about a Somali community event with both Senate candidates, a traditional electoral setup, where a community asks the candidates to respond to demands, one by one.

"On the way in," Nimco says, "Paul turns to me and asks me how to say *yes* in Somali. He didn't want to learn the word for *no*. I told him the word is *ha*. So he gets up there, and the representative asked him the first question, and very calmly, Paul replies, 'Ha.' So then they ask him another question, and he says 'ha,' just a little bit louder. By the third question, Paul was yelling 'ha,' and the entire audience was on its feet. All these little kids in the balcony had Wellstone T-shirts and signs, and Paul was getting a lot of energy out of seeing them. By the last question, he was so fired up that he screamed 'Ha,' like a preacher, before the question was even out. The crowd went nuts."

But beyond Paul's fire, the charisma that invigorated large, diverse communities, people were drawn to Paul because he demonstrated his love for them, over and over, in concrete ways; they knew he had and would throw down for them. Paul worked with hundreds of people from more than dozen African nations, assisting with citizenship and reunification. He spearheaded the Hmong Veterans' Naturalization Act, allowing Hmong veterans, their spouses and widows, to take the citizenship test with an interpreter. As a result, over four thousand Hmong nationwide—including seventeen hundred in Minnesota—now have their citizenship.

That act drew Pakou. As the twenty-five-year-old campaign director for then newly elected Mee Moua, Pakou came to the campaign not only because she believed in the issues Paul stood for, but as a personal thank you. "My grandpa was one of the Hmong veterans of the Vietnam War. He had lived in this country, fought for it, but at the end of his life he still wasn't a citizen. Paul's fight for the Hmong Veteran Naturalization Act allowed him to pass the test and get his citizenship two months before he died. This was so, so important to him and my family. Me working for [Paul] was thanking him for doing so much for us, for Hmong people in Minnesota, for immigrants in general." Other staff people came for similar reasons. Tibetans came to thank Paul for his support of Tibet under Chinese occupation. Latinos because Paul had defended the rights of migrant farmworkers in Minnesota.

## No Magic Bullet, No Kidding

In reaching out to communities of color, the campaign—largely because of its multiracial, multiethnic staff—was well aware of the fact that there is no magic bullet for organizing a range of communities.

Unlike most campaigns, which translate a leaflet to Spanish here or there and call it a mulitcultural day, Wellstone campaign materials were produced in Hmong, Spanish, Somali, Oromo, Arabic, Russian, Tibetan, and French. Staff and volunteers phone-banked in Hmong, Spanish, and Somali. The campaign also paid for advertising in bilingual papers and media outlets by and for communities of color.

Hmong people in Minesota come from a primarily oral culture. Families often exchange "letters" with relatives back in Laos or in other parts of the United States using cassette tapes, gathering the whole family together to listen when one arrives. So the Wellstone campaign recorded a forty-five-minute taped conversation with Paul. Translated into Hmong, this tape was given away in laundromats and sold in Hmong grocery stores—with huge success.

Contrast this with the print-focused strategy the campaign had for engaging Minnesota's predominately Jewish, Russian immigrant community. The volunteer in charge of Russian outreach was told adamantly "the community will not believe anything that is not in print." So the campaign worked to get Paul an interview with the major Russian-language newspaper. The editors ended up liking Paul so much that they turned the whole thing into a huge front-page story.

The campaign also produced an ad on Spanish-language radio, featuring "Mark," a teacher in a St. Paul high school with lots of Latinos. In Spanish, Mark spoke about the importance of education and criticized the plummeting budgetary support for schools. The ad ended with Mark saying "And how do I know all of this about Paul Wellstone? Because he is my dad."

Because a large number of Minnesota Latinos are undocumented, the campaign de-emphasized voting as the major act of political engagement. "We worked with everyone in the Latino community regardless of citizenship status," says Costain. "While non-citizens can't vote, they can still articulate the issues important to the community. They can help mobilize others. They can volunteer. Basically non-citizens can do everything but vote and therefore they are an important part of the effort."

And whereas traditional Democratic campaign wisdom says you reach black people though the church, the campaign's director of African-American outreach, Jasaun Boone, saw it differently. "If all you do is go through the churches, you'll just turn out the same dwindling set of people—the fifty-to seventy-year-old African-American women. They are important, but they are just a tiny slice of the people who can be mobilized."

In order to involve young blacks, the campaign hired James Everett and the Subzero Collective, a hip-hop crew recently credited with having played a significant role in the election of a black woman to the city council. The collective organized hip-hop concerts, where they registered folks to vote and talked about campaign issues. "There would be this sea of Wellstone T-shirts," recalls Boone, "and it wasn't just campaigners wearing them. It was cats from the hood. That legitimized Wellstone for a lot of young people—like, if so-and-so who you grew up with supports Paul, he must be for real." Subzero Collective would go to fast food restaurants at 2 A.M., when clubs let out, and do voter registration as people ordered at the drive-through.

Many young folks of color who came to the campaign had a direct interest in increasing the political power and participation of their people. They were in it for both the "number goals" of electoral campaigns and the relationship-building of community organizing. Says Pakou: "In a traditional get-out-the-vote effort, you only target the people you think will vote for you. The strategy needs to be different for immigrant communities;. With immigrants, the policy should be to mobilize everybody. Everybody. This is how Mee Moua won her election. This is how the Somali community has done it. It's the difference between mobilizing for the short-term versus the long-term, between the election and the political power of our communities in the larger sense. We're committed to both."

## The Devastating End: "We've got to get back out there"

During the 2002 campaign, more than twenty thousand new people registered to vote. More than one hundred thousand people contributed to the Wellstone campaign, with an average donation of fifty dollars. Several thousand people actively volunteered for every aspect of the campaign. And even though they were traumatized and exhausted with grief, four thousand people worked the streets on election day to turn out votes for Walter Mondale.

Communities of color in Minnesota have shown themselves to be important to any politician serious about winning. Even Norm Coleman got on the "immigrant bandwagon" in the middle of the race—paying young Somali boys to wear his T-shirts in public.

It didn't work.

Communities of color voted overwhelmingly for Mondale, and in greater numbers than ever before. In districts with large numbers of Latinos, voter turnout increased by 14 percent and in areas with large numbers of Asians, turnout increased by 21 percent. In several predominantly African American precincts in Minneapolis, voter turnout was 65 percent or more. In one, turnout was 80 percent.

Wellstone staffers will be the first to tell you they could have taken things farther, that they missed opportunities, they took wrong turns. While the work in the African, Russian, Hmong, Latino, and African American communities was dizzyingly successful, Native American and Arab communities were not given the same level of energy or attention. Mostly they wish they had started sooner and engaged more people. "There was a whole spoken-word community that wanted to organize itself in support of the campaign, but we didn't have the energy to make that happen," says Costain. The campaign also had this brilliant idea of sponsoring a huge international soccer tournament—with teams representing all the various immigrant communities. They would play soccer, meet each other, and build visibility for the campaign. "It was a great idea but we were bursting at the seams. We couldn't take on one more project."

The devastating end of the Wellstone campaign—the death of the candidate, his wife, daughter, and three key campaign aides just thirteen days before the election—along with the defeat on election day, has meant that a lot of the innovative, grassroots strides the campaign made have gone—

underrecorded and underreported. But they still live on.

Fortunately, we've still got the Nimcos, the Jasuans, the Emmas, Brendans, and Pakous.

"I think it's really good that so many of us working on the campaign were so young. An experience like that changes you completely. It helps form the way you see the world. It becomes your network and foundation for the future. What we built was not just support for Paul, but broad support for his kind of politics. What we really built was an infrastructure for the future. I can't wait for someone from the campaign to run for office. We're a pretty loyal group—I'd bet that if one of us ran for office, the majority of us would drop our jobs right there and go work for them." —Pakou Hang

[Editor's Note: In the wake of Wellstone's death, several of Paul and Sheila's family, friends, and staffers came together to create Wellstone Action, which teaches Wellstone campaign's techniques across the country. Please visit www.wellstoneaction.org.]

## *Political Sex Survey* — MATTIE WEISS

*Favorite political song, artist, or lyric:*
The Coup—"Heaven Tonite"—this song makes me recommit everything, every time I hear it. It also makes me cry.

And if we win in the ages to come
We'll have a chapter where the history pages are from
They won't never know our name or face
But feel our soul in free food they taste
Feel our passion when they heat they house
When they got power on the streets
And the police don't beat 'em about
Let's make health care centers on every block
Let's give everybody homes and a garden plot
Let's give all the schools books
Ten kids a class
And give 'em truth for their pencils and pads

Retail clerk—"love ballads" where you place this song
Let's make heaven right here
Just in case they wrong

*What candidate would be best in bed? (please explain)*
On a purely technical tip, probably anybody in Bush's inner circle, with the exception of Bush himself. They're utterly uninhibited, attentive to detail, and have twenty sly little moves to every obvious one. (I can't believe I just wrote that . . . )

*Where are you touring this book?*
That sweet strip of Midwest swing states—Minnesota, Wisconsin, Iowa, Missouri, and maybe Arkansas.

*Something you hope to teach people on your book tour:*
About examples of electoral and grassroots organizing overlapping—about the potential for electoral campaigns to get beyond cold hard number goals and actually be a tool for changing folks' lives (something I didn't have a clue about and wouldn't have believed until I wrote the chapter).

*Creative strategy to win?*
Umm . . . actually do what it takes to get all the decent people who have been screwed over, locked up and shut down by our political system out to the polls. It'd be all over.

*Finish this sentence: "The day all of our political problems are solved, you'll find me . . ."*
Blissed out, and working diligently as the Minister of Revolutionary Soccer.

*What actor or public person would you like to see smackdown Ah-nold?*
Frankly, all of them. But let's start with Tanya Harding on his kneecap, Mike Tyson having a go at his earlobe, and one Mrs. Bobbitt working her magic wherever she so chooses . . . (oh no, I didn't!).

# Aya De León is Running for President!
## On a Platform of Partying, Sexiness, and Emotional Transformation
### an interview with Aya de León

[Editor's Note: Aya de León turned thirty-five and she's running for president. Well, not really (we wish) but she is thirty-five, and she's doing a one woman show called, you guessed it, *Aya De León is Running for President!* This is an off-the-cuff interview].

Aya de León: I was visiting my family in Puerto Rico during the 2000 election. I'm Puerto Rican but I'm from California, and so I was not prepared for the way my people put on an election. In Puerto Rico, people treat the election the way we treat the Super Bowl or the World Series. I mean folks put the "party" back in "political party," and there's a sense of joy and celebration and connectedness. They have big parades and people are roller-skating down the streets with their faces painted and blowing whistles. Young people who can't even vote yet are already affiliated with a political party, waving the flag, yelling and screaming. You have young people driving down the streets, setting off their car alarms intentionally to make noise, like "woo woo woo!" Or the other thing that people would do is put their car in park and spin the wheels really fast. I mean, you couldn't sleep around the time of the elections cuz people were just so loud! The night before, the night of, just partying! And ninety-plus percent of the people in Puerto Rico vote! It reminded me of sports teams. People feel an affiliation with their team, and whether your candidate wins or loses, you party.

Puerto Rico is a colony of the U.S., and so most parties are organized around their position on what the status of Puerto Rico should be. The party that advocates statehood is most conservative; the party that wants to keep Puerto Rico a commonwealth connected to the U.S. is moderate; and the party that advocates independence is most progressive. Many Puerto Ricans would ideally like independence, but are hopeless that an independent Puerto Rico could be economically viable. Still, the independence party is given all due respect, even though a small percentage actually vote for independence candidates nationally. With its colonial legacy, in Puerto Rico people really value the right to vote. It also helps that election day is a holiday, so working-class people can actually get to the polls with ease. This level of participation was such an eye-opener for me. I'm also African American and I think that until I was in Puerto Rico for the election I carried an African-American perspective towards voting—the legacy of hopelessness from disenfranchisement and lack of voting rights.

Not only do Puerto Ricans vote, but the Caribbean culture of Carnaval and festivity is at the center of the process, along with the political issues. Candidates get the local salsa or merengue band or disco crew to make a song for them. And then they get huge speakers and put those on trucks that travel through the neighborhoods blasting their songs, and that's what campaigning looks like! Young people hang out at rallies, getting caught in traffic jams with these tailgate parties, with rows and rows of cars and people sticking their heads out the window and waving flags. And this is not just in the city; this is way out in the mountains, too, in the middle of nowhere. Wherever you were, there was a truck going by, at all hours, blasting the anthem of one of the political candidates.

What I learned from the elections in Puerto Rico is that people of color can have a culture of enthusiasm about political participation, but it has to reflect the values that are important in our community. We want to be connected to each other. We want to celebrate. We want to feel powerful. It's not just about, "We have to vote in this one election and hopefully our candidate will win." People in Puerto Rico have relationships to political parties like many people in the U.S. have to sports teams. Many folks in the U.S. can love their local sports team and their team can have a terrible record and never win and never make it to the finals, but people just love their team, you know? And I think that we might want to use more of a sports model around how it is that people get excited about voting, that people love their team and they go all to the games, and they're loyal.

It's the sense of celebration and joy, and the opportunity for people to be connected and be together—that's the missing piece in the U.S.. The Left uses a sense of terror and desperation to try to motivate people to vote. "Oh God, oh no the world is ruined again! Oh terror! Oh desperation!" Believe me, I know there are reasons to be terrified and there are ways that the situation is desperate, but what happens is that only a small percentage of us are motivated by terror and desperation. Terror and desperation are not attractive. Most people just go back into denial and don't want to deal with it. We have to be appealing and we have to create a situation that is desirable, so people want to be part of it, and where people are welcomed into it.

I also wanna say that, for me, it isn't a problem that people like to join and become part of things for a lot of different reasons. Why can't we encourage people to come register to vote at the singles' event, or the emcee battle, or whatever? It's fine for voting to be associated with a lot of the things that are valued in this society, like young, sexy people! Which isn't to say I don't have a critique of that. I'm not saying "have a strip show," but I am saying this: find the places where young people are and politicize those places. Identify the elements of places that attract young people and incorporate those elements into our tactics. Any political event targeting young adult voters should broadcast "this is where a lot of young, fun, smart, interesting, exciting, sexy folks are gonna be." If there's one thing we know, that's where young people want to go! And there are things about that that are problematic, but that's also what's real. There should be voter registration going on in the back of every slam, every spoken-word set, every hip-hop show, every nightclub. There needs to be voter registration right there. And I also think that there need to be incentives for people to actually vote, like if for thirty days after the election you brought your little voter stub to all kinds of different environments and you got a discount or you got a free drink, or you got this or you got that, or you got a friend in free, that would be appealing. People who do marketing know that those are the ways that you market. And, you know, many of our causes don't have the same amount of money that more conservative causes have, but we do have the power of our entrepreneurial and underground stuff, and we need to flex all that—in 2004 and beyond.

In this country—and among progressive folks especially— we're so intellectual and we're so up in our heads, and I think part of the triumph of the right-wing has been to meet the emotional needs of the people. People want to feel powerful! People want to deal with their pain and their stress and their issues. And the right-wing, particularly the far Christian Right, is offering a package to address those needs. I don't like the package they're offering. I don't think it's ultimately a healing for those folks, but they're addressing it. And I think that we've got to start offering some progressive alternatives.

Because, ultimately, it's not about intellectual stuff and quoting statistics. The reason we're able to behave the way that we do towards people in our country and towards people in other countries is a lack of empathy. Children are born with empathy, and they lose it. And we lose empathy because of all kinds of socialization and abuse and terrible things that happen to us as young folks. Whereas the right has figured out how to step in and manipulate peoples' emotional desperation to its own ends, I think that progressive forces need to figure out how to actually do some healing work and restore people's empathy on a wider scale. Our current strategy seems to be to continually work the same twenty people who already have empathy and make those of us who do have empathy feel worse about ourselves because we're not doing enough to change the world.

The other thing that happens is that we on the Left don't know how to have empathy for people that we disagree with. I was at an antiwar protest and some business guy walked up, and he was obviously very uptight. The antiwar forces were blocking traffic and he made some comment and people made fun of him, and yelled at him. This is the wrong way to go. There are reasons to be mad, but why isn't our movement growing? Because that's how we deal with folks who try to engage with us—we don't know how to listen!

Progressive people are angry, but conservative folks are angry, too. But underneath that anger, people are hurt, and they feel discarded. And whoever that guy was, whatever his story was, he was trying to get our attention. If somebody could listen to him and validate, maybe not his thinking, but some of the feelings underneath that, then we could start making those connections. If we don't connect to him, some right-wing organization certainly will. We need to stop missing these opportunities to connect to people. And it's gonna be out of those connections that our movement's gonna grow and develop. Because it's not just that we're preaching to the choir, it's worse than preaching to the choir—we're

www.pocho.com

dumping on the choir! Like I said, there's a small group of people whose empathy is intact, or who, for whatever reason, feel like it's our responsibility. So we keep heaping more and more and more and more responsibility on that small group of people. And so then you say to other people, "Be an activist! You, too, can be underpaid, stressed out, always feel bad about the world, and always be worried!" That's not attractive. And so we continue to have the same tiny group of activists being further and further beleaguered as the right-wing makes more and more gains.

One of my favorite things about hip-hop activism is the hip-hop part of it! The new generation understands that you don't just have an endless series of meetings where people sit on their butt, get stiff backs, feel hungry, have to go to the bathroom, get dehydrated, and stay up in their heads. They understand you have to get off your butt and shake it; you have to get connected. You get to see other people who you find interesting and attractive and visually stimulating and people get to wear bright colors and fly gear. And you know, yeah, capitalism is up in that. There are parts of that we can critique but I think the bottom line is there's a sense of joy and there's a sense of connectedness. And that's what people are desperate for. And that's what the right-wing is offering them. And our activism, outside of hip-hop activism, is so dry and so dreary and so intellectual. I feel like the motto of the Left should be: "Lose and feel bad—but for all the right reasons." And that's got to change.

People are so beleaguered in their daily lives, that if activism does not offer them some outlet of joy and community, folks are not interested. We have to really build a movement, and this movement, it's got to *move*, you know? This movement's got to be fun, this movement's got to be sexy. And we have it. We have all the elements we need in order to do that.

And it's also got to address people's pain, and people's emotional needs, not because we want to be all touchy-feely, but because that's where the actual shifts take place. People will often point to some intellectual reason for holding a bigoted, irrational, or shortsighted point of view. And you can throw well-documented statistics and logical arguments at them all day long and they won't change their position. Because the opinion isn't actually based on the logic they articulate, it's based on a deeper emotional reason, like fear or rage or hopelessness. People are more likely to change if we make an emotional connection. For example, it can be very effective for someone to tell their story. You can have a group of hardcore, uptight, homophobic types and you'll have a queer person come in and tell their story and say "people said this and did this to me and this is how I felt" or "this is what it was like for me," and then once people can create that bond of empathy then they have to start re-evaluating their homophobic notions.

Howard Zinn says that "the purpose of political art is to move people to action." I would remix that to say that the purpose of political art is to move people, period. Many times we need to use art to move people internally, to unfreeze or un-numb them inside, before we can manifest a change in their actions.

Movements need to move people. It's not just intellectual and it's not just about political organizing. It's not even just about the art—the art begins to scratch the surface of the emotion, but sometimes we've just got to go for the emotion. The emotional transformation.

*What's your sign and what does it have to do with politics?*
I'm a Scorpio with a Cancer moon. This means I'll never forgive the Bush family for what they did to this country, but I'm also hella sensitive and liable to cry about it.

*What candidate would be best in bed? (explain)*
Anyone but Bush. He's a lousy negotiator (sex is all about negotiation). He wouldn't know the geography of the female body, and when you were done, he would say something really stupid.

*What might happen if Bush gets another four years?*
He might change the Constitution so he can be president indefinitely! Yikes!!!

*A slept-on group of voters you'd like to see organized:*
Wrestling fans. We would have candidate look-alikes mud wrestle in g-strings to help develop a sports fan fervor for elections.

*Your greatest political achievement prior to helping swing the 2004 election:*
Staging a political coup in my high school and engineering a progressive takeover of the student senate.

*What's up with Aya de León is Running for President:*
I have always identified the 2004 election as the first year I would be old enough to run for President. I just finished my solo hip-hop theater show about women's empowerment in hip-hop *Thieves in the Temple: The Reclaiming of Hip-Hop*. Then in the end of 2004 I'll start my next project about violence against men, *How the Other Half Endures: A Spoken Word Exploration of Male Experience Against a Backdrop of Violence*. I figured the least I could do would be to squeeze in a one-woman show about running for president in order to inspire more political activism among young people. What I'm doing in art, we will begin to see more and more people doing in real life. As the hip-hop generation comes of age, we are going to be the candidates and the columnists and the voters, as well as the artists and the activists. We need to begin to understand that political power can be ours, and step up to make that a reality.

*One politician, big or small, who you think is halfway decent, other than Barbara Lee (and they have to be alive):* Former Congresswoman Cynthia McKinney!

*What superhero is needed to get us out of this situation:*
Super-us!

PART

3

# "Honey, We Got ISSUES!!"
## How We Changed the Laws

*"Dr. Mr. President,*

*What's happenin'? I'm writing you because shit is still real fucked up in my neighbrhood. Pretty much the same way right around the time you got elected. Ain't nothin' changed. All the promises you made before you got elected aint come true. Me and my homies was wonderin' what's goin' on. Holla!"*

—from "Letter to the President,"
Tupac and Outlawz

# Students vs. Court of Public Opinion

By Monique Luse, Jackie Bray, and Michelle Lin

JACKIE BRAY: Monique and I had our cell phones pressed to our ears and two legal pads in front of us. With the press swirling around, we were trying desperately to listen to the D.C. civil rights lawyers, who were interpreting the decision. We would each furiously take a page of notes to give the spokespeople. We were literally rewriting the student body president's statement minutes before she gave it in front of live television cameras. Then we stopped cold. We froze and looked at each other. A tiny smirk came over our faces. Through the madness we had forgotten the obvious. We scrawled on our papers, "Hopwood: null and void."

*Hopwood*, a circuit court ruling from 1996 that affected Texas, Louisiana, and Mississippi, outlawed the use of race in admissions. It had just been overturned. This was huge. We ripped the sheet off and watched as Michelle Lin proudly told all the spokespeople, "Start saying this makes Hopwood irrelevant, start calling for Texas to reinstate race conscious admissions policies." The next piece of paper read, "Today *Bakke* has been strengthened." For years we had all been fighting tooth and nail to hold onto *Bakke*, the precedent setting case on affirmative action. Now we had helped to strengthen it.

The press conference was over, and after the thank yous to the students, Monique, Michelle, and I started hugging. None of us could figure out whether to laugh or cry, so we just buried our faces in each other. As we were releasing our grips Monique said, "Remember this because it's not everyone who gets to start life with a victory. We have to remember how this feels so that we don't stop until we get back here on other issues."

MICHELLE LIN: On February 6, 2000, I got an email announcing that SCC (Students of Color Coalition) had gotten access to "the Tower" of the Michigan Union to protest Michigamua, the elite "secret society" that bastardizes Native American culture. They were occupying the Tower and simultaneously running tours through it.

The lobby area was packed with students waiting to see the Tower. Twelve at a time, we climbed the dark and narrow stairs to Michigamua's "wigwam." What I saw in that room made me sick to my stomach. A stuffed snowy owl was hanging with wings spread full from the ceiling. "Native" artifacts were displayed on a table. In disbelief, I stared at the names of Michigamua members on the wall: "Flipp 'Um Back Ford," "Silver Feathers Fleming," "Great Scalper Yost," "White Eagle Hatcher." I had seen these names before; they were the names of many campus buildings. I started to realize how fused Michigamua was to the foundation of the university. By the time the tour finished, I was enraged.

© 2003, Chris Ho

SCC's occupation of the Tower was the first time I saw what it meant to have solidarity with other students of color; it was both inspiring and alienating. My Asian Pacicific Islander (API) sisters' voices were marginalized as APIs and as women within the coalition, and they ended up leaving the Tower. Monique Luse, a black freshman, was having similar experiences. We saw our big brothers and sisters—our mentors—infighting and, over the course of thirty-seven days, they actually drove each other out of the Tower. Even though Monique and I wouldn't meet each other for the next couple of years, the Michigamua protest planted a seed in both of us. When we met three years later, I found a friend and comrade who understood the power of coalitions. We formed a partnership that help set the stage for our later affirmative action organizing. But first, Jackie Bray had to enter college . . .

JACKIE BRAY: As a white, upper middle class kid from the suburbs, I entered college with no idea what I wanted to do with myself. My parents would disown me if I became a Republican or a hockey fan. With those options ruled out I joined the campus labor group. Soon, I found that substantive conversations about politics and organizing don't happen in formal meetings. Any self-respecting progressive has stayed up way too late, sprawled out on a dorm room floor, eating Cheez-Its, and debating the best ways to unite the Left and take over the world.

It is in such conversations that pivotal moments happen. I befriended Monique Luse and we started to make these conversations a habit. No matter what turns our conversations took, love lives to libertarianism, they found their way back to affirmative action. Our university was at the center of the national debate, yet, there was no student organization to champion it.

The Center for Individual Rights (CIR) is a Washington-based legal arm of a network of right-wing conservative think tanks and foundations, with close ties to the Pioneer Fund, the notoriously racist and openly white supremacist organization that funded studies to show the genetic inferiority of Black Americans. CIR leads the anti–affirmative action countermovement in the courts, and litigated the lawsuits against the University of Texas, the University of California, the University of Washington, and most recently the University of Michigan. Using classified ads to find white applicants who had been denied admissions, CIR chose Jennifer Gratz and Barbara Grutter, who were rejected from UM's undergraduate and law schools, respectively, to become the faces of "reverse discrimination." In 1997, CIR filed suit against the University of Michigan claiming its admissions policies unfairly discriminated against white applicants.

Monique and I wanted to pull people together to strategize about how affirmative action could be framed under a united front. Maybe it was the old vending machine food we had been stuffing our bellies with, or maybe we were just young and stupid, but we decided to put all the campus leaders in a room together.

So what does the campus activist do when she wants to start the revolution?

We called a meeting.

In March of 2001, we held a meeting to introduce Students Supporting Affirmative Action ( SSAA). Our meeting was UM's own Noah's Ark—they came two by two: from the Black Student Union, from the College Democrats, the Asian Pacific Islander umbrella group, the Native American Student Association, La Voz Latina, the LGBT Commission, the American Arab Anti-Discrimination Committee, and so on.

Unfortunately, our ark could not withstand the downpour of ego that followed. Everyone agreed affirmative action organizing wasn't being done. But no one wanted to do much about it, and worse, no one wanted anyone else to do much about it, either. People did not want to create an entity that might be "in competition" with their current organization. Leaders repeatedly told us that their organization "just wasn't ready" to be involved in affirmative action. When would they be ready? When the cases get to the Supreme Court and there's not a single student there? When minority enrollment drops sharply the first year after a landmark constitutional case barring the use of race? How about when we look up and there's a crazed maniac in the White House telling the country that it has moved beyond racism, and that it's okay to bomb countries for the hell of it? They did agree to stay informed and connected. This clearinghouse concept became a basis for later collaboration.

By the fall of 2001, our stubborn persistence built SSAA. A typical student group, it had letterhead, an email list, and was registered with the student assembly, but lacked committed students (with the exception of Monique and myself) and buy-in from other campus organizations. By December, I had decided to shift my attention back to labor issues (in March 2002, we organized three thousand undergrads to walk out in support of the grad student union). And Monique decided to focus on gaining resources and legitimacy for affirmative action by pursuing a role in student government.

MONIQUE LUSE: Student government lent instant credibility with administrators and the media (something students of color desperately needed), and had mad resources (a five hundred thousand dollar budget). I ran for student representative my first year with the "All People's Party," a radical student of color party, dealing with real issues. Our platform included more tenured professors of color, more funding for student of color recruitment and retention programs, and an increased sensitivity amongst the university cops. The goal was to get people of color represented in student government. The campus is 74 percent White, 8 percent Black, 4 percent Latino, 12 percent API, and less than 1 percent Native. We bombed at the ballot box. The Blue Party, dominated by Greeks and careerists, slaughtered us. After the massacre, and despite the fact that I'm neither a white ma, nor paving a path to some brand name law school, I decided to run with the University Democrats—a well-funded, slicker, and significantly whiter party. (I was one of two people of color in party leadership.) We too were blown out of the water. After drowning our sorrows in a keg of beer, we were defeated, drunk, and disappointed; on a campus that votes 70 percent Democrat how could we have lost? We didn't connect with students. We ran on policies that are important, but not deal breakers. Scared to openly support affirmative action, we lost those votes; too intellectual to run on better workout facilities, we lost those votes too.

ANN ARBOR

VICTORY: WE WON STUDENT GOVERNMENT AND DEFENDED AFFIRMATIVE ACTION

Learn from my mistakes? Never! I got involved as the chair of the Minority Affairs Commission (a voteless voice for Students of Color). Jackie, who had continued to be involved with the University Democrats, and I spent the year traumatized by the foolishness of the government.

I felt like a broken record. Whenever something meaningful was before the assembly I gave the same speech: "You are the representative government of the students at the university. It is your job to have an opinion." These people had brought an ethic to the assembly that students, especially in the government, shouldn't have opinions. Convincing elected officials to vote on non-fluff resolutions was like beating my head against a concrete wall. The wall never seemed to mind, but my head hurt like hell. These fools weren't just out of touch with my issues as a Black woman; they were out of touch with anyone who wasn't trying to pad their resumes for Georgetown Law.

With the Supreme Court in our future, I had no time to ponder the evils of elected government. So, when I got called into secretive meetings between folks from the University Democrats and the Blue Party who wanted to start a new party, I went. These folks knew how to get power, but they had nothing greater than themselves to use it for.

I was the only person of color in the room, the only person who had ever lived in a working class neighborhood. I had to figure out a way to get my community into this room and rooms like it. So I swallowed my disgust and shared my vision:

* Student government has the power to make students lives better. If someone has a concern, then those elected to speak/work for her should hear it.
* Student government should not be made up of career politicians; it should consist of leaders from around campus. It is not enough to just run an Asian or Latina on the ticket. You have to choose someone who is involved in her community.
* Everyone deserves representation.

Pretty simple, right? It was like an alarm clock drawing a teenage boy out of his wet dream. These career politicians woke up and put their masturbatory politics on hold.

The Students First Party (S1) was born. I was chosen as our candidate for president. Jackie became one of the campaign managers (SSAA was dormant while we ran the campaign). It reflected both a principled view of government's potential to be activist, and a pragmatic understanding of how to gain control of untapped resources. The plan: join forces with the Greek representatives; put people from different constituencies on one ticket; then get each of the separate communities to vote for everyone on the ticket. Convincing other leaders of the idea was easy; picking a slate with nontraditional candidates was a different story.

It was midnight and the six women doing candidate selection had been fighting all night. There were two art school women who wanted to run on our slate. Brooke Gurber had been on the Michigan Student Assembly for a long time, was in a sorority, and was your average conservative Democrat. Emily Squires was a dynamic progressive activist. She was lively, fun, and tenaciously committed to representing the ideals Jackie and I shared. Cramped inside a tiny upstairs bedroom, we fought over these two women. Jackie and I could not stop pacing back and forth. My heart was pounding, Emily was my kid, Jackie and I had convinced her that she wanted to do this and now we knew she was the right woman for the job. Liz kept saying that Brook was more experienced. Jackie and I would counter that it was exactly those career politicians that we wanted to get rid of. It was ugly.

At three A.M., we were exhausted and split, three to two and one undecided. We had agreed that given a tie Sarah's vote counted more because she was the party chair. Liz put it to her, "You have to just choose, you're going to be the fucking president, so start making decisions." I was nearly doubled over with anxiety, when Sarah finally said, "We're going with Emily, she's the better candidate, and she'll bring more to the party." Jackie and I had won this fight but we had lost others. Still, we came out of candidate selection with a slate we could live with.

Most of the people that vote are freshmen. Freshmen can be found bored in the dorms, so that's where the election is won or lost. We combined a classic electoral plan of talking to as many students as possible with a grassroots tenacity usually reserved for issue based direct action organizing. Would freshman buy into the idea that everyone needs representation, would they accept a party willing to do more than expand meal options? Would the Greek system vote for everyone on our slate or just the Greek candidates? Could the progressive community be convinced to vote for our representative from the Club Sports teams? Could the Muslim Student Association vote for the representatives from Hillel and vice versa? We would run the unlikely candidates; they all had a stake in winning and recognized that they could not win on their constituencies alone.

Take my case, for example. I never actually convinced Black students to vote for Tim Whelan, a white frat boy. I convinced them to vote for me and that he would support my work and I his. One of the biggest lessons to teach about affirmative action is just because somebody else gets something doesn't mean that you don't too. Life is not a zero-sum game.

Our opposition, the Blue Party, had dominated the past six elections and three years of student politics. Over their tenure, the Women's Issues, Minority Affairs, and Lesbian, Gay, Bisexual and Transgender Commissions had all fallen on hard times and the Peace and Justice Commission had repeatedly been threatened with being written out of the assembly's code.

The External Relations Committee had gone from lobbying Lansing for more education funding to being virtually inactive. They were horrible at representing students, but brilliant at getting votes.

Evidence shows that in every election since they first won, the Blues have stolen email addresses and passwords, and voted for students without their knowledge. Blue party leaders pick their successors without the input of their members. While we were tolerating less efficient organization for more democratic input, the Blue Party was rolling ahead. They demanded high party dues and required their candidates to finance their own campaigns. We made a rule not to turn a qualified candidate away due to finances. The Blues would rely on their name recognition, outspend us and then steal enough votes to put them over the top. They were well established, well funded, and well known. We were brand new, took candidates without expendable income, and no one knew what S1 meant. But we knew our constituencies, and were willing to work harder than they were. Most importantly, we had something the Blue Party never did. We had vision.

The decisive votes would come from our newly engaged constituencies. Our candidates talked about what mattered to the people they represented. We didn't avoid the tough issues; our progressive candidates were proudly against the Bush administration; our Black candidates spoke out on affirmative action; and our Greek candidates ran on better workout facilities and more food options. We didn't have to be shy about who we were; we were everyone.

S1 won a decisive victory on March 21, 2002. I, a black radical, with a moderate white Greek guy as my running mate, won on a pro–affirmative action platform, and became president of the undergraduate college. Between the two assemblies, we won twenty-four out of the thirty-seven seats.

I was now one of the "legitimate" student voices on affirmative action. Our Party controlled the five hundred thousand dollar budget and the main student communication line with the administration. Our campaign yielded twenty thousand dollars, an unprecedented amount of money and support from the Michigan Student Assembly, for political work on the April 1 Supreme Court hearing; and I became the "go to" student for press inquiries on student opinion about the university's admissions policy. It was a long detour on the way to putting affirmative action at the center of campus politics, but it was time well spent.

It was January 2003 and the Supreme Court decision was looming over us. Most student organizations still didn't want to touch the issue. The Supreme Court was set to hear the oral arguments on April 1. We didn't have much direct influence on the Supreme Court justices, so we took our case to the court of public opinion. We had four months to change the entire face of campus and form a broad, campus-wide alliance—it was now or never. By now, the three of us were in organizational positions that gave us access to resources and platforms to reach students; Jackie was the Peace & Justice Chair of the Student Assembly, Michelle was chair of the API umbrella organization, and I was president of the undergraduate college.

Jackie, Michelle, and I pulled together a small group—about twelve key people from different communities—who trusted each other. We took steps to formulate our goals, and map out a process together before going public. After two precarious months of long meetings, we decided on a collective of leaders, rather than a coalition of organizations. The collective could bypass the bureaucracies of coalitions, and we didn't have to "steal" members from other organizations. Our collective model allowed flexibility for each organization to tailor its message or educational strategy for its respective community. The Black Student Union held a role-playing/media training session and created packets entitled "Affirmative Blacktion;" the Latino community had dialogues and bilingual literature; the API umbrella group created a presentation to educate its member groups and passed a resolution to support affirmative action, putting forth a unified voice for the API community; the chair of Students For Choice organized an educational event that centered on white women and affirmative action. All the efforts were coordinated through SSAA.

The SSAA collective agreed on five main projects to happen at the end of March: (1) a Jam for Justice, (2) a Student of Color Day of Silence, (3) a Rally for Educational Justice, (4) buses to D.C. on April 1, and (5) a D.C. press conference. By the end of February, we had literature and had set up a mechanism to stay in touch with all interested parties. SSAA was reborn, this time stronger, more strategic and better equipped. Having spent years gaining legitimacy, building a resource base, and acquiring control of student government, we drew on everything we learned.

After spring break, we had exactly one month until the university's most important moment in front of the Supreme Court. There were about ten of us who had committed to focusing on SSAA's five main projects, and we were excited about the work ahead. The work included eighteen-hour days, barely passing classes, and losing any semblance of a social life. Each of these long days were filled with any number of triumphs and tribulations.

JACKIE: Late morning to early afternoon was prime calling time. Most students were in classes, so whoever was in the office would turn our attention from educating and organizing our peers to corralling national organizations. Money had to be raised. Congresswomen and men had to be convinced to come to our press conference. National organizations had to be brought on board. We were one week out from April 1 and everyone was expecting a press conference with Michigan students and congresspeople. The phone in the Peace and Justice office rang and I ran out of the communications office to answer it. On the other end was a staff person from a particular congressional office in D.C.

"I'm calling to make sure that the congressman is upfront at the press conference on April 1."

"Of course! Actually, I've been meaning to check in with you to make sure you got the location we asked for," I replied cheerfully.

Surprised the staff quipped "No one called you? We were unable to reserve space, I assumed by now you had taken care of it. I've got to run."

"Wait a minute!" Now near panic I answered, "Only congressional offices can reserve space, how exactly did you think we were going to pull that off?"

"I'm sorry I really have to go, if this thing still happens he'll be up front right?"

Click. I was left staring ominously at the phone. Defeated, I walked out of the office slamming the door. I plopped down on the sofa to figure out how the hell we were going to hold a press conference in D.C. without a location. Forty-eight hours of worrying later some wonderful senators came to our rescue and got us the Senate Swamp, but each day we were living on the edge of a crisis.

MICHELLE: At a check-in one night, a graduate student working on faculty donations told me that she had arranged a meeting with a professor in the women's studies department for the next day. I was going to meet her to pick up checks from faculty in women's studies and history. I expected a few checks—five at the most—worth sixty dollars each, enough to help with supplies. The next day I ran into the university credit union to meet Professor Carol Smith Rosenberg. She smiled and handed me an envelope while she finished writing another check. I took the envelope without realizing that it was the checks; it was too thick to be what I had come for. It wasn't until she walked away without handing me anything more that I looked inside. Inside were over twenty faculty checks ranging from sixty to two hundred dollars! Over the course of the month, faculty donations raised over three thousand dollars.

MONIQUE: The more I worked on SSAA, the more the Black Student Union rejected me. A producer at Dateline NBC saw me doing an interview on affirmative action and asked if they could follow me around for the month. I invited the crew to come to a BSU meeting. But, when I told the BSU, the responses were all negative: "Who said you could invite people into our meeting?"; "This is not the only issue that we work on;" or, behind my back, "Monique is always caught up with those white folks—she doesn't care about us" and "Monique is so caught up in the camera, she doesn't care about what we think." Shit, these were my brothers and sisters, and they couldn't get over their own egos. From then on, people with whom I had shared my passions, my soul, and my life treated me with distance and mistrust. It sucked, but I put my head down and focused on the work.

JACKIE: By April, all of us who were the main organizers had been pushed to the edge of our own communities because we insisted on working with each other. But we made the decision that on this issue it was that important that we work together.

Over four weeks, SSAA talked to thousands of students. More than five hundred students of color participated in the Day of Silence, with a comparable number of white allies. After years of looking out into the same twenty disappointed faces, we were finally staring into a sea of students at our Rally for Educational Justice, the first pro–affirmative action rally organized by students in six years. Over seven hundred students went on thirteen packed buses to D.C. to join thousands of other supporters from across the country. Our D.C. press conference premiered on CNN. It was a sight to see, hundreds of University of Michigan students singing our fight song "Hail to the Victors," wearing M JUSTICE t-shirts and listening to Senator Stabenow, Congressman Conyers, Congressman Dingell, Congresswoman Lee, Congresswoman Kilpatrick, and Mayor Kilpatrick talk about our place in history as half a dozen news cameras watched.

SSAA helped organize and got invited to speak at many other campuses. At Northwestern, we were asked what special technology we used to be able to organize successfully. In fact, word of mouth was our strategy. We were short on people, short on support, and very short on money but we still insisted on having real conversations with real students about the facts, the feelings, and the substance of affirmative action. We didn't have satellite technology, we had people power. You can delete an email but you can't delete a conversation.

SSAA was in a holding pattern over the summer, waiting for the Supreme Court to announce its decision. Five of us were flown to D.C. by the Leadership Conference on Civil Rights, and were told we had to get on board and learn how to do some seriously good press work before the decision came down. Affirmative action is a slippery issue: phrase it one way and people support it, phrase the exact policy another way and people abhor it. Messaging is everything and SSAA leaders had six weeks during the summer to train over twenty student spokespeople. If the court upheld the principle of race-conscious policies, even if it struck down the process our university used, students had to claim a victory. Press cycles are fast paced wars between two opposing frameworks. For too long, conservatives had been able to frame the issue of affirmative action, and if the university got even a partial victory, the students were in a position to take the issue back.

On June 23, 2003, the decision came down on our side.

MONIQUE: That day my thoughts were on my former Sunday school kids. I went to U of M to fight for an opportunity to match their promise. I had wanted to go to college for those who could not. I chose U of M to win this fight. When I heard the decision, standing in the middle of our campus, I felt like I had fulfilled my purpose.

MICHELLE: I had spent my entire summer working on this one day. While Monique and Jackie interpreted the decision I was herding the media towards the press conference. When I grabbed a minute to look around I was staring at dozens of cameras and hundreds of elated students decked out in our M JUSTICE T-shirts. Immediately, I knew we were getting good coverage; clips of our students were all over TV and SSAA members were quoted by the AP wire service. Our moment had come. That night I got on my computer and slowly the major newspapers posted article after article quoting our spokespeople. Then I saw it, two simple words that let me know we had done our job. Our opponents use *race-based* or *race preference*. We use *race conscious* and those words were dotted on the headlines across the country: "Race Conscious Admissions Policies Upheld." We won the cases and we won the press cycle. We had changed the debate around affirmative action and made it possible for students in the coming years to get off their heels and move forward.

JACKIE: So this sounds great, right? Those fabulous chicks really kicked some ass. But what does that have to do with you? Everything. The 2004 election is crucial. Things are worse than they were three years ago. Get of your asses! Kick that SOB out of office. You have the energy, instinct, and power to change the direction of this country. But you are not going to rock the world by your lonesome. You need allies. We got a lot more authentic work done trusting people's commitment to the issue and letting them do their thing. Suck up your pride; ship your baggage and hope the airline loses it. You have to be real with people and talk to them. Find folks that you need to work with and figure out how you can. We will only win if we win it together.

*Where are you touring this book?*
I'm taking this book to the streets! Well actually I'm taking it to the halls. The hallways of our colleges, our universities, and our high schools!

*Goals for 2004?*
In 2004, I want to see progressives in this country develop a national discourse that moves us away from issue-based movements and begins a conversation about who we are as Americans, what freedom and democracy mean to us and how we can continue to strive for equality in this country and around the world.

*How do we get a progressive majority and how long will it take?*
We don't have to *get* a progressive majority, it already exists! But we do have to organize and articulate it. Organizing all the people in our country who know right from wrong and have some ingrained sense of belief in true democracy isn't easy work, and it is going to take us a long time. However, the first step is believing in our fellow Americans. I believe that there is good at the heart of most of us, that the American people believe in fairness, freedom and democracy. When we act as though our progressive numbers are small and the rest of the country doesn't know what's best, we automatically shut ourselves off from our neighbors. Americans are good people who have been force-fed a politic of insanity rather than sanity, of insustainability rather than sustainability, of greed rather than community. As progressive leaders we've got to get out there and articulate alternative visions and alternative ways of expressing true American values. As for how long it's going to take, a conservative estimate, fifty years. But then again we could cut that in half if we would just start having more sex, well actually more children. We could either do the slow hard work of dialoguing with our fellow citizens or we could get out there and procreate. Perhaps a little of both and we'll get there in our lifetimes.

*Your favorite thing about George Bush?*
My favorite thing about George W. Bush is his smirk. That little smile he gets that tells you one of two things. Either he really truly is a complete idiot or he actually believes the rest of the United States is made up of complete idiots. That smirk has come in handy though, every time I question if it's worth it to throw free time out the window, buckle down and get ready to help kick his ass out of office, all I have to do is picture that smirk if he wins on November 4, 2004, and I am right back in it ready, willing and able to

help make sure that come November of 2004, Mr. Bush is out of a job.

*Favorite political movie:*
By far my favorite political movie is *Bullworth*. Subtlety is not my strong suit and I don't look for it in art. I love how the movie shamelessly breaks it down into easily digestible bites of political truth.

*Finish this sentence: "The problem isn't really Stupid White Men, it's . . . "*
Stupid leftists. The American Left has spent thirty years being nostalgic for a time when we were actually good at organizing. We've forgotten to continue organizing. We spend countless days yelling at each other and some ominous power structure and we totally neglect conversing with our friends, neighbors, classmates, teachers, peers. And believe it or not, in my book that's good news, because I have a lot more control over what I do than what some stupid white men do with their free time. This country's politics are in our reach, it's in our imaginations, if we could only get our heads out of our asses long enough to engage the nation.

*Finish this sentence. "The day when all of our political problems are solved, you'll find me . . . "*
Wasting away in Margaritaville. No seriously: the day when all of our political problems are solved, you'll find me as the Supreme Dictator of the entire world—oops that's not very democratic of me is it. Okay third time's a charm: the day when all of our political problems are solved, you'll find me working at a flower shop in New York City, raising a gaggle of children, madly in love with some other adult who I attend every single New York Knicks basketball game with because we have season courtside seats.

*When we do get SWM out of office, the next challenge is . . .*
We can't see our movement as having neat stages. We can't wait to get Stupid White Men out of office before we begin to prepare ourselves. What I mean is that simultaneously as we're firing a whole slew of mean spirited nasty politicians we've got to be preparing ourselves, our colleagues to step up and lead. Here's a question, if given the power to decide what to do about sewage systems in a decaying rust belt city what would you do? Don't know the answer; well neither do I, but sewage and a whole list of other questions are the bread and butter of running our communities. We talk a lot about how ineffectual the current leaders are and how we have better ideas. What I'm saying is that we better not be bluffing. If we want other people to take us seriously then we've got to take us seriously. And taking ourselves seriously means truly believing that we can and will win, that means having answers to questions about sewage.

# Dirty Politics and T'ai Chi

## By Eli Il Yong Lee

Known as Marty in public, Martin in formal settings, and Martín in front of Latino audiences, Marty Chavez is the Hispanic Democratic mayor in the Democratic city of Albuquerque in the Democratic state of New Mexico.

In this metropolitan area of six hundred thousand, of which 50.1 percent are people of color, Marty catapulted himself on a platform of unfettered development into his first mayoral term in 1993. Marty has married his political career to the success of Albuquerque's Westside real estate explosion, exemplified by his support of Black Ranch, a sixty-seven hundred–acre development by John Black on the far Westside of Albuquerque. Marty's build-it-and-they-will-come philosophy has turned the Westside into the suburban sprawl so lampooned in teen movies of the nineties, with cookie-cutter developments and big-box retail built years, and sometimes decades, ahead of infrastructure such as water, roads, and schools.

Since he's been mayor, he has wanted to extend a commuter highway called Paseo del Norte through Petroglyph National Monument. Petroglyphs are ancient Native American etchings that adorn the volcanic rock in this serene desert. Listed on the National Register of Historic Places, Petroglyph National Monument has been a religious destination for Pueblos and other Native Americans for thousands of years. This national monument contains the largest collection of petroglyphs in North America—more than twenty thousand. This area is still a sacred site for this area's Pueblo tribes, who continue to use it for religious practice.

Which brings us back to Marty. On one hand, the mayor boasts of the "lifestyles and beliefs" of "the area's earliest civilizations" on the city's tourism website. At the same time, he was trying to run a sixty-five million dollar four-lane commuter highway called Paseo del Norte right smack through the middle of this national monument and sacred area—and directly to Black Ranch.

> Uprooting an object, and thereby destroying its foundation,
> will make the object fall sooner.
> —Master Chang San-feng, T'ai Chi Master, 1200 C.E.

Master Chang San-feng speaks of the utility of identifying the root of a problem. This lesson has served SAGE Council well.

As the token Asian, I helped start the Sacred Alliance for Grassroots Equality (SAGE) Council in 1996 (then called the Petroglyph Monument Protection Coalition) with several other young people of color, mostly Native Americans and Chicanas, in order to stop Marty's road. We were all young—in our early to late twenties—but had the blessing of having two elders, Carol and Bill Weahkee, guiding us.

We called Mr. and Mrs. Weahkee the parents of the SAGE Council. It was at their home that we held our meetings. It was in their kitchen that we ate Pueblo bread, red chili, and potato salad, and celebrated victories and birthdays or licked our wounds and prepared for the next round of battle. It was their quiet leadership that balanced our energy and passion so that we could channel our actions wisely.

Mr. and Mrs. Weahkee had been fighting the proposed Petrolgyph road for ten years before we came on to the scene, Mr. Weahkee in his formal capacity as executive director of Five Sandoval Pueblos, an organization representing five tribes in close proximity to Albuquerque. With the help and

## Westside Roads & Unser Middle

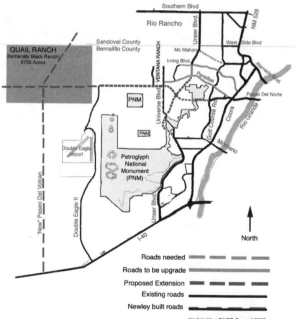

urging of the Weahkees, we began researching the root cause of this Petroglyph problem, trying to figure out how to "uproot" our problem, as the T'ai Chi master advises. What we found was surprising: all roads led to John Black.

John Black is a real estate developer whose family has owned and developed land on Albuquerque's west side for generations. A polite and unassuming man, Black has tenaciously pursued the development of Black Ranch (known as "Quail Ranch" after we campaigned against it), his family's sixty-seven hundred acres, located about five miles to the west of the city. The problem is that he needs a road that can punch through the west side, the volcanic escarpment and the sacred Petroglyph area, to provide the initial access to his proposed development. More importantly, he needs someone to pay for that road.

As we say here in the Southwest, it takes two to tango, and Black needed Marty to move his project forward, a role that Marty has been more than happy to fulfill. Marty has done everything in his power to grease the political wheels for Quail Ranch and fulfill his role as the mini-me of Manifest Destiny.

The SAGE Council recognized right away that the road was and is a terrible idea for so many reasons. First and foremost, destroying someone's place of worship is never a good idea, and one would be hard-pressed to ever justify such an act of sacrilege.

Second, the road, which currently dead-ends at a grocery store, would open the far west side to sprawl unlike anything Albuquerque has ever seen. Quail Ranch would send about forty-two thousand residents through what is now the west side as these new residents drive to and from Albuquerque everyday, where they will work. And, without adequate infrastructure, Quail Ranch would stretch police, fire, emergency response, public school, and water resources even thinner, just as our municipalities and schools are facing their most serious of budget shortfalls.

And third, unlike our dried up Rio Grande, city money is literally flowing away from older, traditional—and yes, people of color dominated—neighborhoods in the heart of Albuquerque to this exurban sprawl.

Luckily, Mr. and Mrs. Weahkee encouraged us to take a step back and look for the root of our problem. When the SAGE Council began holding press conferences about the relationships among John Black, the development community, and Albuquerque's elected officials, we forever changed the public perception of this debate. We framed it as a "profit vs. prayer" issue, which became the name of one of our early campaigns. Juxtaposing the concepts of "religious tolerance and respect" with "developer greed" hit a chord with voters in Albuquerque and drew a stark line in the sand for the campaign, one of the first rules of organizing.

To dramatize the link between developers and elected officials, we filed an ethics charge against City Councilor Adele Hundley, our staunchest opponent. Councilor Hundley co-owned property with our senator Pete Domenici about five miles south of Black Ranch. The development would substantially boost the value of their land. Councilor Hundley had never disclosed her ownership of these thousand acres, but she voted numerous times on the issue. The city ethics committee found Councilor Hundley guilty, resulting in weeks of publicity.

> A victorious army first wins, and then seeks battle. A losing army first seeks battle, then searches for victory.
>
> —Sun Tzu, Chinese General, 510 B.C.E.

Sun Tzu describes the wisdom of planning first and acting later. We did the opposite. When our crew joined the Petroglyph fight in 1996, we jumped in at full speed, fueled by anger and the desire to make our mark. We were a ragtag group of volunteers that picked up the battle flag from the Weahkees and a handful of neighborhood and environmental activists.

After three years of frenetic organizing, public education, and grassroots lobbying, we had succeeded in making this fight the most visible and emotional issue in the city. From our ragtag group, we had developed a 501(c)3 nonprofit organization called the Petroglyph Monument Protection Coalition (we later changed the name to the SAGE Council) with real membership, a real office, a real budget, and three full-time staff organizers.

We generated over two hundred articles and news stories and made the Petroglyphs one of the defining issues in the 1997 mayoral election. Jim Baca, the only pro-Petroglyph, anti-Paseo candidate won. We also built a database of five hundred supporters, and created alliances with predominantly Anglo environmental groups, associations of planners, neighborhood associations, small business owners, environmental justice organizations, and Native American groups.

## ALBUQUERQUE

**VICTORY: WE WON THREE CITY COUNCIL SEATS, AND STOPPED THE MOST POWERFUL DEVELOPER IN NEW MEXICO**

SAGE Council had always had strong relationships with local bands like Red Earth and Stoic Frame. Both did several fundraising concerts for us. We also jumped on the national scene with Rock the Vote. SAGE organizers appeared in a Rock the Vote video and participated in a national media tour on youth organizing and youth voting.

Yet our organizers and members were getting discouraged. Despite bringing over a hundred people to testify at city council meetings; despite organizing demonstrations of several hundred people; despite doing the difficult work of putting the Petroglyph issue on the local and national map and winning large-scale public support—despite all that—we were getting our butts kicked in the public policy arena. We only had the support of two of our nine city councilors, and only one of our five-member congressional delegation. In Sun Tzu's words, we were losing the battle because our initial strategy and planning was not correct.

In 1998, Marty collaborated again with John Black, the developer-driven Greater Albuquerque Chamber of Commerce, and Senator Domenici to push through wholly federal legislation that would esssentially eliminate federal protections for the Petroglyphs. At the time, Marty, Black, and the local chamber of commerce were traveling to Washington to lobby Congress. We wanted to launch a full frontal assault on Congress to stop Domenici's bill. Taking a lesson from Sun Tzu, we took this opportunity to step back and think through our resources and our strategy.

While we did send a few SAGE Council representatives to Washington, including our leaders, Mr. and Mrs. Weahkee, we concluded that our organization did not have the power, relative to Domenici, to defeat his bill in Congress. Moreover, our history, our culture of organizing, and our philosophy was just not suited to federal fights at the expense of locally based solutions. While defeating Domenici's bill may have created victory for us, there existed another path to a win—to defeat the Petroglyph Extension through local city council ordinance.

We took the time to chart our own course, to create our own battlefield and draw our opponents to it, as Sun Tzu advised. We decided to focus our strengths on the local arena and defeat the Paseo Extension by passing new city council legislation.

> Voting is one of the few things where boycotting in protest
> clearly makes the problem worse rather than better.
> —Jane Auer, lesbian author, 1917–1973

The nineties were bittersweet for us. Despite our success in educating the public and organizing our community, we were not able to shift power with our elected officials, never gaining beyond a 2–7 deficit with our nine city councilors.

To make matters worse, our staff organizers, our Organizing Committee, and many of our members viewed electoral politics with disdain. As students of history and taught by the lessons of our elders, we were acutely aware of the compromises regularly cut by politicians ostensibly speaking on our behalf. We had seen how local politicians were beholden to their campaign contributors instead of their communities, which favored cultural respect over developer profits.

Many of us were not even registered to vote. Of those of us who did vote, the vast majority voted just in the big elections. More often than not, we were registered as independents or in third, alternative parties. We were disgusted by the cynical nature of electoral politics. We were much more interested in building powerful grassroots, action-oriented organizations.

But we had to enter into this new terrain. We had to "dirty" ourselves with politics if we were going to have any chance of winning the Petroglyph fight.

We brought together many of our institutional and individual allies, predominantly from community groups organizing in communities of color, to form a political action committee. We named our new, independently financed and structured, federal-level political action committee the Independent Movement Political Action Committee, or IMPAC.

In creating IMPAC, the part that took the longest was discussing how to play in the electoral arena yet retain our values from community organizing. In other words, how could we immerse ourselves in the dirty world of politics, and come out victorious and relatively clean?

We decided that the only way to stay "clean" in our minds was to apply the same principles that had brought us to where we were today—developing homegrown leaders/candidates, working with individuals who came from a base that they remained accountable to and who supported the Petroglyph fight as well as a few other "litmus test" issues like the right to collective bargaining and opposition to school vouchers. And we recognized that what we had to contribute was not money, but volunteers who were trained in knocking on doors and making phone calls, often to people in the very neighborhoods in which we actually lived.

IMPAC was now a force to be reckoned with on the local political scene. However, campaign techniques were becoming more modern in Albuquerque. We could not do enough to push our less well-known and more progressive endorsed candidates over the top. We needed more capacity.

Three years ago, we started a for-profit political consulting company called Soltari Inc. Candidates and nonprofit organizations would contract our company to design and manage issue and electoral campaigns. Four of our past and current staff, including me, came up through the ranks together in SAGE Council, and we brough with us our experience as community organizers. Together, we experimented with electoral tactics in our local races. We also joined existing congressional campaigns to learn the ropes. We quickly realized that electoral politics had things in common with community organizing, like field operations and coalition building. There were many areas that were brand new for us too, like message development, dealing with radio and television, voter targeting, and polling and focus groups.

Since 2000, Soltari has swung two city council races, helped on a third, and also elected two school board members. We've gone from a 2–7 deficit on the Petroglyph fight in our city council to a 4–5 deficit; we removed two of our most vocal opponents and replaced them with equally vocal champions. Retaining our focus on local activity has helped IMPAC and Soltari grow methodically, building a successful track record as we set our sights on adding larger offices down the road. For city council races, Soltari Inc. only works for candidates who have been endorsed by IMPAC.

Capacity-wise, we now have three strong organizations that share a common vision and understanding of the social change we want and how to achieve it. SAGE Council maintains a three full-time staff and an active organizing committee. IMPAC has an active core membership of twenty individuals. And Soltari Inc. continues its campaign work with four experienced staff.

In addition to our local work, we did a massive field operation in 2000 during the presidential election. SAGE Council and Soltari Inc. collaborated on a project to turn out unlikely Hispanic voters in Albuquerque's North and South Valley neighborhoods. Al Gore won New Mexico by just 366 votes, so it's safe to say that our intensive door knocking and phone banking efforts changed the electoral outcome in New Mexico. We turned out 2,016 unlikely Hispanic voters, many of whom may not have voted otherwise.

> Doing too much is the same as doing too little.
> —Master Wong Chung-yua, T'ai Chi Master, 1600 C.E.

At the time of this writing, several developers have gotten together with the chamber of commerce to start their own political action committee focused on local races, and they are making a concerted effort to win back some of the council seats this fall. If imitation is the sincerest form of flattery, then we are indeed flattered by the competition.

The road hasn't been built yet, although we are fighting it every day as the developers and Marty move a step closer each month. We'll keep trying to stay one step ahead of Mayor Marty, John Black, the chamber of commerce, and local developers to create battlegrounds that favor the public's interest. With patience comes victory.

[Editor's Note: As we were going to press, IMPAC's most recent campaign, under the brilliant name "Stop Tax Waste" defeated Albuquerque's Street Bonds 55 to 45 percent. According to their victory email, "it was the first defeat for a general obligation bond in 18 years. This election served as a tremendous momentum-shifter in the fight to stop the construction of a six-lane commuter highway from being built through Petroglyph National Monument. It also greatly damaged our mayor, Martin Chavez, who has been the leading spokesperson for this damaging road. www.stop-taxwaste.com.]

# Justice 4 Youth

## By Piper Anderson

Hey! Are you ready to shut down a prison? Get money allocated for youth detention facilities cancelled from your city or state budget? You want to figure out a way to make the city government accountable to young people in your town? Well read on, I'll tell you about some young folks who've done just that.

First, you need to know what you're up against.

Although crime is way down from its peak in the late eighties, the incarceration rate of youth is going up. The mid-nineties saw the sensationalization of youth crime. With the media playing Pied Piper, politicians dutifully led us all into the sea of zero tolerance of youth, where your first small mistake can send you to juvie. Across the country, school districts began enforcing strict codes of conduct with even stricter consequences for breaking that code.

By now, we've all had a personal experience with "zero tolerance," whether we got into a fight at school, been profiled while chillin' on our block wearing the wrong colors, or witnessed a friend get arrested in a confrontation with a teacher. We all know just how deep it can get and how close you can come to getting thrown into the juvenile justice system. On the Lyrics on Lockdown tour with Blackout Arts Collective, I met a girl in Philly who had experienced abuse most of her childhood and was diagnosed with post-traumatic stress disorder. A teacher grabbed her arm, catching her off guard, and she accidentally hit him trying to protect herself. She was arrested and charged with assault.

I came home and got a call that my eleven-year-old cousin had been arrested for poking a boy in the hand with a pencil. She later told me it was an accident but they confiscated her protractor and took her out of her elementary school in handcuffs. She was held for ten hours before being released. She is in the gifted program at her school and had never been in trouble before. It didn't matter: she was given six months probation.

Zero-tolerance laws unfairly target youth of color. According to the Applied Research Center, Black and Latino youth are far more likely to be suspended or expelled from school then their white counterparts. Once they enter the system, they have a 70 percent chance of returning. Zero tolerance is a failed experiment. Regardless, school districts and politicians across the country continue to champion these provisions.

In New York City, a group of young people decided to fight back.

New York Mayor Michael Bloomberg wanted to balance the budget, so he slashed services vital to the survival of the majority of working people like education, after-school programs, childcare, social services, HIV/AIDS programs, housing—you get the picture.

But in the midst of all these cuts, the mayor proposed to increase spending for the Department of Juvenile Justice (DJJ). DJJ was going to get an extra 64.6 million dollars to expand two of its juvenile detention facilities.

The city spends $9,739 per year to keep a young person in public school and $130,670 per year to lock one up. Besides, DJJ was only operating at 70 percent of capacity. At the same time, formerly incarcerated youth have a 76 percent chance of returning to detention, while young people sent to alternatives to incarceration programs only return 30 percent of the time. Putting more money into the system looked like fiscal mismanagement.

We were blown away.

An informal group led by youth from Sister Outsider, the Prison Moratorium Project, and Urban Mindz got together in June 2001 and decided that this required an organized response. They launched the No More Youth Jail Beds campaign. Pretty soon, you'd see stickers and posters on the subway, walking down the street, in your local record story, at hip-hop and spoken word events. The group was soon joined by other youth collectives throughout the city as well as allies from outside our community like policy advocates, community organizers, and prison activists.

© 2003, Chris Ho

Born on February 14, 2002, the Justice 4 Youth (J4Y) Coalition officially launched on the steps of City Hall. Member organizations from throughout the city were present along with community artists, local media, and city council members. A hundred young people stood on the steps of City Hall with signs featuring Valentine's Day themes: "Why does NYC love jails more than education?" and "Love Education Not Incarceration." Two city council members, Charles Barron and James E. Davis, professed their love for this fierce young movement.

In the months leading up to the official launch of the No More Youth Jails campaign, J4Y met with members of the City Council to build alliances. The first council members they stepped to were those who were closest to the beast: Tracy Boyland and Pedro Espada, whose districts are home to the youth detention facilities Crossroads and Horizons.

Boyland was in favor of the expansion of Crossroads because she thought it would bring jobs to her district. When they stepped to Councilman Espada, it was clear that he had fallen for DJJ's lies. They told him that if these two hundred beds were built, then the infamous Spofford Youth Detention Facility would finally be shut down. This promise has been made and broken many times over the last decade to communities in the Bronx.

Councilmember Yvette Clarke, a liberal democrat from Brooklyn, was an early supporter of J4Y. She chaired the Fire and Safety Committee, which handles criminal justice issues. While she could leverage some power for the coalition, Clarke thought that their most strategic ally would be Councilmember Davis, who at the time was the chairperson for the Subcommittee on the Department of Juvenile Justice.

Davis was a former police and correctional officer with ties to the corrections officers union. He was known for his Stop the Violence crusades in central Brooklyn, and his stance against police brutality. When J4Y met with him,

both parties were able to see that this could be a mutually beneficial alliance. Davis would appear supportive of young people, while the coalition would have an in with the city council.

"Our relationship with Davis was . . . complicated," remembers Dana Kaplan of PMP. Because of Davis's strong connections to the corrections offices union he walked a fine line in supporting the closing of Spofford, one of NYC's most notorious juvenile jails. But Davis was in alignment with enough of J4Y's vision that negotiating for common ground was worth the trouble.

Because of Davis's endorsement, J4Y was able to pull major local and national media attention. The *New York Times* painted Davis as the champion of the No More Youth Jails campaign. Even if he was in the spotlight, J4Y knew this was the price of getting so much coverage for the issue.

With the support of Davis and Councilmember Clarke, J4Y held four public hearings in City Hall on the DJJ's budget. Formerly incarcerated young people from J4Y stood before city council and shared their experiences being locked up. They shared personal accounts of the pain and humiliation they experienced in New York City's youth detention facilities. They used their lived experience to advocate for more funding for alternatives to incarceration.

The Department of Juvenile Justice was no match for the No More Youth Jails campaign. In public education campaigns in schools, community centers, and other organizations, J4Y educated thousands of youth and community members about juvenile incarceration. J4Y sent thousands of postcards to the Mayor's office asking the 64.6 million dollar question: "Why does New York City love jails more than schools?" It also flooded the offices of New York state's chair on criminal justice and the head of DJJ with faxes. The city had no answer. This pressure on key decision makers was amplified by local and national media attention. J4Y successfully kept these issues in the spotlight.

By December 2001, the writing was one the wall. The DJJ spokesperson told *City Limits* magazine that she "didn't see the expansion proposal going anywhere." In June 2002, a year after J4Y held its first meeting, the mayor announced that he was removing 53 million of the proposed 64.6 million dollars from DJJ's budget.

But J4Y wasn't ready to celebrate just yet.

"Even though we stopped the expansion of Crossroads and Horizons, we still did not completely succeed. The fact that the city just removed the money from the DJJ budget, instead of reallocating it into schools and community programs, still shows that they didn't fully understand what we were trying to express," J4Y member Malikah Kelly says.

So the movement to realize justice for youth continues and this is only the beginning.

Young people are finding their power and using it to put their issues on the agenda all across the country. Not just in NYC, but in every region. There are movements of youth who are holding politicians accountable. They are saying: We will no longer go silently into your jails. We will no longer be swallowed by the incarceration machine in this country without fighting back. Right around the time that J4Y was kickin' ass in NYC, movements in other cities were taking shape.

Time to step up your game.

A coalition of young people from over thirty youth organizations in Oakland pressured their county to reallocate funds set aside for a youth superjail. Seventy young people packed a city council hearing, spitting poetry, rhyming, and passionately calling for the reallocation of funds to education and an alternative to incarceration programs. They succeeded in getting the number of beds slashed from 540 to 330.

In June 2003, the Ella Baker Center, which organized the strategy behind the Books Not Bars campaign held a press conference to unveil its Sane Budget campaign and blasted Governor Davis for granting a 7.5 percent raise to corrections officers while teachers across the state where being laid off. The Sane Budget campaign includes a list of proposed changes in the state's budget priorities.

The Sane Budget is a lobbying tool. The Books Not Bars campaign, which at the outset depended mostly on grassroots mobilization and "smart media," is stepping up its game and getting into the electoral arena. "This is how we'll play the game for now. But eventually we'll elect people who will represent for the people. It's all a different game once we have someone in office that we elect," says Mike Molina, organizer for Books Not Bars.

You got a right to be there. Pull up a chair to their table.

The Justice 4 D.C. Youth coalition was launched in 2001 after a mayor's commission recommended the closing of Oak Hills, an infamous D.C.–area juvenile hall. When policy advocates and community organizers realized that the district was going to drag its feet in closing the facility, they decided to build a campaign to pressure the district to finally close Oak Hills.

The coalition is part of the Juvenile Justice Advocacy Board, which decides how money is spent on juvenile justice and forecasts the need for secure beds. While most cities hire architecture and design firms that use their own funny mathematics to determine the number of beds (more beds = bigger profit), D.C. called in the Urban Institute to create an internal process.

So what's next? You tell me!

There are lessons to be learned from the success stories in D.C., Oakland, and New York. They are not the only cities where youth jails are being shut down and expansion plans halted. Young people across the country are gaining inspiration from each victory that the youth justice movement garners and using those victories to fuel our passionate desire for change. The incarceration machine is no longer moving on young people without being checked. As J4Y, Books Not Bars, Justice 4 D.C. Youth, and other movements across the country have demonstrated, the building of a prison in your town can be stopped. Are you ready for the challenge?

www.nomoreyouthjails.org | www.nomoreprisons.org
www.ellabakercenter.org | www.youthec.org | www.notwithourmoney.org
www.nomoreoakhills.org

*What's your sign and what does it have to do with politics?*
I'm a Taurus. We're strong, loyal, and we love time to chill. If I was a politician my crusade would be for a midday siesta where people would do no work: just sit some place surrounded by beauty and talk to each other, create, meditate. That would be my great political innovation in this country.

*Favorite political song, artist, or lyric:*
Bob Marley, "Redemption Song."

*What candidate would be best in bed? (please explain)*
Hmm . . . it's difficult for me to believe that a politician would be good in bed.

*Where are you touring this book?*
Wherever I can but especially at poetry and hip hop venues. Gathering places of young people and anyplace where I can dance, talk about the project, and sell books (that would be great!). I guess I'll also do the more traditional spots like bookstores, and schools.

*A slept-on group of voters you'd like to see organized;*
Young single moms. I'd offer them a week-long retreat at an amazing retreat center where they would all experience spa treatments and get training in radical parenting, self healing, and how SWM contribute to making their lives hell. Then I'd send them all back to their communities ready to kick some ass. Finally I'd help them start childcare cooperatives so that they had time to organize and build power in their communities.

*A political achievement prior to helping swing the 2004 election:*
Organizing a national tour with Blackout Arts Collective to build awareness about the prison industrial complex.

*How long until we get a progressive majority?*
How long will it take? I think it can happen in the next 8 to10 years as long as we're committed to not just getting in the game but also changing the way that the political system is set-up.

*A young person I know who should run for office?*
My little sister, Imani because she's the best fourteen-year-old party promoter I know, and I love the way that she can manage to finesse money out of my parents' pockets whenever she needs some new nonessential designer item.

*How to you convince the brother or sister on the corner to vote?*
Talk to them instead of at them and tap into what they're passionate about
as a starting point.

*What actor or public person would you like to see smackdown Ah-nold?*
Erykah Badu because she's little and cute and really hot and it would turn
me on to see her beat him down.

*If I were starting a political movement it would be called*
"The League of Queer Women Voters" 'cause my sistas have yet to fully realize their political power.

*A political goal I have for 2004. Creative strategy to win?*
To launch the first Get Out The Vote Pajama Jammy Jam the night before
election day. We're gonna throw a fabulous slumber party the night before
the election just around the corner from the voting booth, then wake everyone up to a breakfast of vegan chocolate chip pancakes and send them to the
polls.

# We Got Issues!

The one time I went to try to vote, listening to that voice that blares "Do
what you're told!" I walked across the street from my project building,
into another project building where the booths were. I waited as Doña
somebody looked down on me and up her book for my name, for a good
fifteen minutes, until she finally told me, "Your voting polls are four
blocks away in P.S. Oogalee Boogalee." I told her, "Don't you see it's pouring outside? I live less than twenty paces away from this building!" She
told me "I'm just doing my job. You can't vote here."

—Manuela Arciniegas

I haven't been voting much lately,
Because history is no longer enough
To keep me inspired.
Because things that should make me proud
make me sick to my stomach.
Because my predictably Democratic posture
Makes even me tired.
Because beyond the momentary
"victory" of casting a ballot
I realize, I ain't got a damn thing
to vote for, not one.
And now, after years of putting
my head

in the political sand . . .
I have finally decided,
to do something about it.

—Rha Goddess

I always have thought that this government was never for the people and by the people—at least not my people. My people are black, brown, red, yellow, and white (sometimes). They poor, strugglin', trying to make it check to check or every other one at best—hustlin', locked up, trickin', and politicking. They were here first; they came yesterday; either way shoved into corners and never duly paid. They mamas, daddies, baby mamas, sugar daddies, upwardly mobile, do-gooders, tree huggers, organizers. Either way, they just are and have every right to be.

—Mia Herndon

Helping out a young Boricua man in 1998 who ran a campaign against twenty-year incumbent Assemblywoman Gloria Davis had the granny trying to spank us for "misbehaving" and trying to steal her cushy job. She threw the muscle of the Bronx political machine at us, had me wondering, where is the democracy? Granny snatched flyers out of our hands so fast I thought she was running for a check. She even cursed at the folks sitting on Bronx park benches for responding to our positive messages and a little hope. She just got busted and fired for pocketing money from Bronx government construction deals. She was also the only black woman I saw holding office in the South Bronx.

—Manuela Arciniegas

*We got Issues is an initiative of the Next Wave of Women & Power. We are seeking the voices of young women rapping about the issues they have with the government, voting, America, their school, the hospital down the road, the president, their city council, bling-bling, white middle-class . . . Just issues. We're collecting stories, testimonials, rants, and poems from young women across the country. After we collect these voices we plan on creating a performance piece that will rock America into listening and rock young women into participating.*

www.wegotissues.org

# Dancing All the Way to City Hall

## By Alison Byrne Fields

There's no question. There were more than a few times during the fight to repeal the Teen Dance Ordinance (TDO) that folks from the Seattle music scene felt like giving up and going home. Fighting with the city council just to make sure kids in town could see their favorite bands was a pain in the ass: tiresome and time-consuming. "What was I supposed to do?" asked Dave Meinart, a promoter, "Stop doing music while I'm waiting for the system to change?" Despite the fact that it took a whole lot longer than they thought it would, Dave and others in the Seattle music community stuck with it and got what they wanted.

The Seattle City Council passed the Teen Dance Ordinance way back in 1985. According to the ordinance, if anyone under the age of eighteen was let into a dance or concert and there were more than one hundred and fifty people there, no one over twenty or under fifteen could get in. The ordinance also said two off-duty cops had to be hired as security, the event had to end by two A.M., and if someone left a show, they had to pay to get back in. Oh, and one more thing, the ordinance said the venue had to have a one million dollar insurance policy. As promoter Dave Meinhart put it, "The city was screwing its youth with this law."

The city probably had good intentions. They honestly felt like the law kept young people more safer. But it wasn't the first time (or the last) that adults came up with a rule that seemed a little random and got in the way of kids having a good time.

Because of the TDO, all-ages shows were becoming a thing of the past. And there weren't many venues doing shows exclusively for people under twenty-one because they couldn't make any money on liquor sales. Picture it. It's 1993, you're seventeen and living in Seattle and every music magazine is talking about the "Seattle sound." Bands living in your backyard (Nirvana, Mudhoney, Soundgarden, and Pearl Jam just to name a few) are on the radio all over the world and smaller bands are doing shows all over town. Meanwhile, you can't get near any of it because of a law that's shamelessly anti-youth.

On top of it all, the TDO was being selectively enforced, with some promoters and some venues getting a harder time than others. And remember that rule about hiring two off-duty cops to do security? Well, if there weren't any cops who were willing to work your show, your show wasn't going to happen.

A group of young local musicians tried to do something about the Teen Dance Ordinance as early as 1987. They put together the Youth Defense Brigade but hit a wall when no one would take them seriously because of their age. One of the musicians, Arlie Carstens, says he gave up when he couldn't deal with the "absurdity of it all." "I was a little kid just trying to do my part," says Arlie. Seven years later in 1994, a local activist named Greg Bennick started the All Ages Music Organization. Unfortunately, the group made little progress because they were once again ignored by the powers that be. The Seattle City Council couldn't bother to answer the kids' calls or—better yet—meet with them to discuss their concerns.

Three years later, in 1997, Kate Becker, who was putting on all-ages shows at a teen center in Redmond (about a half hour outside Seattle), dove in and started organizing the young people she was working with. Things started looking good when Kate and the kids held meetings about the Teen Dance Ordinance and one hundred and fifty young people showed up to listen or speak out.

Things got even better when city council members started taking their calls and meeting with them in person. It might have been Kate's reputation at the teen center or the fact that Kate was older and could act "professionally" on the phone. "Young people were calling and couldn't get five minutes," explains Kate. "They were like, 'Oh man, see, nobody cares.'"

Kate may have made the calls, but the kids were the ones who eventually won the city council members over. Most of the council members were downright giddy about having young people in their offices, particularly kids in bands. Despite the lovefest, Kate and the kids couldn't get the City Council to get past the novelty of it all and commit to making a change in the Teen Dance Ordinance. For the third time, efforts were stalled.

A year later, Kate says, "Greg Bennick and I conspired to kick the TDO in the ass for the last time." The duo formed the Teen Dance Ordinance Resistance and proceeded to put together a concert with Fugazi, The Ex and Sleater-Kinney to draw attention to the cause. That same year the Teen Dance Ordinance Resistance got support from Rock the Vote to do another show in town to generate public support. A couple of the more supportive city council members—Richard Conlin and Nick Licata—came out to the event and spoke to the kids in attendance.

Things started to roll from there. The Resistance started putting on community forums around town to allow young people to speak out on the issue, with Conlin and Licata making repeat appearances to hear what the kids had to say. The Resistance also organized public hearings to invite supportive parents to testify about why they thought the Teen Dance Ordinance was a useless and discriminatory piece of legislation.

In October 1998, Conlin proposed that the city council create the Music and Youth Task Force. According to Conlin's resolution, the task force would be responsible for advising the city council and the mayor on revising the Teen Dance Ordinance. Conlin has a background in youth empowerment work, so he understood the need to take young people's ideas seriously.

About three or four months later, in February 1999, all twelve members of the Music and Youth Task Force met for the first time, including Kate, Dave, and Greg Bennick. The other members included representatives from the police and fire departments, the city attorney, city council members' legislative aides, Angel Combs of JAMPAC (an organization formed to defend the rights of artists and music fans), and Stephanie Pure, who, as she puts it, was "just a fan." The representatives from the city had all been appointed, but the members from the music community had to apply by writing a personal statement about why the issue mattered to them.

"We were naïve," remembers Kate. "We thought we'd sit down and we'd explain and they would understand. And then once they understood, they wouldn't think we needed the Teen Dance Ordinance anymore." But it wasn't that easy. While the music community wanted simply to abolish the Teen Dance Ordinance, they soon realized that this wasn't going to happen. They needed to find an alternative because while Conlin and Licata and other city council members saw problems with the TDO, they couldn't deal with the political backlash if they eliminated an ordinance that was intended to keep young people safe. They needed to offer a compromise.

The Music and Youth Task Force met as a group once a month for eighteen months and in subcommittee meetings more times than any of them can count. "We'd be arguing the minutiae," explained Kate, "and couldn't get through everything." One of the biggest frustrations for Kate were the people who would make up stories about things that happened at shows— despite the fact they had no firsthand knowledge. "They had strong opinions about things that went on at concerts, but they'd never actually been," says Kate. Trying to keep the momentum going was an uphill battle. Kate says she thought she'd explode if she ever had to sit through another meeting. "The tedium was really wearing people down."

The task force's negotiations were centered on three sticky issues that tended to pit the music community against the police department. The police wanted age restrictions and the music community did not. The police wanted insurance requirements and the music community did not. The police wanted to require the hiring of off-duty cops to do security and the music community did not.

The one thing that they all did agree on was the need to ensure that the new legislation be written so that someone besides a lawyer could understand what the hell it said. The Teen Dance Ordinance was so thick with "legalese" that Kate and others were worried that new young music promoters would not be able to figure out how to comply.

By late spring 2000, the Music and Youth Task Force put the finishing touches on their proposal for an alternative to the Teen Dance Ordinance. The new law, which they called the All Ages Dance Ordinance, removed age restrictions, insurance requirements, and the need to hire off-duty police for security. Under the new ordinance, "regular" people, as long as they were trained, could do security, promoters would have to pass a background criminal check and a Music and Youth Commission—with members from the music community, as well as reps from the city—would be created to monitor all-ages events.

The Seattle City Council overwhelmingly approved the All Ages Dance Ordinance in August 2000. Kate believes that city council members were supportive because of the dedication and diligence of the young people who were involved. The members of the Music and Youth Task Force, says Kate, "danced with glee" when they heard the news, optimistic that the battle was finally over and the Teen Dance Ordinance was a thing of the past. The joy didn't last. The music community was in shock just two days later when Seattle Mayor Paul Schell vetoed the new law.

Many believe Mayor Schell vetoed the All Ages Dance Ordinance because he was trying to make the police happy. Schell's relationship with the police was less than perfect and the cops loved the Teen Dance Ordinance because it gave them a tool for preventing crime before it happened. (None of this innocent until proven guilty nonsense. Kids are rotten and when they're listening to loud music, they're even worse.)

Anyway, Mayor Schell was on the police department's shitlist for bringing the World Trade Organization (WTO) to Seattle in 1999. For months afterward, the Seattle police had been under scrutiny for failing to take the protestors seriously and letting things get so out of hand. With an election coming up, Schell could improve his relationship with the police by keeping the Teen Dance Ordinance—and the power it gave the police—in place. Schell denies that he was pandering to the police, however, claiming that the police didn't lobby him on the issue and that he made the decision on his own.

SEATTLE

VICTORY: HOW WE BEAT THE TEEN DANCE ORDINANCE

© 2003, Ben Wheeler

Whatever the reason, the music community was shaken, and many organizers began to wonder why they were putting their time and energy into a battle that seemed impossible to win. Kate questioned why she wasn't putting the same kind of time and energy into something else. "There are huge political issues. Is this the most important one?" she had to ask herself.

Around the same time, the Joint Artists and Music Promotions Political Action Committee (JAMPAC), made the decision to file a lawsuit against the city of Seattle, bringing the battle against the Teen Dance Ordinance into the courts. (JAMPAC was a political action committee that had been formed in 1995 by Kris Novaselic, the bassist from Nirvana.) JAMPAC's case argued that the Teen Dance Ordinance was unconstitutional because it discriminated on the basis of age and because it violated antitrust laws by allowing the police department to have a monopoly on security jobs at shows.

The judge disagreed with JAMPAC that the ordinance was unconstitutional, but agreed that the young people of Seattle deserved something better. "The Court has serious concerns about the impact of this ruling on the teenagers of Seattle who, the record shows, need and deserve more opportunities to enjoy dancing to music in diverse venues," he wrote.

When the time came for the next mayoral election—late in 2000—the music community decided to throw their support behind someone they thought was "pro-music," hoping it would help them get the All Ages Dance Ordinance passed. While Kate Becker says that Greg Nickels was "kinda mushy" about whether or not he would support specifically the All Ages Dance Ordinance, the candidate did take the time to make an appearance at shows to indicate his support for all-ages events. Dave Meinart thinks Nickels was pretty smart for reaching out to the music community for their support. "He saw this as a group who was disenfranchised by his opponent." The people of Seattle elected Greg Nickels as mayor in the fall of 2000.

The All Ages Dance Ordinance came up for a vote again in 2002. Things were stressful in those final days, with council members trying to attach amendments to the ordinance that would essentially turn back the clock on all of the negotiating that Kate, Dave, and the other members of the Music and Youth Task Force had done. At the last minute, Kate appealed to Peter Steinbruck, the president of the city council, to do what he could not to shit on the work that they had done.

Kate was worried about about the message that was being sent to young people about the political process. "If the TDO remains on the books and the AADO (All Ages Dance Ordinance) is not passed, I am concerned about what the message to Seattle's young people will be," she said at the time. "I worry that it will inspire them not to be politically active. They have seen people from their community come to the table and work in good faith with city leaders for an extended period of time. They have shown up at council meetings, spoken at public hearings, sent letters to council members, and written songs like 'Smash the TDO.' Even more importantly, they have worked together as a community to be responsible and educate each other about societal expectations of all-ages events. They have done this in good faith, trusting that the city leaders would value their efforts and respond positively. If the All Ages Dance Ordinance goes down in flames, I worry that the message to Seattle's young people will be not to care about their community and get involved in politics. I bet this is not what you want and it's definitely not what I want."

The All Ages Dance Ordinance was passed by the Seattle City Council in August 2002 and signed into law by Mayor Nickels. According to City Councilmember Richard Conlin, "The AADO is based on the philosophy that dance and music are positive experiences, and that people of all ages join together to dance. Having responsible adults around promotes safety, and brings youth into the community rather than isolating them."

Nice story, huh? Classic underdog fights the system and overcomes, despite the odds. It would make a great movie: cool kids, fiery speeches, and a great soundtrack. I'd go see it. Great story or not, there are some lessons that we can all learn from the work that Kate and Dave and the other folks in Seattle did to revive the all ages music scene. I mean, one of the most obvious is that you don't have to look very far to find an issue that needs work. Having a place to see your favorite band may not seem "important" when you think about all the other things in this country that need to be changed. But having a place to see your favorite band because you're not being held down by laws that disrespect you as a young person is *very* important.

What else? How about being persistent? The folks in the Seattle music scene fought for more than ten years to get rid of the Teen Dance Ordinance. Hopefully whatever it is that you're fighting for won't take quite so long, but it won't necessarily happen in a day either. Don't walk away when things get tough and don't get distracted by things that don't move you closer to your goal.

There's another thing. Working "within the system" has its benefits. By changing laws, you're potentially making things easier for people who will come along after you. They may wear suits, they may hold lots of boring meetings, they may have rules and justifications that don't make any sense, but they're in charge and they're the ones that have to be convinced to go along with what you want to do.

Remember that part of the story where the kids couldn't get the politicians to take their calls, but then once they did they were pretty impressed by how on top of things the kids were because it went against their stereotypes of young people? That shows you that sometimes being young works against you and sometimes it works in your favor. Don't accept it when people shut you down because you're young. Call them on it and, while you're doing that, figure out who your adult allies are and put them to work. In addition to adults, the media is also a good ally to have. Get as much public attention as you can. If they think lots of people care, politicians are more likely to listen.

That's the last thing. The battle against the Teen Dance Ordinance was finally won because they managed to get a mayor in office willing to approve the new law. Is there a candidate who cares about the issue you are working on? Get them elected so that they can have the power to help you get what you want. Do it in 2004 and do it every year after that. Let them know that you are a political force to be reckoned with and will not be ignored.

# How We Defended Our Homes with Proposition EE

By Bouapha Toommaly

A ratty-ass office in front of City Hall, on Telegraph and Sixteenth Street, was where we won our Just Cause campaign. It was an ugly old storefront with green paint covering the windows. The space was large enough to accommodate three hundred people. I guess it worked well, 'cause no one saw what we were doing in there. I think the setup of our office frightened some of our city council members. They knew that the campaign headquarters for Proposition EE (Just Cause) was there; they knew we were mad and they knew we had the power to make Just Cause a law in Oakland. But they did not know what we were doing inside and yeah, that scared them.

How or why did I get involved in this fight for renter's rights? I love Oakland. I love that it's a majority of people of color, that there are many politically active people, and that the attitude is so chill here. Oakland pride is strong, but if you go outside Oakland, there's a reputation that this city is dangerous and out-of-control. That scares people. But I feel safe here and that's really important to me.

Something like 65 percent of Oakland residents rent their homes or apartments rather than own. In the late nineties, the dot-com boom pushed a lot of white middle class people into Oakland because San Francisco got too expensive. Many landlords saw this as an opportunity to finally cash in on their property. They evicted tenants, gave them thirty days, sometimes only three days, to get out of their homes, and they didn't even have to give a reason for kicking someone out of their home.

Many evicted residents had been in their homes for decades. They stayed in Oakland through some really rough times, only to get kicked out when times got better. Most of the folks being evicted were people of color, lower income, and families with young children. Elders and immigrants were particularly vulnerable.

Landlords had all the power to decide who would to live in Oakland. Cities nearby like San Francisco, Berkeley, and Hayward have Just Cause laws that require landlords to have a legitimate reason to evict their tenants (like not paying rent or destroying property). But here in Oakland, tenants didn't have any kind of protection, not even this really basic law. Tenants were at the mercy of their landlords . . . kind of medieval, huh?

Our first coalition was formed in back in '97. We tried to collect signatures to put Just Cause on the ballot, but the coalition wasn't strong enough to get the required signatures. At first, we tried to approach our mayor and city council members about having a law like Just Cause to protect renters in the city from unjust evictions, but they paid us no attention. Our elected officials were only responsive to the Oakland residents on the hill, because they own most of the property in Oakland and contributed the most to their campaigns. The mayor and city council members declared their opposition to a just cause measure.

Our first try helped to build a foundation for our success the second time around. We learned a lot from our experiences. The make-up of the initial coalition changed quite a bit. We became more racially and economically diverse—closer to what Oakland actually looks like. Our coalition partners consisted of individual activists and strong community based organizations like Pueblo, Asian Pacific Environmental Network (APEN), East Bay Alliance Sustainable Economy (EBASE), and ACORN.

This second generation of the Just Cause coalition was definitely more structured and organized. We had a steering committee of seven people and other committees focusing on fundraising, media, and field operations. We worked hard to do things democratically and made sure people of color weren't mere tokens.

We redrafted the Just Cause ordinance, got community input and support, held grassroots fundraising activities, and for six months collected signatures every Saturday morning and Wednesday night. The intensity was mad! We needed twenty-five thousand signatures in order to get Just Cause on the ballot. Our tireless volunteers pounded the pavement and collected twenty thousand signatures. Our paid staff collected another fifteen thousand signatures. We had to make sure there were enough signatures this time so there'd be no way we'd have to do over again. When we collected thirty thousand signatures, we also neutralized the mayor and city council members. They stopped voicing their opposition.

After we got the initiative on the ballot, we began to educate our communities and focus on turning out the votes. One of our main strategies for education was the media. We were able to get a lot of free media, because it was such a hot issue here. The media liked the sensational dynamic of David v. Goliath. One of our opponents' funnier ads featured a character called Motorcycle Eddy. Motorcycle Eddy was a boyfriend of a tenant. He had a loud motorcycle and played loud music and threw beer cans all over the front yard. But the landlords would not be able to kick him out because the Just Cause law would have stripped away their power to protect their property from such hooligans.

If they wanted to talk about Motorcycle Eddy, then we would talk about your grandma. We showed the public the faces of people who were getting evicted—the senior citizens who were losing their homes. Even the lawyer for the landlords admitted that they could have never beat Just Cause after those ads because everyone has a grandmother, and no one wanted to see their grandma out on the street. An effective media campaign is always helpful.

An example of a more direct educational strategy was implemented by APEN's project: Power in Asian Organizing (PAO). PAO's organizing strategy was on a much more one-on-one level. As Vivian Chang, the organizing director at APEN, puts it, "It was important to us that our work on Prop. EE build toward our bigger goals. Relationship building was really important to us, because organizing means having relationships with people. We did house meetings, door knocking, and phone banking. Our members and leaders downloaded voter rolls, translated surnames, and entered their phone numbers into our database. We were in awe when we had a total of 412 phone numbers and committed 'yes' voters. Out of the 412, we turned out 400 'yes' votes. Our members were fiercely working around the clock, speaking Cantonese, Mandarin, Vietnamese, and English."

We won by 1,542 votes out of only 45,000 voters total, so this is significant. Our biggest opponents were the rich people in the Oakland Hills who owned a lot of properties in Oakland. "It was literally a fight between the hills and the flatlands," says Vivian. "They outspent us 7 to 1! And still the flatlands won. We did all this through our emerging leaders and members." This was the first time PAO had ever worked on an electoral campaign.

"The impact of our victory on the larger Oakland community and on PAO was huge. We knew that Prop. EE was not the be all, end all in this fight toward affordable housing, but it was a truly significant step towards our bigger strategy. I mean when you work on something like Prop. EE, you have to have a bigger perspective, because it does not address the root causes. We know that for as long housing is a profit driven industry, there will never be enough affordable housing," says Chang. They went into this campaign knowing that there would be another fight right behind it. "It was hard, but our involvement was crucial because we were the only ones to organize in the Asian Pacific Islander community. Most organizations don't have this capacity, especially in terms of language and cultural understanding. We

OAKLAND

VICTORY: WE PASSED
A BALLOT MEASURE
TO STOP EVICTIONS

were able to model how to organize in an immigrant community across the whole city."

The coalition's strength lies in our diversity. We had diversity racially, strategically, and talent-wise. Housing was a crosscutting issue that brought together people who wouldn't have otherwise worked together. Not to say that the process was all peaches and rainbows, because within the coalition there were two camps of people (1) a group that wanted to win at all cost—Prop. EE was the be all end all campaign for them—and (2) base-building groups that had a longer term community-building focus. This caused a lot of tension.

Our diversity was a beautiful strength, but also super frustrating at times for folks of color. We had the double duty of working the campaign *plus* educating and struggling with internal oppression within the coalition. I remember having to explain to a white guy why it was important to make people of color feel welcome and safe at meetings, and he just didn't seem to get it. I wanted to quit so many times out of sheer frustration.

We didn't give up, even when things got ugly. Like when Mayor Jerry Brown put out his 100 Cops measure claiming that more cops would make Oakland safer. Safer for whom? It was a big sham and the coalition knew it. People United for a Better Oakland (PUEBLO), a strong community-based organization and a coalition steering committee member, which have had a long history of working on both affordable housing issue and anti-police brutality issue, decided to pick up the campaign against the 100 Cops measure. They asked the Just Cause coalition to support their campaign against 100 Cops, because they saw the connections between the two initiatives. PUEBLO was met with a lot of resistance by the older, white, middle-class folks who weren't down to publicly come out against the 100 Cops measure. They would say: "Of course, I'm against 100 Cops personally, but I don't want to jeopardize Just Cause's chances of winning. We have to win at any cost." We argued and debated about the 100 Cops issue for a long while. At the end, for the sake of continuing the campaign, we decided to run separate campaigns.

Even while struggling through whether to support PUEBLO or not, we continued to stay busy mapping out our universe (which precincts we'd walk and phone bank), doing mad fundraising, meeting with as many churches, unions, and organizations as we could to get their help. PUEBLO understood the deeper political, racial, and class issues at work within our campaign as well as in Oakland. I watched how they conducted themselves and their high level of integrity. The fact that they stuck with the Just Cause campaign really motivated me and I accepted the fact that there are no perfect alliances.

On the last get-out-the-vote weekend, PUEBLO brought out about one hundred people to do the precinct walk, and the same coalition members who were against supporting PUEBLO's campaign had the nerve to ask PUEBLO for help to get some of Just Cause's literature out. In spite of the hypocrisy, PUEBLO did agree to help with leafleting. They demonstrated what political courage and integrity is all about. No games or pettiness. PUEBLO knew it was the right thing to do. Personally, that was the moment that defined the whole campaign for me. In the end, PUEBLO defeated 100 Cops.

But it was worth it. Just Cause also won. It was a really tight race. We won by only a few hundred votes! Every phone call, every window sign, every conversation, every aching foot, sweat and tears made a difference! What Prop. EE or Just Cause did was put the burden of proof on the landlord, requiring them to have a valid reason for eviction. We still have a long way to go, because Prop. EE is full of loopholes. For example, homes that have less than three units are exempt, and buildings built after 1983 are also exempt. But it is still a big step in the right direction. Everyone involved with the campaign was pretty much a volunteer! A collection of very different people, coming together had made a difference in our community. It was beautiful and real.

We always talk about how people of color should organize together more, but it's really hard and I feel overwhelmed by the obstacles this government has built to keep us down. But then I remember my elders and their work and how it's both an honor and a duty to keep on this path. But you know, in addition to struggle, sacrifice, and long meetings, this work really needs to be fun, healthy, and positive. You can't build shit otherwise.

## *Political Sex Survey* — BOUAPHA TOOMMALY

*Favorite political song?*
India.arie, her song "Video," about not having to meet up to the social standards of what beauty is and feeling fine about it.

*A political achievement prior to helping swing the 2004 election?*
I was part of a coalition that won the living wage in Richmond, California.

*Favorite political movie?*
Erin Brockovich.

*What actor or public person would you like to see smackdown Ah-nold?*
I would have Martin Sheen run for governor and have a battle of the super-stars. I think people already have this subconscious idea of him being a political power. I'm gonna tell him to run in 2006.

*If I were starting a political movement it would be called The League of _____ Voters:*
Conscious voters. It's like the turkey voting for Thanksgiving. I mean how are you going to support someone when he wants to privatize your job? How are you going to vote for him if you are a blue-collar worker and he is going to send all the manufacturing jobs overseas in a race to the bottom? Sure, there are tax breaks, but if you don't have any income coming in, how are you going to get a tax break?

*Creative strategy to win:*
I think I like the turkey idea. We should take that on the road, like a show and we should get some spoken word artists and everything and it would be a big carnival, an educational process. State to state.

*A political goal I have for 2004:*
It would be dang good if we don't sign anymore "free trade" agreements. That's my focus right now.

*What's been your experience voting?*
I've lived in the U.S. for twenty-five years, since I was four. But I can't vote because I'm not a U.S. citizen. I pay taxes but I don't get to vote on how my money is being spent! It's taxation without representation. It's pretty frustrating. To become a U.S. citizen, I'd have to pay $350, wait a year, and go through an interview process—so it's already too late for me to vote in November. People who can vote need to remember they're representing a lot of people who can't vote or live with dignity in this country because they're quote unquote illegal.

*Do you vote in Laos?*
I don't have any citizenship. When my parents left Laos, they stripped our citizenship. My people are Khmmu (it's not a written language so there isn't an English spelling). We're indigenous people from the hills, same as with the Hmong people. My father and uncle and grandpa were all part of the CIA army. When the Communists took over in 1975, they escaped Laos by swimming across the river into Thailand. My family was a part of the old government so they had a vested interest in protecting the power structure. The U.S. used us to fight, but afterwards they didn't help us. We were living in a refugee camp in Thailand for years and finally the Catholics brought us over to the U.S., not the government, which I think is the reason why my family became Catholic! (laughing)

*How do you convince your Republican uncle not to vote for Bush?*
My uncle's generation, they're still involved in homeland politics and they think the Republicans will help them get Laos back. So I would talk to him

about the new Medicare bill because we have a grandma. My uncle is the primary care for grandma. He has to bear the medical expenses and there are more bills like that coming down the pipe. That's how my sister and me could convince my mom and uncle that being a Republican is not beneficial for them.

*A slept-on group of voters you'd like to see organized:*
College age people who are in the workforce who work two or three jobs. They need to be told that they do have a stake in the election: at least you don't want to be beat down even more when you are already down. So many people have given it up because so many people have not benefited from who has been elected. I don't think what they realize is that it can get worse.

*"I need to organize my friends and family starting with_____"*
My mom, my grandma, and their friends. My mom does hair for a living so I think it's the perfect opportunity for her, because they chat. I think that's how my mom became politicized; one of her customers came in and they began to chat. And my grandma, because she is so cute! She wants to be involved. When I used to organize in California, my grandpa and grandma would come and testify in front of city council. It would be a family affair.

# I Served My Time— Let Me Vote!
## By Robin Templeton

During the Joe Gotta Go campaign (see chapter 6), Yvonne Cardona was thirty-two and a single mom with two kids. As 21st Century's office manager, she stayed way behind the scenes.

"The movement was always in me—my mom was one of the high school students who marched out of school and across the bridge for civil rights—but I was never out in public. I didn't even plan to stay in Selma," Cardona explains. "Racism was in full force here. I thought this town wasn't going to make it. I couldn't see a future for me or my kids in Selma."

Mayor Joe Smitherman changed Cardona's mind. She spent a lot of time holding a Joe Gotta Go sign outside the mayor's office. "I was standing there one day with some young people, waving a sign, when the mayor rolled by, leaned out his window and said, 'You know I'm gonna win this campaign, and I'm gonna win it with your people's votes.' Smitherman had been in office my whole life and that whole time he was buying Black people off with beer and fish sandwiches. I decided that day that I couldn't let him make fools of us any more."

Cardona made a commitment to herself to be a visible community organizer in Selma and to register people to vote.

But when she started hitting the streets to mobilize voters, Cardona confronted an obstacle that outraged her more than Joe Smitherman's arrogance. "It seemed like every other brother I tried to register told me he couldn't vote because he was a felon."

Like poll taxes, literary tests, and grandfather clauses, felony disenfranchisement laws were designed to paralyze the voting potential of formerly enslaved African Americans. But unlike those other vestiges of Jim Crow, felony disfranchisement laws are still on the books in forty-eight of fifty states.

Across the United States, felony disenfranchisement laws rob 4.65 million people of the right to vote. In many southern states, one-third of the adult male African American population is legally disfranchised.

Until recently, Alabama permanently disenfranchised two hundred and forty thousand of its residents. Cardona was one.

"When I was seventeen, I refused to snitch on my cousin's friend who was into drugs. They waited until I was nineteen and charged me with an adult felony." She never did any time, but Cardona explains, "In many ways, my life was taken away. Here I was unable to vote, when my mother had dedicated herself to the struggle for civil rights. And any time I went to apply for a job, this question about having a criminal record would come up."

Joe Smitherman lit Cardona's fire to organize her community to get him out of office. Her own private experience of being disfranchised, however, helped sustain her passion. "No one in my community knew that I was an ex-felon, not even some of the people closest to me. In fact, on voting day, I'd wear one of those 'I Voted' stickers even though I couldn't go into the voting booth. Because I couldn't vote, it became my mission to make sure that everyone who could, did."

Today, at least theoretically, a lot more Alabamans are eligible to vote. In 2003, after a statewide grassroots organizing effort led by the Alabama Restore the Vote Coalition and championed by the state's Black Legislative Caucus, the governor signed into law a bill that allows the vast majority of those with felony convictions to apply for a certificate of eligibility to register to vote.

Cardona, now state field director with Black Youth Vote and a member of the steering committee of the Restore the Vote coalition, is calling everyone who once told her they couldn't vote. "Over the years, whenever someone told me they couldn't vote because they had a felony conviction, I told them 'That's OK, someday you'll be able to.' I took all their names and numbers and [put] them in a folder. By now this has grown into a pretty big base. I'm going let every one of them know about the certificate of eligibility to vote form."

The Restore the Vote coalition is launching a statewide public education campaign, complete with radio and television public service announcements, to let people know about the new law.

David Sadler, coordinator of the Restore the Vote Coalition, has a story and a passion not unlike Cardona's. Sadler copped a plea and got saddled with a felony conviction in Pennsylvania when he was nineteen. Not long after, he moved to Florida to start his life over. But Sadler found himself ineligible for student aid and unable to secure employment in the Sunshine State because of the felony conviction on his record.

Not knowing what else to do, in 2002, Sadler ran, literally, from Florida to Pennsylvania to petition the governor for clemency.

It took Sadler thirty-two days to run the 1,178 miles on highways and back roads from Orlando, Florida, to Harrisburg, Pennsylvania. Sadler wasn't connected to any particular organization at the time, he just sent out a few press releases, said a prayer, and started running.

An Orlando radio station, 102 JAMZ, got one of his releases and posted an online petition in support of Sadler's cause. The founder of the Orlando-based organization Mothers of Incarcerated Sons called to check on Sadler along the way, when his cell phone was in range.

Word of Sadler's effort reached Jerome Gray, an old-school civil rights organizer in Alabama, who recruited "the Running Man" to help start the Restore the Vote coalition.

"I couldn't see myself doing anything else," Sadler says about organizing for re-enfranchisement. "This is my life's mission. There are so many people out there who lose hope. But people who get caught up in the criminal justice system can rebound, and they need to know this."

In addition to his work in Alabama, Sadler is consulting with the Florida

Rights Restoration Coalition on how to organize a run for voting rights from cities and towns up and down the peninsula to the state capital.

The Florida Rights Restoration Coalition is heading up an effort to let as many as 30,000 people with felony convictions know that they now qualify to have their civil rights restored. After the Florida Justice Institute, the ACLU of Florida and other civil rights groups sued the Florida Department of Corrections, a judge found in 2003 that the department must provide assistance to thirty thousand Floridians with felony convictions to help restore their voting and civil rights.

Courtenay Strickland, coordinator of the Florida Rights Restoration Coalition, explains: "As for how the re-enfranchisement of thirty thousand people could affect the outcome of future elections, no one can say for sure. Judging from the 2000 Presidential election, which was decided by less than six hundred votes in Florida, it could be significant. But the most important thing is that thirty thousand is a drop in the bucket when you consider that more than five hundred thousand people in our state have permanently lost the right to vote even though they've served all their time."

Cardona and Sadler are living their lives as testimony. They refuse to allow the runaway growth of the U.S. prison system unravel the civil rights movement's accomplishment of giving people of color a vote and a voice.

As Latosha Brown explains, Cardona, Sadler and the next wave of civil rights organizers know that voting is not everything, but it is something. "They're letting people know that voting is one way to get free." ·

[Editor's Note: Robin Templeton is the director of Right to Vote: the National Campaign to End Felony Disenfranchisement, which includes eight national civil rights organizations. For more information, go to www.right-tovote.org. She was previously an organizer with the Ella Baker Center for Human Rights, www.ellabakercenter.org.]

# Takin' It Back to the Old School

## By Alma Rosa Silva-Bañuelos

 I remember when I was a little girl, I would wake up early in the morning to get ready for school and I would go to the kitchen to the smell of warm milk, pan dulce, and coffee. My abuela's home, in northern New Mexico, was made of adobe so it was always warm in the morning from the sun or the nice wood fire my abuela would build. On some early mornings, my abuela would be in the kitchen talking to one of the local politicos at the kitchen table, pouring him coffee and offering him warm pan dulce. They would always talk about my abuelo that had passed on and what a hard working man he was. The politicos had been coming over for years to have coffee with my abuela and abuelo, my tia would tell me. My tia would show up on her way to work to say hello to my abuela and she too would stay, drink coffee, eat pan dulce, and talk to the politico.

Sometimes they would talk all the way up until they had to take me to school about what was happening at my tia's work, with the vecinos, la comunidad, and the local government (or at least that's what they would tell me). I really didn't know why it mattered talking with the politico but he would come over enough that I thought of him as a part of la familia. The politico would always be at the birthday parties. He was even at my quicianiera (my fifteenth birthday party). I think he is my brother's padrino and he was definitely at my sister's baptismo. The family events always had one of the politicos, even at the matanzas where my papa, tios, and abuelo would cook the pig underground. And, of course, my abuela, mama, and my tias would always cut up the carne and we would all eat beans, rice, chile, torillas, and the carne that just came out of the ground. Those were always special memories and how can I forget that the politico would always bring my abuela biscochitos around Christmastime and just visit.

Then I started to grow up and I began to take the bus to school and one day I couldn't remember the last time I had seen the politico at my abuela's house. Then I noticed that things in my barrio began to change. As I began to learn about the changes that were happening in our barrio I would ask my tia about what we could do. My abuela was getting older and I overheard one day that the property tax was going to go up and my abuela was not going to be able to afford her house anymore. Our family had been there for generations. How could this happen? My tia pulled me aside and asked me to go with her to visit one of the politicos that used to come by the house. This was the first time I realized why the politico had once become part of the familia. Now we had to go see the politico in some large building that didn't smell like my abuela's house and felt so unfamiliar. This was the moment when I understood why things had changed. This is the moment when I understood why the politico stopped coming to visit us.

It was money.

The politicos no longer had time to visit the gente in our barrios because they were too busy trying to raise money to compete with politicians sponsored by the big businesses that use money to manipulate elections.

As I grew older, I continued to think of how to bring it back to the old school ways of representing the gente. Then I found out that in my own backyard in Albuquerque, New Mexico, there were two organizations, Re-Visioning New Mexico (RVNM) and its sister Progressive Alliance for Community Empowerment (NM PACE), working on something called campaign finance reform. I had no idea what this meant or how it would help us, but I did understand their slogan: "Let's take big money out of New Mexico politics."

As I learned more about what campaign finance reform really meant, I understood that through public financing of elections, big money could actually be taken out of politics. This meant that the people I grew up with—whether it was my vecino, my primo, my tia, or tio—could run for office without having to raise an amount of money that could build a new school. I learned that with voluntary public financing ordinary people could run without having outrageous sums of money.

One of the things I liked best about public financing of elections is that anyone running for office would have to go to their barrio, introduce themselves, and get five-dollar donations from two to three hundred gente from their district. To me, that is clean money. And when the gente from the barrio give their five dollars, it's because they believe that you will represent them on another level. With that five dollars (which means a lot in New Mexico—we are the third poorest state in the union), I am giving that local politico my vote because he came to my home and we spoke face to face. Now this was sounding more like true democracy and a way to bring back the old school ways of representing people in each barrio.

But then came the challenge of how to get this passed in our state legislature, where the laws of the barrios are made. This is where the experience of an old-school organizer, Santiago Juarez, now co-executive director of NM PACE, came in.

Santiago gave me a job at RVNM as a community organizer doing relationship building. I was part of holding house meetings and making sure that the gente from my barrio were given information about public financing of elections. With the backing of the gente, we were able to put community pressure on the politicos that helped to create a fire in the belly.

Santiago would always tell me, "It's about the relationship and the trust we build from these relationships." Relationship building is the main point of organizing. Each relationship must be nurtured. The relationship building foundation is for long-term movement building. This comes in the form of respectful and conscious interactions—in this case, with our legislators and elected officials. All the leaders we worked with had a seed planted in them from the old school days. As Santiago Juarez continued to organize in the round house, we were working on the ground level.

## Raza in the HOUSE . . . and the Senate!

The fight for public financing of elections had been going on for about seven years before I entered the ring. Santiago explained to me that the leadership of the public-financing campaign (also known as "clean money" campaign reform) was in white folks' hands and leadership. The fire in the belly had been missing, not to mention that we had a conservative governor at that time and nothing progressive was getting passed. But in 2002 we had a different kind of leadership that reflected the faces of the families that had been living in New Mexico generation after generation. We had people of color in leadership and they were the ones that took the front lines and fought to pass public financing of elections. Now this was not an easy task and don't forget that relationships take time and nurturing. But that is what Santiago Juarez had: relationships. Back in the day, Santiago had grown up with, worked with, and just developed relationships with the gente that today sit in the state house and the senate. He also had built relations with leaders down south in Las Cruces and in Roswell where he grew up for some time in his life. These rural places are what make Nuevo Mexico beautiful, but also create a challenge to organizing.

Santiago and I were preparing to enter the legislative session in January 2003. We were sitting at the table with New Mexicans for Campaign Reform, preparing the details for the clean money bill. Maine and Arizona were the only two states that had successfully passed laws to allow public financing of elections. Massachusetts passed a law but it got tied up in court. The big business interests will fight you tooth and nail to stop public financing from

NEW MEXICO

VICTORY: BIG
MONEY OUT OF
STATE POLITICS

being passed. So instead of going for public financing for the whole state all at once, we decided to start with the Public Regulation Commission (PRC), an elected office that regulates all public utilities, insurance, transportation, and corporations. Sounds pretty powerful, and it is. Remember the California brown outs? Well, in New Mexico our utilities were deregulated to supply California at Cali prices leaving New Mexicans barely afford the utility prices as they tripled.

The beautiful piece of the organizing was that, through the relationships Santiago had been building and was continuing to nurture he was able to get the fire in the belly started for Manny Aragon, the Senate majority whip, Ben Lujan, speaker of the House, Richard Romero, president pro tem. of the Senate, and Dede Feldman, senator. The seed that Santiago had given light to was the energy from the old-school days of the politicos going and doing home visits and relationship building, just like I remember when I was a little girl. The fire in the belly came from remembering the days when each one of these leaders walked the streets to meet the gente and go to family events to nurture those relationships. So the idea of taking big money out of politics sounded great. It truly became a non-partisan bill. We had support from the Democrats and the Republicans and, of course, the Greens, Independents, and others. Public financing of elections was changing the face of politics and takin' it back to the old-school ways.

By the end of the fight, we had organized people of color on every level one could think of to really bring this bill home. Locally, the Albuquerque City Council endorsed the bill 7 to 2, and when it was time, Linda Lopez, chair of the Rules Committee, made sure the bill made it out of committee. This was of course with the help from womyn of color like Shirley Baca, a public regulatory commissioner, Rebecca Vigil-Giron, secretary of state, and Patricia Madrid, the attorney general testifying in committee on behalf of the public financing of elections bill. We also had the support of David King, a Republican and one of the public regulatory commissioners, which proved to me that this was definitely not a partisan issue. To ensure that our representatives were aware that the gente from the grassroots were in support as well, we made sure that when it was time, they received about sixty calls a day from the gente. We also had the gente send letters, emails, and faxes. This was truly a movimiento of people of color from our communities and barrios. With the local pressure and voice of the people, our representatives and senators could do nothing but fuel the fire in their belly, and I watched as they fought to pass the bill on the floor. Some would ask what moved Manny Aragon to fight so hard for this bill and Santiago would answer that "this is a Raza issue" and he remembers the old-school ways. During the battle, we had support of all five of the elected members of the New Mexico PRC. Linda Lovejoy was one of the first commissioners to step up to the plate and begin open public statements in support of public financing of elections. She is Dinè from the Navajo Nation, and to see a sister of indigenous blood fight to change how elections are run for our communities was powerful and inspiring, especially for other young womyn of color. With her passion, we were also able to get the endorsement of the major newspapers in New Mexico.

We created quite a stir in the round house this legislative session. When it came to the final vote, we had an overwhelming success. The House vote was 40 to 24 and the Senate vote was 20 to 11. New Mexico has now become the third state to provide full public financing of elections. People watching the fight saw the fire in the belly speak and couldn't understand why all of the leaders were so impassioned. I just remembered back to the mornings at my abuela's home, and the smell of warm milk, pan dulce, and coffee.

[Editor's Note: PACE and RVNM are currently working to win full public financing for all elected offices statewide. Many other states have clean elections campaigns.]

## *Political Sex Survey* — ALMA ROSA SILVA-BAÑUELOS

*Where are you touring this book?*
I would love to tour my hood, the Southwest, but I am willing to go wherever needed to motivate and mobilize young people to get out to vote and take back our country. Let's have street parties and make it fun!

*What might happen if Bush gets another four years?*
We will run out of water, we will begin to wear gas masks as accessories to our outfits, there will no longer be jobs in the United States. They will all be sent to other countries for slave labor.

*How do you convince your Republican uncle not to vote for Bush?*
This is too close to home . . .

*A political goal you have for 2004:*
I want to start voter registration on public transit and get so good that the bus driver hands a voter registration card to each person that rides the bus and make sure the buses are *free* on the day of elections!

photo by Sophia Wallace, ©2003

*What states/cities deserve the most attention in 2004 and why?*
Everyone talks about Ohio, but I think New Mexico and it's not just cuz I am from here but we always get played and it's time to become a solid progressive state! And we can't forget the Midwest belt and watch out for Cali—I don't trust the Terminator . . .

*A political achievement prior to helping swing the 2004 election?*
I was also a part of a lock-down at a Texaco station where eight people locked themselves to the gas pumps on a Monday morning so that there was no business as usual.

*The day when all of our political problems are solved, you'll find me . . .* In the garden, planting more trees and vegetables. And telling stories to my grandchildren, expressing how we couldn't have done it without their help.

PART

4

# Pimping Satellites for Change:
## How We Freaked It on the Internet

*"No single person can liberate a country. You can only liberate a country if you act as a collective."*
— Nelson Mandela

# Free Advice for the Democrats: You Need a Whole New Strategy

## An interview with Davey D

[Editor's note: If the Democratic Party had a brain, they would hire Davey D. In the meantime, he's gonna chastise you (and progressive folks in general) till you step up your game and learn your lessons from hip-hop, mass media, and corporate marketing. Just remember y'all, when you're reading this interview: he means it with love.]

*When was the last time you left a crowded nightclub and were handed a well-designed flyer dealing with issues you'd like to see politicians address?*

*When was the last time you went to a sold-out concert and saw a politician, or even a campaign worker, waiting to shake your hand and ask for your support?*

*When was the last time you saw a commercial with someone your age breaking down the reasons why he or she was backing a particular candidate?*

The Democrats are totally out of touch. During the 2000 presidential election, I tried to get Gore or one of his people on my radio show. At the time, it was the most listened to show in the Bay Area. I tried to get Bill, Gore. Their people never called me back. I called the Greens. Ralph Nader did my show. I called the Republicans and they called me back right away so I ended up having a Republican on the show but no Al Gore.

This is the reason why people are leaving the Democratic Party in droves. During the California recall, if you turned on KMEL or the Beat or any of the urban stations in California, you did not hear anybody who sounded like you saying "Vote 'No' on the Recall." But you did have Republicans buying airtime. I realize they have more money, but airtime on radio is not that expensive. On most urban radio stations, the 2 A.M. commercial block shows up at 2:40 A.M. If your club gets out at 2 A.M., 40 minutes later you're in your car driving; the first commercial you hear should be the political ad. I told people in the Democratic Party this. They looked at me like I was crazy. You can get those 2 A.M. spots for fifty bucks! That means fifteen hundred bucks will buy you multiple ads after the clubs let out Thursday, Friday, and Saturday nights.

You can buy a commercial on TV that shows up in one market for a couple hundred bucks. In California, there were no "Vote 'No' on the Recall" commercials on BET or MTV, during shows like Comic View or Punk'D. Did you see any commercials? No. They're out of touch. In a state that has as many young people as California, Gray Davis did not have one young person in his commercials. The Democrats have not made a serious investment in young voters or hip-hop voters.

## Hip-Hop Republicans

It's not a cool situation. The Republican cats, they understand the dynamics of the people they're trying to reach. I love to watch O'Reilly. He'll say: "I'm for the working class." He ain't nowhere near working class. He'll say: "I understand your pain. Your problem is Ja-Rule. He got those diamonds. How come you can't afford them? Lil' Kim is on TV in a big house." And then he'll say: "They want affirmative action." He's planting a seed. The Republicans come across as someone who's gonna fight for you. Bill O'Reilly looks like someone who's gonna fight for you, who's gonna go to the mats for you.

The Republicans are good at going to the people where they are. They go to little county fairs and cow-tipping programs or whatever in the country. They go to the high school football game, like: "I'm gonna show up and make people be like 'That's hella cool he came to a little high school football game.'" Now they're doing it in urban communities, and capitalizing on the void left by the Democrats. Howard University now has hip-hop Republicans on their campus! Why does Howard, a black university, have hip-hop Republicans on their campus when 90 percent of the people vote Democrat? The hip-hop Republicans get funded from the Republican Party. Where were the Democrats to set up the hip-hop Democrats on Howard's campus?

The *New York Times* had a big-ass story about it called "The Hip-Publicans" where they talked about how the Republican Party was doing all these things that I've been talking about: Going around, making themselves appealing, going to beer drives, frat parties, hanging out, and just being on the spot. The Republicans have a "Go Team" mentality. Where's our "Go Team" mentality? There are fifty thousand people at a football game. Did you go there with your No on 54 campaign? No. Will I see an anti-Bush commercial in Murder Dog? Will I see one in XXL? Progressives need a whole new strategy for reaching people where they are.

Bakari Kitwana, the former political editor of the *Source* and author of the book *Hip Hop Generation* predicts that will begin to change during the 2004 election. He points out that many politicians are beginning to realize that the hip-hop generation—those born since 1964—are a sizable minority or even majority in many communities. He points to recent efforts by Al Sharpton, Dennis Kucinich, and Howard Dean to court hip-hop voters. Today I had Chuck D on my show, plus Dennis Kucinich and Paris.

Local groups need to get smart about media. Do you know the morning, afternoon, and evening news directors for the local station? What are their names? Have you met with them? Have you tried to set up a meeting so that they understand you exist? What's been the result when you ask for those meetings? Do you have friends in these places who hook you up and advocate for you in those meetings?

## Style Over Substance

You have to understand that the average person has been indoctrinated and is continuously being indoctrinated to accept style over substance. And that means you have to be creative without compromising your principles. For example: If I need to bring attention to . . . let's use the California recall. Schwarzenegger already had a relationship with the community, because of his movies. So what do I do? I can go door to door, knocking and go, "Hey, you need to vote against the recall, yada yada yada yada." Or I can be creative. Me, because it was such a short period of time, I'd be: "Let's sit down and cut the deal. What do we need? Let's find ten brothers who are political but look like Tyrese, and let's send them out to every hair shop, nail salon, and every nightclub where you find women between eighteen and thirty-four and let them pass out petitions and signs and information about why they should vote no." I want people to go "Daaaamn he look like Tyrese, you know, what are you doing brother?" "Well, here's some information, I'm telling people to vote no on the recall." "Oh really? Lemme take a look at that."

Now is that exploitation and manipulation? To a certain degree, yes, but is it bad? I don't think so. I'm playing a game because I can't get on TV. I can't get on Jay Leno. So I'm gonna get Tyrese to walk down the street, or a Tyrese look-alike, with some information, so that you go, "Ooohh, who's that?" You know, because, ask any corporation—attractive people get the job done. If I need to get some brothers off the basketball court, then I'm gonna find an attractive woman to stand in some of their haunts and be: "Hey, how you doing, I'm working this campaign to tell you vote no." "Really, what's your name?" "Well, here, brother, take a look at this information." You know, make them be like: "Who's the Denzel-looking guy? Who's the J. Lo-looking person?" Political campaigning is like trying to win over a love interest, you know, there's no one way to do it. Depending on who she is and what she's about, you're gonna have to adjust your game accordingly.

A guy named Danny Goldberg who's in the music business says the same thing. He's like, "Yo, you guys are not making yourselves relate-able," and it's almost like, even though we're talking about the Democrats, to a certain degree a lot of activists haven't broken out of that same activist circle, and there's a whole bigger world. So, you know, you could say the same thing to activists: Who went to the last Raiders game? Who went to the last 49ers game? Who went to the last Jets or Giants game? You know, when we go to the Zulu Anniversary party, who's gonna be there? The 50 Cent party, who's there? You see what I'm saying? The Eminem concert, who's there? And I mean, if you're not at those places holding up a sign or passing stuff out then you're out of touch.

You know who does all these techniques now? The army. They bring hummers. They do freestyle battles. Go to any basketball game, see if the army ain't there. Go to any concert, see if the army ain't there. They got models; they got everything. You wanna know how to beat Bush, watch the army. The army guys was coming out playing basketball, got their three-on-three teams, doing all those different things, you know, recruiting at high schools. They hang out everywhere. You know: "Brother you look like an athlete, you look like you got some skills, you look like you could box a little, you should just come to the army, man, you could kick some ass, man, that's how so-and-so became champ, he was in the army, and we'll put you in the boxing program."

The bottom line is you've got to make a commitment to understanding the lifestyle and worldview of the people you want to reach. And if you're not doing those type of things, then you can't be surprised when people don't relate to you because of the rule of style over substance. I would add that, you know, when you show up at certain places, you have to dress the part. If you talk to women who aren't activists, they notice like what type of purse you carry, they notice all these little things, so maybe you just need to have the new Prada purse, just to be like "Oh shit, she has the new Prada purse, let me listen to what she say." You see what I'm saying? Have the nice bag and the nice gear that make people like, "Damn, where did you get that bag?"

Why don't the Democrats show up in nightclubs? You've got everyone from phone companies to soft drink companies there trying to sell their products. Just like Republicans make an investment in NASCAR dads, you need to make an investment. But there's a certain type of elitist attitude that goes on, not just in the Democratic Party, but among some activists. You've got people in the bleachers who don't pay rent and spend their last dollar buying a Raider's ticket. Those are people you want to get passionate your cause; it's in their interest.

## Are You Adding to People's Stress?

You have to have a healthy respect for the lives of working people. I have a 9 to 5 job now. Shit, I've never had a 9 to 5 before. By the time you come home, you don't want to hear about "Bush did this, Cheney did that." I'm not trying to hear it. You're adding to my stress.

That's something activists have to look at: are you adding to people's stress? Not everyone can get to the meeting, to the school meeting. I gotta cook and take care of my kids and I'm too tired. The ordinary Joe is in bed by 11 P.M. He's got a wife and kids to deal with. He's got a million things to distract him. To do my DaveyD.com newsletter, I have to get up at 3:30 A.M.! If you want to reach someone who works all day, you've gotta be hella entertaining, and you have to come with an attitude of service. How do you accommodate single parents? Do you have babysitting there? Someone said the most revolutionary thing you can do is raise kids. Well then the most revolutionary thing an activist can do is to support people who have kids and work all day. That's where it needs to be: "How can I serve you? How can I help you out? Can I go to the PTA or city council meeting and tell you what they said or bring your views there?"

There are a lot of cats who work in the corporate world, but still want to be down in the community. There's a lot of cats who are dissatisfied with the corporate world. Shoot, they hate the corporate world more than you do! After three months of doing this, I can see what people's working lives are really like. They're isolated. After work people say, "Let's go to a bar." Well, Billy ain't invite me to a bar. He's out protesting. And then you get to the bar and people say, "Bush isn't that bad." And these people become your friends. They're here for you, supporting you. People at work are at war, psychological war. You have to remember that people are going through that. Every day they're experiencing a silent psychological war. I have it real easy cuz, man, I like my job. But I can't do stuff like I used to be able to. Arianna Huffington was in town speaking at noon. By the time I got there, it took me twenty minutes to find parking. By the time I found parking, I had to leave.

We need everyone. The woman who works behind the desk in financial aid who makes sure you get financial aid for college. You have to remember that everybody has value. You have to know how to tap into it. You have to value people and support them on their own terms. Like I was telling you earlier, I think you need to have more people in this book. The cat with the gold teeth needs to be able to open this book and see himself reflected in here. See his perspective in here. The quote unquote gangbangers or thugs need to see themselves reflected.

This is what I try to do with DaveyD.com. I get people more acclimated to talking about things of a political and social nature, with hip-hop as a backdrop. Yes, ok we're gonna talk about 50 vs. Ja Rule, but 50 vs. Ja Rule reflects the type of disunity the exists among black churches, where you have five churches on one corner and none of the preachers get along so they never do anything together. 50 vs. Ja Rule reflects the outside interests that play a role in that disunity, having a historical basis in which they're doing this from, meaning that they did it a generation ago to the Black Panthers, and they did it a generation ago to other movements. Talking about 50 vs. Ja Rule lets you talk about all of that.

*Who do you know who should run for office?*
Russell Simmons, Chuck D . . . I'd like to see
Ras Baraka, who has already run, get to the
next level. I think Sista Souljah would be
incredibly sharp if she ran. In the Bay Area,
I think Latifah Simon would bring a certain
pizzazz and sensibility and get the job done.

*Elected officials you respect other than
Barbara Lee (and they have to be alive):*
Charles Barron, in New York. I have a
tremendous amount of respect for him. I'd
like him to run for a bigger office. Maxine

Waters I've always liked.

*Favorite political songs:*
Chuck D's lyrics to the song "Son of a Bush" are pretty good, you know,
especially the last verse, when he talks about he's the son of a bad man, he's
the son of a bad man, son of a Bush, and the way they flip that, especially
the last stanza where he talks about Bush being a CIA child, you know, "CIA
child, that shit is wild, CIA child, that shit is wild." He laid down the legacy of both Bushes in four minutes.

*Creative ways to swing the election in 2004?*
Get some money, get about sixty thousand, no, one hundred thousand dollars, and start having freestyle battles on what's wrong with Bush. If I wanted to beat Bush right now, I would get three hot artists as judges: Dilated
Peoples, Jurassic 5, Talib Kweli, maybe, and I'd be like "We gonna do a ten
thousand dollar freestyle contest in every city about who can beat Bush and
who can come up with the best freestyle as to what's wrong with President
Bush." Now you got cats talking! Oh, now you gonna put money in my
pocket? We gonna have three, no we gonna have ten first place runner-ups,
a thousand dollars apiece, and the grand prize is ten thousand dollars. And
we're gonna put you on a compilation album as to how we're gonna beat
Bush.

Some of Davey D's favorite hip-hop political websites:
Blackelectorate.com | Popandpolitics.com
Urbanthinktank.com | Hiphoppoliticalconvention.org
Hiphopsummitactionnetwork.org | Rapstation.com
Future500.com | Guerillafunk.com
Allhiphop.com | Hiphopactivist.com
Okayplayer.com | Playahata.com | DaveyD.com

# Move the Crowd: Inside the National Political Hip-Hop Convention
## Fuck 'Fight the Power.' These kids are going to be the power.
### By Cherryl Aldave

[Editor's note: Many of the hip-hop organizers in this book are coming together under a new umbrella, from Malika Sanders in Selma to Davey to Ras Baraka in Newark. Here is a snapshot of the new project and some of the people behind it.]

It's been said that the hip-hop generation is a "sleeping giant." Shit, you'd be tired too if the Man always had his foot in your ass. We are criminalized like no other generation in American history. Our educational system is fucked up. Our employment options are few, and the problems go on and on. Why?

It's all a matter of P-O-W-E-R. Or rather, the illusion of it.

Mass media would have us believe we don't have any. They'd rather cover our violent deaths than our peaceful protests. Politicians treat us like we don't have any. They don't court our votes or fight for our issues because they think we're stupid and lazy.

What if more of us were aware that, despite our buffoonish portrayal on WET, there are underground networks within our ranks who are ready to say, "Stop for the booty-shaking! It's time for institution building!"? Okay, maybe not stop the booty shaking completely, but come on!

And what if all of us knew that, right now, the hip-hop generation makes up a mighty 25 percent of the American electorate, and if we actually used that power, we could swing elections across the country and put some real, non–corporate lobby ass-kissing politicians in office?

Forget fighting the power, we'd be the power. So what's stopping us? We have the numbers. We have the talent. We have the hunger. And now, thanks to the savvy team of organizers behind this year's National Hip-Hop Political Convention (June 16–20, 2004, in Newark, New Jersey), we have the beginnings of a workable, long-term strategy.

The Man better start packing his shit.

"I felt betrayed at the highest level!" says a heated Baye Adolfo-Wilson, thirty-five-year-old convention organizer, husband, and father of two. "I was actually willing to give my life for the country, and they're out here killing people for oil!"

In 1986, Baye graduated from one of the poorest school districts in Patterson, New Jersey, and chose the military because "when it was time to graduate I knew I needed to leave home but college wasn't an option because my parents didn't have any money." Sound familiar?

Fresh for '88, Baye was back in Jersey where he enlisted in the reserves and enrolled at Rutgers University. It was the first year of George the First's reign; across America, joblessness and violent crime was on the rise and hip-hop, the cultural revolution birthed in response to these issues, was now as mature as Baye and the millions of other youth who grew up living it.

In this electric atmosphere, the primordial ooze of modern hip-hop activism, Baye discovered an ugly truth about the Persian Gulf war and he began "organizing demonstrations and speaking out against the war." "I started joining organizations and going to study groups on campus," he explains. "I joined the BSU and we organized programs around black history and supported teachers who weren't getting [tenure]." In the midst of all this, tragedy struck. Baye's "best friend from high [school's] baby momma" died as a result of Gulf War Syndrome. "I'd heard enough!" recalls Baye, the sting of the memory shoving his voice up an octave. "I decided I had reached my point of no return and I was gonna be an activist and organize as long as I can."

In May 2002, Bakari Kitwana, a former editor at the *Source*, published a book called *The Hip-Hop Generation: Young Blacks and the Crisis in African American Culture* in which Bakari raised questions about why we don't have political power as a generation, when there is already an infrastructure and a movement that's emerging. Later that year, Bakari was invited to speak at Harvard's Hip-Hop Community Activism and Education Roundtable. "I said, 'We need a national organization and we need a national political convention. And I'm willing to work with any and everybody who wants to work on that.' After that Ras came up to me and he said, 'We do need that.'"

Here's where the dots connect. Bakari had profiled Ras and Baye Adolfo in *The Hip-Hop Generation*, along with Conrad Muhammad, Lisa Sullivan, and Jesse Jackson Jr., in a chapter on hip-hop activism. Another friend of Baye and Bakari's, writer and publisher Hashim Shomari, author of *From the UnderGround: Hip-Hop Culture as an Agent of Social Change* was also in the house for the Harvard roundtable and came on board as well.

They immediately reached out to their individual networks, and before long the crew of four turned into a dream team of thirty or so grassroots organizers, political activists, intellectuals, and journalists, all wanting to do something, anything, about getting the hip-hop generation organized to become more of a political force.

Acclaimed speaker and WBAI radio personality Rosa Clemente worked in the New York state assembly for four years under different assemblymen, including George Pataki and Carl McCall. As an internationally known public speaker, owner of Know Thyself Productions, and organizer for the Malcolm X Grassroots Movement, Rosa Clemente lives and breathes to "reclaim [the] media for the people."

In Cleveland, Ohio, the swingiest of swing states, Angela Woodson helped the first female mayor, Jane Campbell. An organization she co-founded, Blacks United In Local Democracy (BUILD) "kinda became a dangerous force in Cleveland," after they oversaw the victorious campaigns of three underdog city council candiates. sssWING!

Savvy young politicos on the verge. Ballers. Organizers who, just like Baye, got bit by the activism bug while in college during the tumultuous late eighties and early nineties and are now grown-ass adults who still love H.E.R. and are each doing their thing in local politics.

The dream team was ready to lay the groundwork for a movement.

They met on a breezy Chicago day in March 2003. After intense exploration of the problems facing the hip-hop generation, lengthy critiques of several historical models like the Niagara Movement and the Harold Washington elections of 1983 and 1987, many hours, and sweaty handkerchiefs came the breakthrough.

"We realized our generation doesn't even have a political agenda," says Baye. "[So] we decided that we were gonna do this convention based on the Gary convention."

Ahh, the Gary convention! The unprecedented, 1972 meeting of the greatest black minds in literature, activism, and politics at the time, coming together to re-energize the African-American leadership built by the sixties civil rights movement. And I do mean greatest. Bad meaning bad not bad meaning good. Baye's lifelong mentor, Amiri Baraka was on the steering committee, while such politically diverse figures as Carl Stokes, Jesse Jackson, Walter E. Fauntroy, Richard Roundtree, Bobby Seale, Louis Farrakhan, and Barbara Jordan also participated. After the convention there was a quadrupling of the number of elected black people in office over the next decade.

Politicizing the hip-hop generation ain't gonna be easy. If it was, some person or group would have done it by now. The group who has gathered to organize the national hip-hop political convention represent our best hope in a generation. They're created a local organizing committee structure in which each state sends delegates to the convention. Each delegate needs to have registered fifty people in order to cast a vote at the convention. "But," says Angela Woodson, co-founder of BUILD, "the real work will begin the day we step out of Newark."

www.hiphopconvention.org

# How a Twenty-Year-Old Revolutionized the Internet
## By Andrew Boyd

"Do you know what completely blew me away?" This is how conversations would usually begin with friends who had read my August 2003 cover article for the *Nation*, "The Web Rewires the Movement." I was figuring (hoping) that it was my brilliant analysis of X, my insight into Y, my diligent research of Z. No. No. No. They said. "I had no idea that Eli Pariser was only twenty-two!"

Eli Pariser (pronounced "Paris-er") is only twenty-two. He's tall and shy and the campaign director for MoveOn.org, arguably the most significant online political organization in the world. My friends had been receiving emails from one Eli Pariser at MoveOn all through the war in Iraq, reading every word as if it was gospel, and participating in most of the actions he invited them into, all the time assuming he was a mature thirty or forty-year-old veteran activist. The Internet is funny that way.

Born in Maine to parents who protested the Vietnam War, Eli took on their progressive ideals but not their alienation from America. In 2000, soon after graduation, Pariser and a handful of friends toured the country in a fixed-up school bus as part of the American Story Project, interviewing Americans of every stripe and creed, trying to suss out what kind of politics made them tick. This experience affected Pariser deeply, giving him insights into and an abiding faith in ordinary Americans. The day after September 11, Pariser, who was twenty at the time, sent out an email petition to a few dozen friends calling for a restrained response to the attacks. It ricocheted around the world and within a week one hundred and twenty thousand people from one hunded and ninety countries had signed his petition. He had discovered a powerful new tool. Soon after, the folks at MoveOn.org came calling. They merged lists and Eli came on staff.

MoveOn itself was founded well before the war, or even Bush's presidency, as an effort during Bill Clinton's impeachment to push Congress to censure the president and "move on." Their petition also went viral, gathering half a million signatures in a few weeks. After that, the group used its list to raise money for progressive Democrats. By the time Bush was threatening war, MoveOn had become a well-oiled machine.

During the war, with only four other staffers in addition to Eli, MoveOn initiated a phenomenal series of organizing actions. They raised millions of dollars online to run national TV spots, as well as print ads in hundreds of local papers; delivered a petition of one million signatures to the UN Security Council; and called a "Virtual March on Washington" in which two hundred thousand people phoned D.C. on a single day. In addition, MoveOn facilitated leafleting efforts in cities and small towns across the country and coordinated volunteer-led accountability sessions with almost every member of Congress. None of this stopped the war, but it did help put antiwar sentiment squarely on the political map—and made the case for how powerful the Net can be in mobilizing social protest.

"You could say that MoveOn has a postmodern organizing model," says Pariser. "It's opt-in, it's decentralized, you do it from your home." MoveOn makes it easy for people to participate or not with each solicitation—an approach that embraces the permission-based culture of the Internet, and consumer culture itself. "If Nike hadn't already taken it," Pariser says, "our motto would be 'Just Do It.'"

MoveOn has set the threshold for involvement so low that it has provoked skepticism among some activists—as well as jokes on the *Daily Show*. Nevertheless, this organizing model has allowed MoveOn to play an important role as a campaign aggregator, inviting people in on one issue—say, the war—and then introducing them to additional issues, from Bush's tax plan to the deregulation of media ownership. "We're helping to overcome the single-issue balkanization of the progressive movement," Pariser says.

By now, many well-funded advocacy groups (Common Cause, Environmental Defense) have developed email lists topping one hundred thousand, which they typically use to run traditional, tightly controlled campaigns, using email as they would direct mail or a phone bank to mobilize their base to lobby legislators. Within the more radical global justice movement, on the other hand, there are a multitude of resource-poor grassroots groups whose email lists are relatively small (five to fifty thousand), but who use their websites to foster self-organizing, putting their organizing kit online and trusting their activist base to run with it.

"What MoveOn has done," says Tom Matzzie, at twenty-eight the AFL-CIO's online mobilization manager, "is to bring the core elements of these two models together for the first time."

MoveOn has a huge list that it carefully manages, and it also provides web tools that enable members to organize themselves. In the past eight months, as antiwar organizing exploded, their membership more than doubled, to a global total of more than 2.1 million.

A good email list is not something you can buy or borrow. "Every MoveOn member comes to us with the personal endorsement of someone they trust," Pariser says. It is word-of-mouth organizing—in electronic form. Email is cheap, fast, and easy to use, and it has made mixing the personal and the political more socially acceptable. Casually passing on a high-content message to a social acquaintance feels completely natural in a way handing someone a leaflet at a cocktail party never could.

This "tell a friend" phenomenon is key to how organizing happens on the Net. It gives people who feel alienated from politics something valuable to contribute: their unique credibility within their particular circle of acquaintances. A small gesture to these friends can contribute to a massive multiplier effect. It is a grassroots answer to the corporate consolidation of media, which has enabled an overwhelmingly conservative punditry to give White House spin real political momentum and the semblance of truth, simply through intensity of repetition.

MoveOn is often criticized from the left for not attempting to build permanent local structures or on-the-ground leadership. "They're great at getting new people involved, but it's not true self-organizing," says Leda Dederich, web director for United for Peace and Justice. The criticism is fair, but MoveOn's strength lies elsewhere, in providing a home for busy people who may not want to be part of a chapter-based organization with regular meetings. And given what MoveOn is doing—activating people on two or three different issues at a time, often for short durations as legislative targets change—it's hard to imagine a more appropriate model. By combining a nimble entrepreneurial style with a strong ethic of listening to its members, via online postings and straw polls, MoveOn has built a responsive, populist, and relatively democratic virtual community.

CYBERSPACE, MF

VICTORY: WOKE THE DEMOCRATIC PARTY FROM ITS COMA

Although MoveOn does not track member demographics, anecdotal evidence suggests that its base is disproportionately white. This reflects the persevering digital divide, in which, according to a recent Pew survey, a full 24 percent of Americans are totally offline, and those who are online still tend to be younger, whiter, suburban, better-off, and better educated. But defying online trends, the majority of MoveOn's active volunteers are female. And staffers say its members are diverse in other ways, with thousands in each state, ranging widely in age and income.

Zack Exley, a union organizer and MoveOn's organizing director, says that the group reaches deep into politically disaffected middle-class constituencies, what he calls America's "silenced majority." Unlike the traditional Left, he says, "we trust people. We don't think Americans are crazy or stupid or brainwashed or apathetic. We're not trying to drag them kicking and screaming over to our view. We know that there are millions of Americans in every community and walk of life who already know that something is terribly wrong with our country and who are as angry as we are and who are mostly just looking for a meaningful way to do something about it."

According to Pariser, most MoveOn members do not define themselves as activists. Rather, MoveOn is often their first step into political action—and what inspires them to take that step is usually an email message. "A lot of 'Take action now' emails feel like they were written by a focus-group e-newsletter robot," says Madeline Stanionis, who as a senior consultant for San Francisco-based Donordigital has developed scores of online advocacy campaigns. "MoveOn emails feel personal and fresh. They write from their hearts." The emails about the global vigil came directly from Pariser. His voice was strong yet levelheaded. There were no ideological digressions. He got to the point early and kept it action-oriented. It was easy to trust.

Pariser says he crafts his messages with an eye toward taking MoveOn members on a journey, by providing a narrative that connects them to an ongoing social movement. As each campaign proceeds, short email updates build excitement and a sense of community ("50,000 of you have already signed up . . . here's a typical response from a schoolteacher in New Mexico . . . "). This feedback loop is an example of how the Internet, when used well, can extend the shoulder-to-shoulder solidarity one feels on the street to fellow participants across the nation and around the globe.

This kind of solidarity was dramatically in evidence on March 16, on the eve of the invasion of Iraq, when with a wave of candlelight vigils, followed the dusk west across the Earth, involving an estimated one million people in more than six thousand gatherings in one hundred and thirty countries and every state in the nation. Even with MoveOn's one-and-a-half-million-person email list, this global action could never have come together (in only five days) without a piece of web software known as "the meeting tool."

The meeting tool allows anyone anywhere to propose a meeting time and place in his or her own neighborhood and makes it easy for others to sign up. The day before that Sunday in March, I went to the MoveOn website, entered my ZIP code and learned that three vigils had been scheduled in my neighborhood of Park Slope, Brooklyn, including one outside the apartment of prowar Senator Chuck Schumer. The website told me how many of my neighbors had signed up for each. It was already well into the hundreds, and I made it one more.

That Sunday evening, I joined fifteen hundred of my neighbors. Someone handed me a candle and lit it for me; at some point a rabbi and a pastor spoke to the crowd. But otherwise, there was no obvious leadership, and it didn't seem to matter. There had been no meetings, no leaflets, no clipboards, no phone calls; we were all there, essentially, because of an email we trusted.

Returning to the MoveOn website a couple of days after the global vigil, I was able to browse through photographs and personal commentaries from vigils all over the world: Kazakhstan, Korea, and Kenya, as well as the one I attended in Park Slope. All in all, some ten thousand photographs were uploaded that week. Through the Internet we had found our way into the streets, and the streets had then found their way right back onto the Internet. Our local protest was immediately reflected back to us as part of a larger story of national and global resistance.

The AFL-CIO's Matzzie says all this activity is impressive, but could prove irrelevant in the general election if it doesn't take place in the right precincts. He notes that in 2002 only ninety-four thousand well-placed votes would have given the Democrats control of Congress. He cites recent studies from Yale's Institute for Social and Policy Studies demonstrating that email on its own—just like direct mail and commercial phone banking—does not increase voter turnout.

"Anyone who gives you his email is already with you," says Matzzie. "The trick is to get those people to talk to their neighbors, friends, and colleagues offline. Those are the people we need to mobilize." He's been building the AFL-CIO email list by hundreds of thousands in the past few months with this goal in mind. But he'll combine online work with shoe leather and door knocking.

Matzzie is not the only organizer rejecting Internet hype for a more measured view of its capabilities. "The Internet has been an enormous boon to grassroots mobilizations," says Leslie Kauffman, a staff organizer for United for Peace and Justice (UFPJ). "But it can't replace old-fashioned face-to-face organizing, especially when you're trying to build something as delicate as a multiracial coalition." The polarizing debate about how to take up the issue of Palestine, for example, which roiled the UFPJ listserv in May, was handily resolved in the more goal-oriented and accountable setting of the coalition's June conference.

In some ways, the debate over whether online organizing is as "real" or as effective as face-to-face organizing misses the point. What's interesting about MeetUp.com and MoveOn's meeting tool is how they leverage the Internet to get people together face to face in ways (and at speeds and costs) that were simply not possible before. As with the phone, television, or computer-generated direct mail, the Internet won't replace traditional organizing, but it does alter the rules in important ways.

Because email is near instantaneous and costs just fractions of a penny, one can communicate very quickly with a lot of people at the speed of word of mouth. Because it is browsable from home, at any hour, it provides a much easier first point of contact between a campaign and interested participants. Because it is a peer-to-peer tool open to all, it allows geographically dispersed people to find each other easily and coordinate. Because it is still an open-publishing model, free from the constraints of corporate-owned media, it can carry the channels of alternative information essential for sustaining social movements.

Although it replaces some organizing structures (email makes for a far better phone tree than phones ever did) and invents whole new ones, like the campaign web hub or the meeting tool, the Internet is no silver bullet. But what organizing tool ever is? Rather, contemporary social movements will, more and more, straddle both worlds, in a synthetic feedback loop, at once real and virtual, online and off.

Last December in South Korea—the most densely wired country on the planet—a grassroots revolt streaming rich media across high-bandwidth connections helped elect an outsider human rights activist as president. Where will our own Internet-fueled movements take us?

In the first month after MoveOn installed its meeting tool on the Dean campaign website, supporters self-organized more than a thousand local events—testament, perhaps, to the stirrings of a democratic revival, in which large swaths of disaffected Americans are finding forms of political participation that feel fulfilling, effective, and connected. MoveOn's Zack Exley asks us to imagine a political landscape, five years from now, with fifty MoveOns, each tapping different political currents, with a whole new ability to mobilize grassroots power.

Whatever else it has done, the Internet has helped to level the playing field between entrenched government, corporate, and media power, and an insurgent citizenry. The future might indeed be up for grabs.

# Beyond Our Borders—
# South Africa and Brazil

## Mattie Weiss

It's hard to write off electoral work as "sell-out" politics when you look out-side the United States. In a number of countries and time periods, electoral politics have been tightly, inextricably tied to people's grassroots organizing movements. South Africa and Brazil are two dope examples of this.

In South Africa a massive countrywide resistance made it too politically and economically costly for the white supremacist government to maintain con-trol. In 1960, the country's white supremacist regime banned the African National Congress—the major resistance party—forcing its leadership to strategize and organize as best it could from abroad and behind bars. Out of this political repression, a new, broader, and more creative resistance bloomed: across the country people played their part in a strategy of "ungovernability"—rioting, burning their identification "passes," and refusing to pay taxes and rent. On the flip side of ungovernability was the increasingly organized nonviolent resistance involving massive student-organized marches and school boycotts, block-by-block neighbors' associations, "people's courts," women's organizations, and a labor movement able to pull off massive work stoppages and rallies. The resistance also developed an armed wing, Umkhonto we Sizwe, to hit at government targets, particularly those connected with the policies of apartheid and race discrimination.

These grassroots efforts, combined with international boycotts and political pressure through the 1980s, forced the white government to unban the ANC and negotiate with its leadership. In 1994, the people of South Africa went to the polls and, in free and fair elections, voted Nelson Mandela, their long-jailed leader, into office. The ANC has held majority power since then, but in a system of proportional representation has shared it with other parties—including even right wing parties.

Brazil is an even more recent example of the marriage of grassroots organizing and a strong electoral strategy leading to vast and real social change. In 1980, Brazilians on the Left, in the labor movement, and within progressive churches put their differences aside. They decided they had had enough of the poverty, hunger, and disease that came with their government's slashing of basic services and ass-kissing of foreign investors. They formed the socialist Partido dos Trabalhadores (Brazilian Workers Party; PT). Over the next ten years the PT ran—and elected—thousands of members to local offices, on its pro-woman, anti-racist, and often anti-homophobic platform of real reform and "people's power."

One of the best examples of this people power approach is the PT's budget process, where thousands of people in each city meet to decide how to spend half of the municipal budget. The result has been an extension of water and sewer connections to 25 percent more of the homes in one city, new public transportation routes and affordable housing in another, a quadrupling of the number of schools in a third. One major city turned down a five-star hotel investment on the site of an abandoned power plant, and instead built a public park and convention hall.

# Smart Mobs for President
## By Annie Koh

No longer the Hermit Kingdom, Korea is now the Land of the Always Connected—it boasts the most advanced mobile phone system in the world. And thanks to broadband DSL, 70 percent of households in this nation of nearly fifty million people are always online.

All Koreans tote around cell phones. Hundreds of street vendors peddle cell phone charms; customize yours with a plush miniature schnauzer or maybe a hand-knit phone sweater. And young South Koreans are part of "the thumb family," their opposable digits punching in messages to friends at blur-speed. In any given Starbucks, a good percentage of the caffe latte sippers are tap-tapping away, preoccupied with some urgent note to a friend stuck in the subway.

Young South Koreans live online. High school students spend real cash on virtual outfits and accessories for digital personas and kick it in enormous fantasy worlds instead of hitting the mall. The ubiquitous group websites at café.daum.net allow loosely connected friends and former study group partners to stay in touch. In the quarter million PC bars that have mushroomed around Korea, chain-smoking college students and young professionals team up to obliterate their opponents in Starcraft, Counterstrike, and other Doom descendants. South Korea is, after all, the land where PC gamers get their own channel and you can watch the top competitive gamers play for big cash prizes.

Korean media focus on the negative aspects of this new culture. The twenty-four-year-old who keeled over and died after eighty-six consecutive hours of game playing is the first martyr of the internet age. Psychologists who specialize in internet-related behavioral disorders estimate 10 percent of all Koreans are addicted to their machines. The TV talking heads like to groan about the loss of traditional family culture, with one furious father even tossing the computer out of a fourteenth-story window. Because even if most young people continue to live at home until marriage, their busy online lives keep them separated from their parents watching a sappy drama just one room over. But is the internet just an escape from the real world? All the web personas and gory games and pop music fan sites are just more evidence for the disaffection of today's young people right? The more time you spend on your virtual life, the less time you actually do anything worthwhile in real life, right?

In 2000 two important URLs were registered. Ohmynews.com. And nosamo.net. These two websites would change Korean history.

In 2000 Roh Moo-hyun was a little known politican with little success. Out of principle, he had continued to run unsuccessfully for the national parliament from his hometown Busan. The human rights lawyer even had a failed bid for mayor. His nickname? "Roh the fool." The biggest city in the economically developed southeastern part of Korea, Busan was an extremely conservative town at odds with Roh's liberal views. He ran under the banner of the Millennium Democratic Party (MDP), even though his party's stronghold was the economically neglected and historically activist city of Kwangju in southwestern Korea. The country split politically along geographical lines. He was an MDP man from Grand National Party territory.

www.ohmynews.net

Roh was an oddball in other ways. Although he had passed the rigorous national law exam, he only had a high school diploma— Roh had never gone to college. His regional accent marked him as a provincial, not someone who had been groomed for power along with the sons of businessmen and generals in the capital city's elite prep schools. After he lost the parliamentary election for the third time, young idealists attracted by his stubborn integrity formed an organization called Nosamo, an acronym for "People who love Roh Moo-hyun" in Korean. They weren't spontaneous cheerleaders for fourth run for the parliament, these activists thought that Roh should run for president of South Korea. "Roh the fool? For president?" Weary of politicians who relied on regional and party loyalties to win elections and never made bold stances of their own, Nosamo's founders thought that they had found the one—an oddball with integrity and a willful unwillingness to play by regional politics. Nosamo.net became the nerve center for progressive politics over the new few years, as previously disheartened young folk nationwide hurried to his support.

The mainstream media in Korea is largely the preserve of the old guard. Seventy percent of readers subscribe to three newspapers which all come squarely down on the anti-reform side of "don't rock the boat." All of them first rolled off the presses in the late nineteenth or early twentieth centuries—predating the formation of South Korea by several decades. At two P.M. on February 22, 2000, Oh Yeon-Ho and three other writers declared the end of twentieth-century journalism and launched Ohmynews.com. A thirty-something former progressive magazine reporter, Oh saw the internet as a worthy challenger to the print defenders of traditional thought. The concept? The reader as a producer, not a passive consumer of what is deemed appropriate. A new term—citizen-reporters—signaled this shift, as ordinary Koreans all over the country generated articles about local issues or personal pet peeves. They were not paid much, less than twenty dollars for a headline article. While several other internet news ventures preceded Ohmynews, they were often spinoffs from already existing papers, or purely business and market focused news outlets.

While the bulk of stories are now reported by the beefed-up staff of forty reporters, the core of Ohmynews continued to be the underreported elsewhere, the little stories with larger ramifications. Hoaxes and irresponsible rhetoric slipped past the editors from time to time, but readers continued to flock to the site because it provides stories and viewpoints they don't find in the pages of the major daily papers. The focus is on what regular people experience, from the decline in Thanksgiving bonuses to the ever-spiraling usage of English words, with an emphasis on the personal not the corporate.

A mere three years and two blinks later, Ohmynews is now the most popular news site in Korea, reaching an estimated six million readers a day. That's nearly 20 percent of Koreans over the age of fifteen. Ohmynews also publishes an offline weekly that reaches readers with an aversion or inability to access news online.

If 2000 was the start, 2002 was the year.

During the 2002 World Cup, a well-organized internet-based fan club called the Red Devils instigated the transformation of the capital Seoul from a city of twelve million separate lives to a roaring red-clad sea of soccer fanatics. Over the summer, hundreds of thousands of Koreans filled up city centers and plazas to chant and holler and sing in tandem while they watched the Korean national team on enormous projection screens; they held up their mobile phones to the sound of the crowd for family members watching the games from home.

SOUTH KOREA

VICTORY: HOW THE INTERNET SWUNG A PRESIDENTIAL ELECTION TO A HUMAN RIGHTS ACTIVIST

That same summer on June 13, an American military armored vehicle ran over and killed two Korean junior-high school girls. The story was largely ignored in the mainstream media, which tended to be pro–U.S. and pointed to the Korean War and the subsequent years of aid and continued military support as proof that the American government was a true friend and ally. But the new generation, who lost friends and classmates when U.S.–supported dictators violently suppressed pro-democracy protests, viewed the U.S. more negatively. The young generation had a media outlet this time, and due to the dogged persistence of a few citizen-reporters, the deaths of the two girls became the major story at Ohmynews, forcing print media to follow suit months after the accident.

Massive candlelight demonstrations against the U.S. military presence ensued, sparked in part by one Ohmynews reader's call for protests. The enormous turn-out made it clear to the U.S. that the presence of thirty-seven thousand troops, with seven thousand soldiers parked smack in the center of the capital, was not welcome. While some in the peanut gallery say that young Koreans were just looking for a new excuse to gather en masse in front of City Hall, the truth was that Korean distaste for American saber-rattling and faulty foreign policy that ran roughshod over the rest of the world had reached an all time high. In 2003, the South Korean and U.S. military commands announced plans for a massive troop redeployment out of Seoul and into the countryside.

What about Roh Moo-hyun, the perennial underdog? In early June of 2000, one hundred people crammed into an internet café in a city in the central Korea for the first Nosamo general meeting. Ohmynews was there, providing live internet coverage of this organization with this most unlikely of presidential candidates. A little over a month later, nearly eight hundred "People who love Roh Moo-hyun" had popped up, including one movie actor who was elected Nosamo's first president.

On New Year's Day 2001, a middle-school teacher and two students left Kwangju headed to Busan. They called their winter cross-country trek "Mending the east-west divide, step by step, stitch by stitch." Dozens of Nosamo members tagged alongside the three as they walked, and hundreds more cheered them on via Nosamo.net. It vividly symbolized the belief that Roh could be the politician to end the decades-long schism between western and eastern provinces. When the walkers finally arrived, they brought dirt from the site of a 1980 massacre of Kwangju students and residents by Korean military troops and mingled it with earth from a public park in Busan. Ohmynews was there as well.

In May, the first Nosamo college chapters began flourishing, eventually spreading to over fifty campuses. In general, Korean college students are notorious for demonstrating for any number of causes, big and small, and especially in regard to democracy and national politics. In the early 1990s, it was not uncommon for riot police to search undergrad's backpacks for the makings of Molotov cocktails. By the early 2000s, however, cynicism with corrupt politicians and regionalism made even the most idealistic turn their back on electoral politics. But via Nosamo.net, the belief that Roh was really unique—a politician clean of scandal and independent of party bosses—had spread like a virus. Once the epidemic hit, college students shed their apathy and began strategizing. By the end of 2001, the "Roh wind" blew so strong that even slow-to-notice MDP party honchos started wondering if this thrice-failed politician might actually be the right person to run for president.

By 2002, millions of readers were already bookmarking Ohmynews for its citizen-reporters' fierce commentaries; their coverage made Roh a household name. In April of 2002, the Millennium Democratic Party held its primary, the first presidential primary in Korean history to accept a small percentage of online balloting. Although Roh still had little support from party leadership, Nosamo's groundwork on his behalf easily won him the primary and avoided being tangled up in the rigidity of the party system. By now Nosamo claimed thirty-two thousand members with hundreds more joining the organization every day.

Nosamo used the internet to vault over the ignore-or-belittle tactics of old media, which supported the more conservative candidates. The smallest contributions were welcomed. Nosamo distributed yellow piggy banks to collect donations in loose change. In the end, the little website gathered eighty thousand members, and helped raise millions of dollars for Roh's campaign in spite of the scare tactics of some media magnates who insinuated, or sometimes flat-out thundered on their op-ed pages, that Roh spelled ruin for the country.

Roh's explicitly oppositional stance to U.S. foreign policy and his avowed desire to continue talks with North Korea won him the support of young people disgusted with American international bullying. Anti-Bush and anti-war banners festooned college campuses. Even though the faltering economy kept unemployment at over 7 percent for young people, they turned their efforts from finding a paycheck to getting Roh into office. One Nosamo member admitted that he hadn't paid attention to previous presidential elections. People who had been anti-government activists in college in the eighties and nineties had generally practiced democracy in the streets and on campuses not at the ballot box. This time these former activists, now parents of toddlers, reconnected with the electoral process. All of a sudden, through an online community, young progressive voters discovered that far from being shoved to the ineffective margins, they were a powerful part of Korean politics.

Political discussion had been limited to how to best economically develop the nation. Issues that had once belonged to the beleaguered fringe, environmental protection, gender equality, human rights, and other young people's issues concerned with the long term, moved the forefront of public debate. Nosamo grew and grew and supporters smelled the heady scent of possibility. Roh became a character much like any other politician packaged for election, but with an unusual (for Korea) emphasis on his plain background. A photo of him shopping at a discount department store was circulated as proof that he was down-to-earth.

As one Seoul National University sociology professor phrased it, Roh was not and is not a "member of the gentleman's club"—not part of the establishment, not part of that elite group who run the nation's industrial conglomerates and populate the parliament. Just a few companies dominate the Korean economy and the owners' sons and daughters tend to marry one another. Years of military dictatorship resulted in a very tight cabal of military and business leaders who sent their kids to the same schools and expected their children to become the next generation of leaders. Roh's opponent Lee Hoi-chang was more of the same. But Roh lay completely outside of that system.

Seven hours before the election in December of 2002, the former candidate Chung Mun Jon publicly withdrew his support for Roh Moo-hyun. Chung was an executive of one of the largest conglomerates and had bowed out of the race early on, urging his supporters to vote for Roh Moo-hyun. Now in the last hours, he claimed that Roh was too radical. The conservative papers literally stopped the presses and reran the early edition to crow about the deadly blow this had dealt the Roh campaign. Morning polls indicated that Roh trailed his opponent by a few percentage points. The establishment was certain that Chung's withdrawal of support had ensured the conservative Lee Hoi-chang's victory. In the meantime, initially disheartened supporters of Roh realized that if all their friends made it to the polls, Roh might still be able to win . . .

Via email and cellphone text messages, Nosamo members entreated their normally apolitical friends to head to the polls. "Don't treat today just as a day off to spend shopping or at home," pleaded one. One Roh partisan sent such a flurry of text messages that he ended up paying several hundred dollars worth of phone fees when the bill came. Although it was illegal to use media websites or other public portal sites to campaign for a particular candidate, young people managed to make the point "vote for Roh" through use of code or suggestion. By some measurements, three million, or nearly 10 percent of the eligible electorate, had logged onto the Internet because of the election that day.

On election night, when Roh's victory was announced, the conservatives were in panic and shock. How could he have won?

Roh won by just 2.2 percent, just a few percentage points difference in an election that saw nearly three-quarters of the available electorate turn out and vote. No one can know for sure exactly how many people voted because this last minute internet and cellphone-assisted push—one Internet site reported a 600 percent increase in activity on election day—but nearly all accept that Roh rode the Internet wave into office. Ninety percent of twenty-year-olds were Internet users, compared to forty percent of forty-year-olds.

Young people in their twenties and thirties voted for Roh two to one over his opponent, the more conservative Lee Hoi-chang. In the previous presidential election, the ratio was only one to one for the eventual winner Kim Dae-jung. This concerted action by young voters also counteracted the decades of regionalism and brought victory to a candidate who campaigned on a reformist platform that promised to clear out the corruption and listen to the voices of the people. Young people from the most conservative provinces in Korea turned out in favor of the reformist party—voting an unprecedented 40 percent in favor of Roh. The president-elect recognized the power of this internet revolution and snubbed the established media by granting his first postelection interview to Ohmynews.

After this demonstration of political potency, the conservative papers decried the danger of democracy dominated by young whippersnappers, pointing to banks with financial problems due to young managers. Pundits continue to grumble about this "War of the Generations" and tsk-tsk that a country politically divided by generations will be ungovernable. Others chastise the newly energized young people for being too emotional and impractical, and for wanting equality without merit. Tenured scholars at the top universities, glum at the idea that they had been rudely shoved out of the center of the political arena by a bunch of text-messaging twenty somethings, muttered dire predictions.

Upon his arrival in the Blue House, Korea's presidential residence, Roh pulled together a truly progressive administration, incorporating professors from provincial universities and activists from the labor movement and the feminist movement as advisors. Issues like worker welfare, workplace discrimination against women, and foreign policies independent from American wishes were no longer just topics bandied about on Ohmynews but policies researched for implementation. Roh increased property taxes to slow down the real estate bubble and help narrow the widening gap between rich and poor, which had been mostly driven by an absurd real estate market that sees apartment prices in upper-class neighborhoods near-ly double from year to year. He has maintained the increasingly beleaguered Sunshine Policy with regards to North Korea and its possible nuclear arsenal and refused to ratchet up the rhetoric to match the American president's playground posturing. Unfortunately, his presidency is also plagued with scandals and crises, some left over from the previous president and some manufactured in house. It's unclear if Roh will be able to honor the trust of the millions of young people to keep politics clean, but what is not in doubt is the ability of those young people to put a president into the Blue House.

This new network of young people in politics isn't a one-hit wonder that died out after the Roh campaign. Technology is linking people together ever closer. The two biggest telecom companies in Korea are scrambling to build a wireless network so phones and laptops can receive the latest news, text messages or email blasts anywhere and anytime. A coalition of young voters is gearing up for the next national election with a get out the vote movement that grabs the attention of even the most cynical with the slogan "Running out of bad words? Then VOTE!"

No one can deny that young people are a force in Korean politics. Their internet and phone habits, labeled as useless and escapist, have suddenly and unexpectedly combined into an information juggernaut that could set agendas and make presidents. It's as if all those sports fans who play fantasy baseball on Yahoo, or download the latest celebrity scandal video, suddenly formed an online community that reshaped the face of electoral politics. All it took in Korea was two little websites that could and the volunteers that would.

In the United States, Asian Americans are known as the most wired ethnicity. While second-generation immigrants usually pay little attention to their parent's home country politics, perhaps the twentysomethings that spend the off minutes at work updating their Friendster profile will get infected with that virus of hope. That hope that politics as usual can be thwarted, that the issues that matter to them could be addressed, that if they just spent a little bit of time and money on politics they could actually elect politicians they believed in. Like the Melissa worm or the latest urban legend hoax, that hope can spread like this (snap) through the Internet.

*My first memorable experience with electoral politics:*

When I was in the fourth grade student council our student council president was a charming young fellow with a winning smile. Fred Savage went on to do the Wonder Years the following year, if I remember correctly. I'm ok with that trajectory. Elected office and then Hollywood. The reverse, however, is more troublesome. Politics in America have devolved to the level of a middle school student council election. Do you have enough money to trot down to the neighborhood copy shop and make pretty color posters that read "VOTE FOR ME! I'M CUTE AND POPULAR!" or converted to electionese, "I've got name recognition and you can project whatever fantasy you may have onto my bland but always smiling visage." Nerds like me never get elected to be student council president.

*How do you convince your Republican uncle not to vote for Bush?*

Let's start with my Republican dad. (Growing up he'd always get the holiday greeting card from the Bushes, while I was getting swamped in environmental action direct mail.) My Republican dad remembers the Korean War, so has a healthy skepticism of U.S. military hijinks abroad. I think laying out in careful detail exactly how Bush has made the world a less safe place will be sufficient.

*A slept-on group of voters you'd like to see organized (who they are and how you'd do it):*

Cocktail drinkers. I mean, generally cocktail drinkers/bar-goers end up reading bathroom ads and promotional napkins. Maybe if we can get political napkins. Or political ads in bar bathrooms. Slightly drunk people are more open to suggestion, right? I think politics could be injected into the hook-up scene.

*My greatest political achievement prior to helping swing the 2004 election?*

Using my U.S. Senate ID badge (from my two-month internship during high school) to make a fake ID.

*Something I hope to teach people on my book tour:*

How to have hope.

# The League of Pissed Off Voters and You

## By The League of Pissed Off Voters

Raise your hand if you've taken a pay cut.

Raise your hand if you've lost a job, if your family members have lost jobs.

Raise your hand if you are coming out of high school or college and can't find work worthy of your education.

Raise your hand if you're in debt or can't find the funds to get more education.

Raise your hand if you've been forced to do things you didn't want to or served jail time just to survive.

Raise your hand if you know someone who is incarcerated because they need medical and psychological care.

Raise your hand if you or someone you know can't work and is no longer eligible for welfare.

Raise your hand if you can't figure out how you will support your parents when they stop working.

Raise your hand if you consider yourself middle class but are two checks away from broke.

Raise your hand if you or someone you love can't afford health care.

Raise your hand if you can't swim in the nearest body of water because it's polluted.

Raise your hand if you know someone who's been sent over to the Middle East.

Now look around you. How many other people do you see in the same situation?

Feels like waking up from a dream, huh?

That would be the result of the American Dream.

We want children to grow up in loving homes and yet most of us are children of divorce or unhappy marriages. Most parents judge and criticize children into shells. But we find a way to grow up anyway.

We love this country, and yet we abuse then enable it every day, letting it become a horrendous monster without sending it to therapy.

We want to be monogamous, clean, stable and kind, in good with some God somewhere, just in all decisions, known for our big hearts. And yet we cheat, we get dirty, we fall apart and we're mean. Still, we are loved, and we love.

Something in us moves the greater powers to let us survive one more day each day.

We are moved to breathe, to think, to build, to communicate, to connect.

We are moved to change and adapt and evolve.

This is progress.

We are progressive.

We are not about the reactionary, the gimmick, the symbolic. We want real solutions and we want them now.

If SWMs do not volunteer these solutions, then we will create them, and we will take over, and we will implement them.

How?

Well clearly we've already started.

It's very strange to us that no one has done a book like this before. It's such an obvious idea: telling the real life stories of young folks who've actually won or swung elections and changed laws.

A twenty-four-year-old black woman in the Georgia state legislature? A twenty-five-year-old Green mayor? The Bus Project in Oregon? A Chicano community organizer elected to Congress? Native Americans swinging a Senate seat?

VICTORY: HOW WE'RE GONNA SMACKDOWN THE LIARMAN IN 2004

Who knew any of this was going on?

And have young progressives been winning elections all along, under the radar, unrecognized? Could this book just as easily have been written five or ten years ago?

Or did we stumble onto an historical moment?

If you look back through the book, you'll notice that every major victory (with the exception of Tammy Baldwin) happened in the past two or three years, many in the past year.

What's going on here? Why is this happening now? Are these stories a blip on the political radar, or are they part of some sort of larger trend?

We see a simple explanation: there is a youth movement now.

Six years ago, in 1998, there was no visible youth movement in the U.S. The youth anti-prison movement was virtually nonexistent. United Students Against Sweatshops was a brand new idea. Spoken-word poetry was hard to find outside a few major cities. The peace movement consisted of a few nuns over the age of fifty. Indymedia.org hadn't even been thought of yet. And no one in Seattle had ever heard of the WTO.

In the past five years, there's been a youthquake of political organizing all over the country—from the Southern Girls Convention to the explosion of DaveyD.com, MoveOn.org, and Pocho.com. For the first time in a generation, there is an undeniable critical mass of young people who are aware of ourselves as part of a growing national—and international—movement.

It's already happening, the ground is rumbling beneath our feet.

Look down.

The fissures that pattern the foundation are not chaotic, they are not without purpose; those are the new paths we must walk, this mad rhythm is how it feels when those paths become clear to us. They are paths our feet recognize because we walked them in past lives. We read them in the words of our grandparents. We dreamt of these paths to rise up for our lovers and friends. This is a revolution we know intimately.

This is a revolution we know commercially. This new political movement shows up in advertising, movies, and in the lyrics of popular songs. It is discussed regularly in the pages of the business press. How many people has this movement touched? No one knows for sure. Harvard's Institute of Politics found that 35 percent of U.S. college students reported having participated in a rally or protest in the past year. On February 15, 2003, more than a million people in the U.S. participated in hundreds of antiwar rallies in cities, towns, and suburbs across the country.

Our movement is maturing. And we're realizing that even though we hate electoral politics, we can't afford to ignore it anymore. We disregard the divisions of our predecessors—we're doing politics our way—beyond partisan, nonboring, with a long-term vision.

"All this time, we've been playing marbles," says Van Jones, who has been fighting prisons and police abuse in California for a decade. "We've gotten good at playing marbles. We spend a lot of time talking about how to play marbles. What color the marbles should be. And that's all fine. The problem is, we're on a football field. And there are these other people who are playing football while we're still playing marbles. And that's why we keep getting run over."

The Zapatistas do electoral politics. The Landless Workers Movement in Brazil does electoral politics. Even Russell Simmons and Jay-Z do electoral politics. Why can't we?

The Bush boys want to ignore us when we protest? It's time for us to show those fools something they can't ignore.

Oh, you think you're just gonna declare war on the world in our name and turn us into the Roman Empire? You think you're going to put our entire generation in debt so you can give tax cuts to the top 1 percent?

No, actually, asshole, you're not.

If you do not stop, we are going to make you stop. We are going to vote you out of office and take away your job. What are you going to do? Put us all in prison? Spy on us at the library? Unlike you, we don't have anything to hide. We're not afraid of your little Ashcroft and his henchmen. Bring them on, motherfucker! We're not intimidated by you. You're just a bully. Bring. It. On.

Well.

Ok that might have been a bit rash—technically we are cowering just the slightest bit in fear. No one wants to be surveilled on the toilet, it's just not cool. No one wants to be disappeared, mysteriously suicidal; it reeks of a bad TV movie. And yet that's the kind of government we've got right now. And that's wack!

John Ashcroft, you hear me? You are a petty little bully and you may scare us now, but we will ultimately defeat you and run off victorious to the strings of an triumphant underdog TV movie theme song!

No wait—to a really fresh Afro-Cuban hip-hop from Detroit theme song.

Boo-ya!

Cause see, this is not just a book. We're building an organization, the League of Pissed Off Voters, that teaches our generation how to implement the strategies in this book.

## Lose Your Fear of Power

We had the power to intervene in the last election and we didn't use it.

We sat there and let "Bush the Lesser" (as Arundhati Roy nicknamed our dear chap) walk in, don someone else's title like it was his inheritance, and walk off with it, taking our surplus with him.

We sat with our mouths agape.

The power to change the course of recent history was within our reach, but we were too scared to touch it. Perhaps it was too dirty a thing at that moment, and we were scared it would corrupt us.

And yet are we not corrupt now, against our collective will? Our backs bend with the weight of doing nothing or not doing enough, or not being allowed to do enough.

And within our borders is the single black hole; every other inhabited surface glows with the desire of people wishing they could vote in the next United States election.

We have to realize what this power means for young Americans.

Each story in this book is about living in power.

That means the power to be young.

Keep in mind that America has been sweating the opinions of youth for years now.

How else can you explain white boys across the nation sippin' pimp juice—white boys created neither pimps nor juice. But (and we may not be proud of it) that is the reach of our power. Young people decided that "pimp" was not going to be the derogatory exploitative word on the street, it was going to indicate power, cool, wealth.

Oprah, Donald Trump, J-Lo, the Puffster, Russell Simmons, Martha Stewart, Robert Johnson, Bill Cosby: pimps.

Bill Gates? Shawn, the Napster dude? Britney Spears? Ashton Kutcher? Pimps.

And we can't overlook the militant political pimps—Reagan was a laid back in the cut pimp, Cheney is a big fat P.I.M.P. Rumsfeld is a super pimp, he's got all the gov'ment bitches lined up ready to kiss his left shoe.

That would make Bush and Condaleeza and Colin . . . You guessed it: sex workers without a union or healthcare plan. If only! Wouldn't that change some things?

Anyway, we empowered the vocabulary of pimpdom.

We also brought jazz, rock 'n' roll, hip-hop, jeans, sneakers, and the Internet to power.

Now we're the ones who determine the success of damn near everything. Opening weekend for Lord of the Rings or the Matrix, you saw lines of us out there, contributing to million-dollar revenues. We are the pot of gold at the end of the Skittles rainbow. Jay-Z or 50 Cent drops a CD and it will be a hit if and only if we are waiting there to buy it.

Now we need to pimp power for change.

We want to see 50 and Jay-Z—and Eminem and Missy and Nas and Trina and Talib Kweli and Common and L'il Kim and Gwen Stefani and Coldplay and the White Stripes and all those folk—endorse a candidate.

But to get there we have to exercise our right as young people to throw a national tantrum, and demand what we want.

Just like with TV, sugar, and toys, we will get it.

As usual, youth is in this season.

Youth are cool.

Being cool wins elections.

That's right! The true winning strategy behind a remarkable number of the winning candidates in this book is that they are cool people. It sounds silly—by being dope I could be president?

Why, yes.

Wellstone, Baldwin, West, Segal, Thomas, Grijalva: they were all cool before they held office. They were able to show people themselves in a way that could be absorbed. They each thought about the character of things in determining their actions. They each came to politics after trying their hand at other expressions of themselves.

They didn't come at politics for the cash—West and Segal's salaries are smaller than the smallest donations to some of the folks we're trying to escort out of the big building.

They certainly didn't come at it for the sheer fun of sitting in rooms with a majority–radical Right system and trying to battle for small victories.

They were just righteous, dude.

And back in the day, try if you can to remember, George W. used to be pretty cool too. Did we just say that?

In school he was the kind-of-lazy cool kid sliding through on the merit of his papa. We all knew kids like that in college, privileged but shirking all that power stuff. Dubya just wanted to chill. And people wanted to chill with him. He got picked for exclusive clubs; people wanted Dubya around, he was the dude cracking jokes that weren't quite funny but he'd buy everyone in the house a drink for laughing and he was always down for a line before trig. Dude could party allllll night!

But the pressure on George to become super uncool has been intense. Being the president's son made poor Bushie the tool of a truly evil puppetmaster—Karl Rove (the czar of pimps, no less)—and that would pimp-slap the cool out of almost anyone.

And Bush had a dream. He wanted to manage a baseball team. He loves baseball; he was truly happy, and successful, with that team. Boys and girls, can you imagine how much better off we'd be if Georgie had stuck with his dream?

Luckily most of us aren't in that situation. Progressives tend to not have legacies of absolute power to inherit. We can maintain our cool all the way to Congress. We can live the lives we dream.

What were you born to do? Are you doing it? Why not? Make it your profession. Stop cheating yourself.

Some of you must have a governor, senator, representative, or even president in you. Join the ranks of collective-minded, cool power-wielders!

Still scared? Try and understand your fear.

It's a given in America, a talk show boon in fact, that we are hurting, bored, insecure, lacking a spiritual center, consumed with materials. Yet we punish people for all of this. Of course it's scary to strike out with an earnest step, this country is a hard place for people to be themselves, know themselves, think of themselves as powerful, divine creatures. We are constantly criticizing and judging folks and ourselves for those natural responses to the world we created.

Humans have this whole hyperego self-hate thing going on, and America is the peak of that tide.

And so far, any path out of Ego Ocean has been met with excuses—we're scared of power, we're scared to win, so we raise our noses and act like those paths are wack.

Activism gets a bad rap as something, you know, over there, for the crazies.

But the point is this: you have a powerful effect whether you intend to or not. There are pro-money activists, anti-art activists, pro-war activists, pro-apathy activists. You are what you live for these days, and we are unintentionally becoming desks, computer screens, cash, DVDs, nifty T-shirts, commercials, spreadsheets, and copying machine/fax/scanners.

Voting gets a bad rap as being too dorky and in-the-system, playing the game of the oppressor.

But we're only ever going to be able to throw off the weight of oppression once we're in decision-making positions. If you have some better-than-voting revolutionary way to realistically change the power structure in this country, call us; we'll be there.

Until that phone rings, we must embrace our inner cool-dorks. We must be the voting activists launching an electoral revolution.

We must remember this crucial fact: we gave Bush his job.

## Organize the Choir

Now you may be thinking "So what if a bunch of people who read this book get excited about voting? They already agree with you. The people you need to reach are the undecided voters. You need to reach the forty-five-year-old white guys in the suburbs. You're just preaching to the choir!"

But guess what? Take an informal poll of your friends and acquaintances. *Half the people in our so-called choir don't vote.* How do you think the Radical Christian Right built its power base? They organized their choir. They mobilized their choir into an electoral army.

We have to do the same. We have to organize our choir. We need to organize the choir in order to organize the congregation. And once we organize the congregation, then we can go out and start knocking on doors. And then, Hallelujah, we will see the liiiiiight!

This is what the evangelical Christian movements have done. It's a four step process: Choir, then Congregation, then Community, then Country. C-C-C-C.

The right-wing has bought their choir new robes every year, made sure they had pizza at choir practice and a special choir retreat for the big hymn competition each year. Progressives, we like to take our choir for granted. They get the hymnals with the pages missing, the irritable choir director, the untuned piano.

It's not that we're too stupid to organize our choir. Our choir is much harder to organize than the right-wing choir. We're not all excited to wear the same outfits and act like robots. Our choir isn't a bunch of followers. Our choir ain't tryna be told what to sing. Our choir likes to make up its own songs. And the songs we sing must incorporate many voices, many rhythms, many histories, including those of smart and stupid white men.

How many people are in our choir, Deacon? Well, Reverend, no one knows for certain.

There are different ways to estimate how many of "us" there might be.

About sixty million U.S. adult citizens—roughly a third—identify themselves as Democrats. Another third identify as "independent" or unaffiliated.

Sixty million is the approximate number of people of color in the U.S..

About fifty million Americans are "cultural creatives," generally liberal on most issues.

Over fifty million people voted for Al Gore in 2000.

About thirty million adults say they disapproved of George Bush even at the peak of his "popular approval" after 9/11.

According to polls, if the election were held at press time (November 2003), roughly eighty million American adults would choose any of the Democratic front-runners over Bush—if they make it to the polls.

Those are numbers for the congregation.

The numbers for the choir are much smaller. For our purposes here, we will define the choir as people who are connected to some identifiable movement network, issue, or organization: antiwar, schools not jails, workers' rights, environment, education, LGBT and gender equality, global justice, alumni networks of liberal colleges, and progressive online communities, plus hip-hop, punk, spoken-word, and rave scenes.

We estimate our "movement" personally touches at least one million young adults between eighteen and thirty-five nationwide. At least. Probably two to three million. Maybe as high as five million. From organic farmers to immigrants' rights advocates, graphic artists to graffiti heads, progressive church groups to Food not Bombs, we believe there are *at least two million young people who we can reach through existing social change networks.*

Based on our informal surveys with this group of people, only about half of us vote. Half don't. That means there are at least five hundred thousand eighteen- to thirty-five-year-old non-voters who we as a movement could easily reach. Easily! We're not talking about random people. We're talking about people we are already connected to. We're talking about our friends. We're talking about ourselves.

Think of all the people in your phone book right now. Think of all the people you went to school with. Think of all the interesting, sexy young people you've seen at events. Think of all the phone numbers you've gotten and never called. Think of all the people who emailed you that movie about the Meatrix.com or Blackpeopleloveus.com. If you get together with a few friends and go through all your phone numbers and emails and have a brainstorm session, we guarantee you'll come up with at least five people who don't like President Bush but who might not vote on November 2 unless you pester them.

Fine, you say, I can talk to five friends. That's not going to swing the election.

Here's where it gets interesting. Between the fifty or so people who are most involved in the League of Pissed Off Voters, we know at least twenty thousand of those people *personally.* The twenty thousand who we know, in turn, know the vast majority of the two or three million. Who knows why we are all so popular. Maybe it's just our style or the way we walk into a room. But the bottom line is that we are within two degrees of separation from the entire U.S. social change movement (including folks in isolated rural areas, and by the way, you). In short, *we know everybody* and we're building an online platform to invite all of our friends to join us in creating a powerful new political force.

Will we swing the presidential election this year? Maybe. Maybe not.

Most political strategists are predicting it's gonna be squeaky close again. According to Gloria Totten of Progressive Majority, "The 2004 election could look just like the 2000 election. It could come right back down to Florida and end in a recount."

Or it could come down to any of the other seventeen swing states. There are going to be a lot of unknowns and surprises in the final months. Republicans are going to play the Gay Marriage card. We're going to play the Supreme Court card and the Environment card and the Deficit card. Iraq is a wild card. Bush's lies and the media are wild cards. The economy is a wild card. The Democratic candidate is a wild card. The Greens are a wild card. The lunatics in Bush's cabinet are a deck of wild cards. We just won't know until the last poll closes on Tuesday, November 2.

What we do know is that Bush has divided the nation. And what everyone on both sides agrees is: This election will not be won in the media. It's gonna be won block by block, dorm by dorm, precinct by precinct. This election is about which side can implement the most effective field campaign to register their people and turn them out on November 2.

Liberal donors and unions are pouring hundreds of millions of dollars into turning out Democratic voters. Suddenly, the Democratic Party has begun to wake from the dead, energized by the antiwar movement and Moveon.org.

What the liberal and progressive big-shots don't understand yet is us: The five hundred thousand-plus eligible and pissed-off seventeen- to thirty-year-old nonvoters. They have written our generation off. They're focused on the same old union members, churches, environmentalists, and womens' groups.

They will be happily surprised if we pull something off on November 2. In fact, they'll be shocked. But, honestly, they're not holding their breath. It's up to us to organize ourselves with no money and prove them wrong. This is our planet, our country, our legacy on this Earth. We need to pull out all the stops. And we can win. Not definitely, not probably, but can, just like Chicago's Thirty-fifth Ward, just like Austell, Georgia, just like Shannon County, South Dakota, and just like every other uphill battle in this book: We can win. And if the race is close, we could be the deciding factor.

Let's look again at the numbers.

In 2000, New Hampshire was decided by 7,211 votes; Oregon by 6,765; Wisconsin by 5,708; Iowa by 4,144; New Mexico by 366; and have we mentioned there's this little state called FLORIDA?!?!

# 537.

How would you feel if you and your friends helped to swing an election? How would you feel if you helped to redirect trillions of dollars, make thousands of hiring decisions about who controls the world's most powerful government, and appoint up to three Supreme Court justices? Would you feel powerful? Would you feel like you can do anything? Would politicians take your phone calls?

You better believe it.

Choir, if we get organized fast enough, we can swing this election.

And even if we lose the big one, we can win a lot of smaller ones. From the bottom up, we can begin our realistic thirty-year plan to build a progressive governing majority in our lifetimes. Every two years, we can do a new version of this book with twenty more success stories initiated by people like you who've never cared about electoral politics.

How do we do win this election, you ask? Good question, choir!

Voter Organizing 101: Studies show the best way to increase voter registration and turnout is through peer-to-peer organizing. This isn't about convincing anyone to vote. In the 2000 presidential election, only 32 percent of eligible eighteen- to twenty-four-year-olds actually voted, down from 42 percent in 1992. But a recent study by Harvard's Institute of Politics found that 57 percent of young people are "definitely planning to vote" in the 2004 election and another 26 percent are "probably" going to.

We just need to make sure they follow through.

There are all kinds of stupid little reasons why people don't vote. We forget. We scheduled something else that day. We were on the road. We have a job (most states mandate that you be given two paid hours to vote as long as you give your boss proper notice). We've got kids. We forgot to get a babysitter. We attend night school. We have drama in our lives. We move around a lot and we don't know who to vote for where we're from or where we live now.

But the biggest reason most of us don't vote is cuz we don't have someone in our life who asks us to vote. Someone who makes sure we don't oversleep that day. Someone who makes sure we mail in our absentee ballot by the deadline. Someone who makes sure we know where the polling place is. Someone who gives us a voter guide. We need a lot of those someones. Together those someones can create a culture of voting within our two- to three-million-person choir. That's our first step: for the two or three million of us to change our antivoting culture into a provoting culture. This was the Christian Right's first step.

It's so simple. So basic. So obvious.

And yet no organization has existed to organize "the choir." No organization exists to teach our generation to do electoral politics on our own terms and on a massive scale. That's why we had to start the League of Pissed Off Voters.

## November Surprise

Our short term plan is to organize a November surprise at the polls. We have a whole strategy laid out for every day and every week leading up to the election. Think of how many people are reading this book right now. Together, we can move tens of thousands of new voters to the polls. Tens of thousands who care like you do. Tens of thousands who can swing the entire election if it's close.

The second strategy is our book tour. Naw, we don't have a bus and a bunch of celebrities to come with us. We don't need em. What we have is the twelve kick-ass artists and organizers who created this book and who will come to your town or college, especially those in swing states, and help you strategize how to do this.

The third strategy: IndyVoter.org.

IndyVoter.org will revolutionize the way young people do politics. It will revolutionize the way young people who don't do politics do politics.

Like MoveOn.org and MeetUp.com blew up Howard Dean.

Or Ohmynews.com and Nosamo.net blew-up Roh Moo-hyun in South Korea.

Indyvoter.org is going to create a platform for hundreds and eventually thousands of Danis and Shanas (see final section) to create their own voter guides, and circulate them like crazy in the weeks before the election. You and your friends can make one. You can print them out and hit up high schools, colleges, cafés, beauty salons, basketball courts. Sign people up. And once your results are compared against voter files, we'll have a certified network of local progressive voting blocs all over the country that can run candidates, swing elections, and hold politicians accountable.

We believe this voting bloc strategy will capture the imagination of a generation of young non-voters and enable us to do electoral politics on our own terms. In a tight race, we believe this voter bloc effect could help swing the election.

But enough about us. Time to give you some homework, fun homework.

Get to a computer, go to www.indyvoter.org, click "join," and let us know how you want to get involved. While you're waiting to hear back from us (it shouldn't take long) call and email everyone you know who could possibly vote in a swing state. Or swing district. Or anywhere. Make them sign up. We only have a few months to get everyone signed up and to build critical mass to swing the election.

Then we as a generation are gonna go out in force.

Registering.

Working voter lists.

Teaching people HAVA, the new Help Americans Vote Act.

Translating.

Reinstating the voting rights of former prisoners.

Knocking on doors. Wearing buttons. Talking to folks at bus stops.

Preparing people to use the new voting machines.

Learning local issues and key races.

Making our own media.

Finding mentors.

Creating and distributing voter guides.

Making signs. Making art.

Chalking sidewalks with arrows pointing to polling places.

Calling everyone on November 1.

Emailing our entire network a Go Vote reminder on election day eve.

Pajama jammy jams the night before.

Calling everyone on November 2.

Taking people to the polls.

Pushing wheelchairs.

Driving.

Poll watching.

Babysitters Against Bush!

Voter parties before, after, and during the election, blasting merengue from your car! Setting off car alarms. Tailgate parties. Kids rollerskating with face paint.

Fighting for our lives with everything we've got.

And then a moment later. Just one moment later:

Polls closed. Tired and spent. All eyes on the TV set.

Living room. Everyone's here.

Eating. Laughing. Drinking beer.

Can't watch. Can't eat. Can't drink. Must watch.

Red state. Blue state. Red state. Blue state.

Numbers. Reporting. Nails. Biting.

Arizona. Tension. Wisconsin. Tension. Pennsylvania. Tension.

And then . . .

Disbelief.

A gasp.

A jaw drops.

The room stops.

ECSTASY

# Shana's Voter Guide for the Pissed Off

I moved to New Orleans two and a half years ago and finally felt at home. I love my life here and don't plan on leaving unless the big one comes to wash me away. The voter guide you have in your hands really is a love letter to this city. I made it because my friend Billy was talking about tactics people were using to make voting more effective. I made it because I was mad as hell and not going to take it anymore. I made it because I protested the war, supported cool organizations, voted once in a blue moon—but didn't feel like I had any political power. I made it because an election was coming up and the ballot was going to be the longest one in recent memory. The state of Louisiana even imposed a three minute rule for how long you could take to make up your mind while you were in the little box though there were twenty-seven separate things to vote on. I made it because (once again) I didn't know who or what to vote for.

I spent about a month of my free time researching, writing, printing, and distributing it. I talked to everyone who would talk to me; I read everything available. I spent $118 to make three thousand copies. Everyone I know who was interested got fifty copies; they gave them to people they know, posted them, left them at their neighborhood bars and coffee shops. A few super-stars passed them out at concerts and events. Strangers found out about them and asked me for stacks to give to their friends and family. I felt like a rock star, except I didn't have an entourage or leather pants.

So, did the voter guide work? Were the masses swayed, did the revolution happen, did all my dark horses come in? Well, some of my picks won, many of them lost. I am not sure where it made a difference. I haven't yet learned how to analyze election data to figure out how many votes were generated. It would be conjecture for me to guess.

What I do know for sure is that the voter guide was seen by about three thousand people, many of whom used it and contacted me to talk more about it. It worked as a voter organizing tool: folks who were not going to bother voted because they felt more informed. There were sightings of guides being taken into the voting booth. A friend in Cincinnati, Dani McClain, heard about it and made a voter guide with her friends (it took about a week). And I'm hoping that you, dear reader, see how cool it is and get fired up to do one your own self, whether you blanket the city with them or give one to the five people closest to you.

For me, it was the most powerful voting experience ever. I learned more about local politics and the electoral process than I could have in class or from a book. I feel more invested in what happens in my home, and more capable of doing something about it.

I am psyched to do it next year, and I have talked to people who want to collaborate. And when I am allowing myself to dream that big, I see a time, some years from now, when everyone in New Orleans just expects to see the little-homemade-voter-guide-that-could at election time. I dream about a nonpartisan voter guide that isn't about just one person's point of view, but that is collectively created by a strange and wonderful cross-section of people in New Orleans who have enough in common to vote together and wield their political power like a club, um, I mean a beacon.

## Ballot for the Primary Election — Saturday, October 4

*special note — if there is no new challenger a nasty incumbent, I suggest writing in Kermit Ruffins

Governor - Claude "Buddy" Leach #11 — one of the folks in this race rock. I surround it down to Foang or Leach. Foang is a conservative gay who is a pretty conservative Democrat. Leach is a kooky old union guy who is a pretty liberal Democrat. Foang has the endorsement of the mayor and The Gambit and The Louisiana Weekly. Leach has got the endorsement of the Tribune and Rep. Ed

Lieutenant Governor - Mitch J. Landrieu #12 — No-brainer. Only Democrat on the field. Supports juvenile justice reform and local reform.

Secretary of State - M. Fournette #27 — The incumbent Republican. McKeithen, a lefty Democrat. But I am worried about election stuff being in the hands of the Republican Party post Florida 2000 - weird.

Attorney General - Charles C. Foti, Jr. #39— MAASHURE We must vote for Foti his opponent, herself, is scary and keeps trying to get elected.

Commissioner, Agriculture and Forestry - Bob Odom #33 — Probably a crook but not much clean here.

Commissioner, Insurance - Dan Kyle #38 — A fundamentalist Christian Republican! Not this simple. CPA, but's likely to rise to a higher elected post, and is the only one of the field to sign a pledge to not take insurance money (the position regulates the insurance industry).

BESE, 1st District - Barbara Ferguson #44 — Only Democrat on the field, former school principal and attorney

BESE, 2nd District - CC Campbell-Rock #45 — founder of Parents for Educational Justice, journalist, and grassroots activist

### State Senator

| | |
|---|---|
| 1st Senatorial District - Wayne Landry | 5th Senatorial District - Diana Bajoie |
| 2nd Senatorial District - Ann Duplessis | 6th Senatorial District - write in Kermit Ruffins |
| 3rd Senatorial District - James Devills | 7th Senatorial District - write in Kermit Ruffins |
| 4th Senatorial District - Paulette Irons | |

### State Representatives

| | |
|---|---|
| 82nd Rep. District - write in Kermit Ruffins | 94th Rep. District - Eddie Gaskard |
| 86th Rep. District - write in Kermit Ruffins | 97th Rep. District - Arthur Morrel |
| 91st Rep. District - Juan Aubrom | 98th Rep. District - Randy Roppel |
| 92nd Rep. District - Leo Bouchard | 99th Rep. District - Charmaine Marchand |
| 93rd Rep. District - write in Kermit Ruffins | 100th Rep. District - Diana Henry |
| 94th Rep. District - Jean Lawless | 101st Rep. District - Cedric Richmond |

Judge, Criminal Court, Section B - Gregory Hugo or ??
Clerk, Criminal District Court - Johnny Jackson, Jr # 81

### Constitutional Amendments

| | |
|---|---|
| 1. for | 8. for | 15. against |
| 2. for | 9. for | 16. for |
| 3. for | 10. for | 17. for |
| 4. against | 11. against | 18. against |

*** Partly with Progressive - but Nadine Gassig is the Progressive, she's not ***
Ruben Gassig is my favorite punch, but I know what I doesn't win a continued neighborhood; it a good way to destroy a neighborhood. the proponents have been manipulate and incentive to their example.

---

## Shana's Voter Guide for the Pissed Off

Hey New Orleans.

This is my love letter to you. Like a good lover, though, I'm gonna prove my love—

Here's what I did: I spent a few weeks researching the folks asking for our votes this Saturday and tried to figure out who was mostly telling the truth, who mostly cared about us, and what propositions make the most sense. Here's who I am. I am a waitress who believes in these things:

1) Social and economic justice in our public schools.
2) Real rebel beyond tap dancing and waiting on tourists. The ones you'd actually want to work.
3) People have the right to control what they do with their own bodies.
4) More prisons and bombs are not the answer to all our problems.
5) Our city and state and country belong to us, not to corporations.
6) The Constitution and Art
7) Politics is about doing right by people, not about personal power or greed. (thanks Paul Wellstone)
8) It all ends in tragedy. Sure, we're all gonna die someday. Things fall apart. But, we can decide who we want to be in the meantime.

So, I guess that makes me a liberal, progressive, radical, populist, feminist, independent, anarchosocialist, democratic, bleeding heart something. If you believe in some or all of the above, this is your handy, dig'n save voter guide to take with you into the polls on October 4th, to use alongside your own best judgment.

I'm not usually hanging out at traffic lights trying to get people to vote, but I'm ready to start. People with scary, mean agendas are now running this country - and it happened because most eligible voters didn't (and don't) vote. I want politicians that give a damn and can't be bought. I want regime change right here in New Orleans. Yeah, I know how you feel. Politics is so dirty, boring, confusing, heartbreaking, irrelevant, enraging, overwhelming. So, what are we gonna do about it?

Any and all mistakes, errors in judgment, bad calls, or flippery in general are mine and mine alone. It's my first attempt at what I hope will become a bigger, better, more effective, helpful, and inspiring voter guide. So, give me some feedback. If you want to work on stuff like this and/or help organize voters, let's hook up. Cuz... "No single person can liberate a country. You can only liberate a country if you act as a collective." (Nelson Mandela).

Contact me at:     P.O. Box 19742 – New Orleans, LA 70179-0742     or
redanvoter@yahoo.com

You'll get out of bed to watch the Saints lose, for Chrissakes! So get out of bed to vote.

Love,

P.S. Sources consulted: Bureau of Governmental research (www.bgr.org), Public Affairs Research Council of Louisiana (www.la-par.org), League of Women Voters of New Orleans (www.lwvla.org), Secretary of State web site (www.sec.state.la.us), The Times Picayune, The Gambit, The Louisiana Weekly, The New Orleans Tribune, Project Vote Smart, Green Party, Democratic Party, The BOLD ballot, The Louisiana Family Forum (creepy), Indymedia (www.neworleans.indymedia.org), Alliance for Good Government endorsements, New Orleans Coalition endorsements, candidate's web sites, my friends and neighbor, activists, politicos, artists, academics, cronies, and upstarts around town. PPS. No group or individual paid me to do this.

For voting information in Orleans, call the Registrar of Voters: 565-7153 or register online.
Last day to register for the November 15th Run-off Election is OCT. 15th.

# The Political Power of the Internet is about to Flex

MoveOn.org's two million members raise serious money for the progressive cause and stop bad laws from getting passed just by forwarding e-mail to each other. This is just a hint of the democratic promise of the internet.

Power for political change in this country traditionally requires money, ideas, and people out in the streets spreading the message and getting out the vote. Where do we get these resources if we are not a political party or a PAC? From our friends: our social networks both online and offline.

The internet is all about people connecting with each other. We talk about fucking and selling shit. We forward endless bad jokes to each other. Indyvoter is an attempt to spread the virus of meaningful political dialogue throughout the consumerist hook-up fest that is the internet.

We use this fledgling internet to build communities, emailing our friends, posting on web boards and blogs, and spreading our art—pictures, videos, songs.

These communities are arenas for public dialogue about music, culture, survival strategies, common values, politics, and social issues that are important to us as individuals. How do we bring that energy and passion offline into the realm of meaningful political change?

Steve's friend Olivia is running on a progressive slate for a position on the school board. He's throwing a fundraising house party to help pay for printing some stickers, flyers, and mailers. He puts the call out to his friends who donate a soundsystem, vegan appetizers, and some art to auction off. He pulls it off in forty-eight hours; planned completely online, it came off tight and raised five thousand dollars just by people showing up to a house party.

Alejandro is a rave promoter just getting into local electoral politics. He raises money through parties to print up a voter slate for the San Francisco Late Night Coalition, detailing which politicians are friendliest to the rave community. Using indyvoter.org, he publishes his voter slate online. Within a few weeks, thousands of people who have never met Alejandro have pledged to vote the SF Late Night Coalition's slate.

IndyVoter.org is an online tool that aims to revolutionize democracy through the use of social networks: to strengthen our online and offline communities through sharing resources and building voter blocs with everyone we know.

IndyVoter.org is a public trust, a collective community written using open source software. We build it together. Our communities contribute to the way the website looks and works. Check out the preliminary design for a candy-raver version of IndyVoter.org:

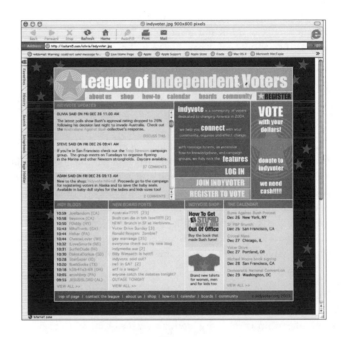

# 13 Slick Moves to Swing the Election
## Take It to Bed, and Wake up with a Winner

1. IF YOU HAVE FRIENDS . . .
- Give them a copy of this book.
- Organize a book club–style conversation about it.
- Tell them what you think and what you're planning to do for 2004.
- Ask what they think. Ask what they're planning to do. Strike match. Boom!

2. IF YOU HAVE A HOME OR LIKE TO THROW EVENTS . . .
- Organize a fundraiser, party, BBQ, or brunch. Download our shit. Pass it out.
- Make your next event or chill session a Local League event.

3. IF YOU'RE A COLLEGE STUDENT . . .
- Write a paper on local electoral politics. Get school credit!
- Get an internship with an organization working on the 2004 election.
- If your college is in a swing state, organize a local voter registration drive.
- If your college is not in a swing state but attracts out-of-state students, do a local registration drive *and* a swing state absentee voter drive.
- Organize a speaker/trainer to talk to your college about voter organizing. We'll help you find good speakers/trainers. Hello.
- Organize a conference on voter organizing on your campus. We'll help you!
- Intern for the League.

4. IF YOU'RE A HIGH SCHOOL STUDENT . . .
- Write a paper on local electoral politics. Get school credit!
- Get an internship with an org working on the election. Get school credit!
- Organize eighteenth birthday parties for seniors and register people to vote.
- Create your own voter guide and Remind Fools to Vote campaign.

5. IF YOU'RE AN ARTIST . . .
- Create a rap, song, album, flyer, poem, piece, video, website about the election and give www.IndyVoter.org a big fat shout out!
- Perform/screen/post/paste it everywhere!
- Organize a "Pissed about Politics" talent show, art show, or open mic.
- Become an Artist Partner to a League Affiliate in your area.
- Incorporate the League of Pissed Off Voters and www.IndyVoter.org into your next tour.

6. IF YOU HAVE A JOB OR SKILL . . .
- Donate your goods and services to a local League Affiliate or some other local progressive organization working on the election. From free food to legal counsel to office supplies we need it all!
- Mobilize your professional/workplace connections.

7. IF YOU'RE A TEACHER OR PROFESSOR . . .
– Pass this on to your students.
– Help them to connect with local political internships.
– Create assignments that allow students to learn about local politics. Encourage them to create, disseminate and post their own local voter guide on IndyVoter.org.

8. IF YOU'RE INVOLVED IN AN ORGANIZATION OR GROUP . . .
– Talk about what you want to do about the election.
– Organize your people to register, vote, and turnout their people.
– You or your members can create your own local voter guide and voter bloc in your living room without endangering your tax exempt status.
– Need someone to come and talk about voting strategy? We'll hook you up.

9. IF YOU KNOW HOW TO USE THE INTERNET . . .
– Tell everyone you know about Indyvoter.org. Get them to join before it's too late.
– Write about it on your website, blog, or e-newsletter.
– Put a www.IndyVoter.org link on your email signature.
– Put a www.IndyVoter.org link or banner on your website.
– Bumrush chatrooms.

10. IF YOU LIKE TO TALK TO PEOPLE . . .
– Make your own IndyVoter.org flyers or stickers.
– Survey people at upcoming events about their plans for the election.
– Set up a table at a local event.
– Collect stories and rants. We will showcase them and feed them to our partner organization, the Next Wave & Women in Power for their major touring performance *We Got Issues.*
– If you register fifty people, you can become an official delegate at the National Hip Hop Political Convention. www.hiphopconvention.org

11. IF YOU LIVE SOMEWHERE . . .
– Become a precinct captain. Walk around your block, talk to your neighbors, and make them vote.

12. IF YOU SPEAK MORE THAN ONE LANGUAGE . . .
– Translate voter guides and other materials.
– Organize and support people who speak languages other than English.

13. IF YOU WANT TO STEP UP YOUR GAME . . .
– Start an informal group, or to create an unofficial or official local voting guide or local voting bloc at IndyVoter.org.

# The People We Will Dance in the Streets With

This project has been a snowball—one flake of an idea gathered speed, volume, and shape and power to become the avalanche you hold in your hands. Major gratitude goes out:

To George W. Bush and company, for making this time so ripe for us to find ourselves and our community and organize to move forward.

To our behind-the-scenes editors: James Bernard, who sat with the pieces and returned to us a product that we could mold into a book. Your vision, clarity, mercilessness, and dedication was crucial and well timed. Anna Lappe, who made the novel suggestion of chapters to us as we sat with our twenty plus stories and dreams. Sarah Greenwalt, for her twenty-fifth-hour edits of purpose and vision without which the book would be entertaining but, perhaps, convoluted; Naina Khanna for her finishing touches. And to Soft Skull's brilliant copy editor Sarah Groff-Palermo, who backed over the manuscript with a truckload of red ink.

To our publisher, Soft Skull Press—for the most extraordinary support waaaaaay beyond the call of duty. Richard Nash—you believed in us and this project from day one, before we were even sure we could pull it off. Tennessee Jones—dynamo of publicity—Ammi Emergency, and the entire Softskull fam.

To the co-authors: Annie, Malia, Piper, Davey, Bouapha, Marisol, Mattie, Alma Rosa, Jackie, and Aya. Your leadership and innovation inspired this book, your writing filled it, and now we're counting on you to spread your gifts and teach young people everywhere that we can do this!

To the writers: Yahonnes Cleary (who'd like to thank Tracey Luszcz, Ras, David Muhammad, Trevor Phillips, and Rachman Muhammad), Adam Smith (who'd like to thank Karynn Fish and Jefferson Smith), Gary Dauphin, Kari Lyderson, Miriam Markowitz, Monique Luse, Michelle Lin, Robin Templeton, Cherryl Aldave, Andrew Boyd, Alyson Byrne Fields, Adam Klaus, Seth Donley, Eli Lee, Alejandra Ibañez, Amanda Klonsky. Thank you for your brilliant stories and patience with the editing process.

To the most kick-ass of all photo editors: Margarita Garcia and Sophia Wallace and their crew: Daniel Liao, Michelle Matos & Christina Wallace and all who contributed visuals: SFifty5, Amy Woloszyn, Ben Wheeler, Hugh Gran, Chris Ho, Cherisse Domingo, Una-Kariim Cross, Jessica Pinkham, Sophia Wallace, Courtney Hull, and to Pete Miser for the World's Illest Logo.

To the miracle worker of design, Amy Woloszyn (www.amymade.com). Amy Makes. The World Takes. When you movin' back to Brooklyn?

And to the entire League crew and advisors and supporters working behind the scenes, building this movement: Kyle Stewart, Sarah Greenwalt, Laura Livoti, Karynn Fish, Adam Smith, Naina Khanna, James Bernard, Malia Lazu, Meighan Davis, Donna Bransford, Mahea Campbell, Shana Sassoon, Nimco Ahmed, Alyssa Erickson, Wendy Volkman, Gavin Leonard, KJ Carter, Foster Gamble, J-Love, Wendy Day, Shalini Kantayya, Ellen Furnari, Maricruz Badia, Margarita Garcia and Daniel Liao, Cary Davidson, Jordan Heckman, Bodil Fox, Willy Becker, Ibrahim Abdul-Matin, Eddie Codel, Marc Powell, Jo & Schuyler, Leah Markos, Cherryl Aldave, Rha Goddess, Lenore Palladino and United Students Against Sweatshops, Pete Miser, Yahonnes Cleary, David Perrin, Sally Kohn, Mario Yedidia, Jess Pinkham, Molly, Erin Markman, Rowan Garret-Moore, Charlotte, Maria Bacha, Manuela Arciniegas, Mia Herndon, Lenora Pace and Next Wave of Women & Power, Gloria Totten, Teresa Van Deusen, Cathy Doggett, Portia Pedro, Becky Wasserman and United States Student Association, Jane Fleming and Brian Elms, Ben Quinto, Catilla Everette, Angela Angel, Dani McClain, Rachel Durschlag, Toni Blackman, Hallie Montoya Tansey, PJ Urquilla, Ian Simmons, Jee Kim, Mandie Yanasak, Sarah Shanley, Daniel & Isaac Souweine, Kalpana Krishnamurthy, Gita Drury and Active Element fam, Emily Nepon, Jason Gillis Lemeiux and Eggplant Active Media, The Ladiez of 456 SVN for their love and support, David Jacobs, Jenny Overman, Katie Gunther, David Perrin, Jamie Schweser, Malika Sanders and the Sanders family, Tarana Burke, LaTosha Brown, Tanya Diaz, Marta Drury, Tim Freundlich, Stephan Rechtschaffen, Adam Stenftenagel, Shannon Service, Courtney Hull, Resource Generation crew, AYE crew, Dan Carol, Tom Hayden, Greg Nelson, Nzinga Kone and CTSG crew, Grant Garrison, Andre Carothers, Drummond Pike, Idelisse Malavé, Tod Hill, Mark Richie and National Voice peoples, Jehmu Greene, Hans Riemer, and Rock the Vote crew, Sarah Ellis, Nancy Hale, Malissa Janasik, Reverend Sekou, Van Jones, Ocean Robbins, Claudine Brown, Jane Yett, Gavin Leonard, Jeff Chang, Jessica Tully, Diana Puente, Kevin Harris, Julia Butterfly Hill, Kofi Taha, Jordan Bromley, Baye Adolfo-Wilson, Bakari Kitwana, Hashim Shomari, Rosa Clemente, Shoneli Saba, Dennis Kucinich, Tyler Askew, Angela Woodson, Breeze Luetke-Stahlman, Taj James, Lisa Russ and Movement Strategy Center, John Sellers, Donyale Reavis, Eli Pariser, Dan Comstock, Adam Gold and Mamie Chow from OMAC, Harmony Goldberg, Rona Fernandez and crew at SOUL and YEC, Sofia Santana, Janine de Novais, Pam Costain and Wellstone Action, Reggie Moore, David Muhammad, Ebony Barley, Karl Carter, Lisa Nevins, ShaRhonda Knott, Teddy Kott, Robert Sherman, Rob McKay, Mary Manuel, Abby Lopez, Ludovic Blain, Dirta Edwards, Lisa Simms, and Nicole Johnson from Listen Inc, Maya Enista, James Bernard, Rhea Vedro, Anna Lappe, Kimo Campbell, Melanie Campbell, Adam Luna, Bob Borosage and Campaign for America's Future,

Tracy Sturdivant and Black Youth Vote! The Brown and Wimsatt families, April & Autumn Brown, Bill, Elsa, Miro, and Marguerite Horberg, Cynthia Renfro, Erin Potts, Jon Voss, Adam Werbach, Thenmozhi Soundrarajan, Rima Anosa, Daniel Brito, Celeste Espinosa, Marlena Sonn, Windy Atien, Veronica DeLaGarza, Camilliano Juarez, Third World Majority.

And many many more!